POEMS FROM ITALY
edited by
William Jay Smith and Dana Gioia

POEMS FROM ITALY

edited by

William Jay Smith and Dana Gioia

A New Rivers Abroad Book

New Rivers Press 1985

Copyright © 1972 by William Jay Smith
Copyright © 1985 by William Jay Smith and Dana Gioia
Library of Congress Catalog Card Number: 84-61826
ISBN 0-89823-060-8 (paper)
      0-89823-061-6 (cloth)
Book Design by Daren Sinsheimer and C. W. Truesdale
Typesetting by Peregrine Cold Type

Some of these poems and translations appeared in William Jay Smith, editor, *Poems from Italy*, published in 1972 by the Thomas Y. Crowell Company. We are grateful to the publishers for permission to reprint that material here.

The woodcuts illustrating this anthology are from *Hypnerotomachia Poliphili* by Francesco Colonna, Venice, Aldus Manutius, 1499. The editors are grateful to the Chapin Library, Williams College, Williamstown, Massachusetts for their use here.

Acknowledgements for specific translations used in this volume are listed at the end, starting on Page 453.

Publication of *Poems from Italy* has been made possible by grants from the Italian Ministry of Foreign Affairs, the Arts Development Fund of the United Arts Council, the McKnight Foundation, and the First Bank System Foundation. The editors also wish to thank the Istituto Italiano di Cultura of New York and the Library of the Casa Italiana at Columbia University, New York, N.Y.

New Rivers Press books are distributed by

Bookslinger   and   Small Press Distribution, Inc.
213 East 4th St.   1784 Shattuck Ave.
St. Paul, MN 55101   Berkeley, CA 94709

Poems from Italy has been manufactured in the United State of America for New Rivers Press, Inc. (C. W. Truesdale, editor/publisher), 1602 Selby Ave., St. Paul, MN 55104 in a first edition of 2,200 copies (of which 200 have been bound in cloth).

To
David Emerson Smith

and
to the memory of
Filippo Mariano Gioia
(1892-1970)

POEMS FROM ITALY

PREFACE

In 1829 Leopardi wrote: "After reading a passage of true poetry of our time, whether in verse or prose (but the most powerful impressions come from verse), one can say, even in this prosaic age, what Sterne said about a smile: that it adds a thread to the short canvas of our life ..." Leopardi was indeed correct in speaking of "this prosaic age," for the period in which he wrote was one of the most unproductive for Italian poetry, and he stood out like a giant alongside his contemporaries; but true poetry in Italy has throughout the centuries added many threads to the short canvas of life: it has provided a rich tapestry without which the literature of Europe would be very much poorer.

Italy is, as Harry Levin once said, "the traveler's endless museum, the expatriate's second homeland." The list of poets who have responded to her enchantment is long. The English poets, Shelley, Keats, Byron, Browning, Lawrence, the German poet Goethe, were all drawn to Italy. It was not merely her climate, her landscapes, and the beauty of her cities that delighted them. "The pleasure of Italy," Luigi Barzini writes in his book on the manners and morals of his countrymen, *The Italians*, "comes from living in a world made by man, for man, on man's measurements." The Italians realize, he says, "that everything in their country is governed by their experience, the product of their industry, imbued with their spirit. They know that there is no need, really, to distinguish or to choose between the smile on the face of a cameriere and Donatello's San Giorgio ..." because both are "works of art, the 'great art of being happy' and of making other people happy, an art which embraces and inspires all others in Italy, the only art worth learning, but which can never be really mastered, the art of inhabiting the earth."

Hand in hand with the art of living has gone the art of poetry. Song to the Italians is as natural as breathing: their folk songs are rich and varied, and they have produced some of the greatest lyric poetry of the modern world. The images of

Petrarch's love poetry come right down to us—in a debased form, of course—in the popular songs of our own day. The humanity that characterizes the finest Italian poetry is implicit in one of the earliest poems, written when the Italian language was beginning to emerge from Latin, in the celebrated canticle of creation of St. Francis of Assisi. This poem, with which this anthology opens, is a joyous acceptance of the universe in all its varied aspects. What makes it especially moving is the utter simplicity with which St. Francis addresses all living things. All are made to seem intimate and human: "earth, our mother and our sister," "the sun, our master and our brother," "our sister the moon," and "our brother the wind." Dante's great poem, which reflects the spirit of St. Francis, came to be called the *Divine Comedy*, but it was as much human as divine, for in it Dante attempted to encompass not only the entire theology of his period but all human knowledge and experience. He chose to write it not in Latin, which was the one language then accept-able for poetry, but in the language of the people, which has become the Italian of today. Dante's concern for the people of his time, their achievements and their failures, and for the whole of his country, then so divided and broken up, makes him the last writer of the Middle Ages and the first of modern times. He remains, as T. S. Eliot has said, "the most universal of poets in the modern languages."

The most important influence on early Italian poetry was that of the Provençal poets. In the courts of southern France in the eleventh century, poets developed a highly cultivated type of poetry whose main theme was the celebration of love. So famous was the work of these troubadours that they were asked to visit the Sicilian court of Frederick II. Imitations of their songs flourished in Sicily in the twelfth century, and lyrics influenced by them began to appear in the Tuscan language in central Italy. Dante and Petrarch were both familiar with the Provençal poets; the names of many of them appear in the *Divine Comedy*. It was from the work of these imitators that in the thirteenth century there developed in Tuscany the sweet new style (*dolce stil nuovo*). Of those who employed this style the most famous was, of course, Dante. Indeed Dante's *Divine Comedy* may be said to contain the whole range of Italian poetry from the forthright, often coarse and vulgar, language of the *Inferno*, through the plain speech of the *Purgatorio*, culminating in the sublimity of the *Paradiso*.

Readers of this anthology may be astonished to find that almost two thirds of the poems included were written before 1700. We have resisted the current fashion of anthologists to over-represent the present at the expense of the past. Of the nearly eight centuries of poetry represented here the greatest work is clearly from the earlier period, especially the Renaissance. Modern Italian poetry is rich in achievement, but no other period can compare with the flowering of Italian verse between the late thirteenth and sixteenth centuries which produced Cavalcanti, Dante, Petrarch, Boccaccio, Ariosto, Michelangelo, and Tasso as well as scores of superb minor poets as diverse as Cecco Angiolieri (the Italian Villon), and Gaspara Stampa, perhaps the finest woman poet of the Renaissance. During this period Italy dominated the poetry of Europe as it never has again, and any attempt to represent the particular achievements of Italian poetry must begin here.

Because the united Italy of which Dante dreamed and wrote did not become a reality until 1870, this venerable national literature abides in a political federation only half the age of the United States. For centuries Italy was a disunited, occupied land, further divided by local dialects spoken in each region. In a politically and linguistically partitioned country the role of a common literature is hard to overestimate. It was the language of Italy's first great poets, the Tuscan dialect of Dante, Petrarch, and Boccaccio, that provided the common tongue for a divided people. And for centuries the mere act of writing poems in this common language affirmed a national identity denied in the political sphere. Not surprisingly a dominant theme in Italian poetry, especially from the end of the eighteenth century until the unification in 1870, was patriotism.

This political rebirth was soon followed by a poetic *risorgimento* led by three writers who helped restore Italian poetry to the mainstream of European literature: Giosuè Carducci (1835-1907); Gabriele D'Annunzio (1863-1938); and Giovanni Pascoli (1855-1912). Carducci, who was awarded the Nobel Prize for Literature in 1906, was called "the first poet of the new Italy," and indeed his work revived the great public poetic tradition of his country. But it was D'Annunzio, borrowing from French and German poets, who created a bombastic but intoxicating new style that took Europe by storm. His overpowering language, technical virtuosity, and heroic poses

19

dominated the age, and many of the subsequent movements of modern Italian poetry were formed in reaction to his rhetorical excesses. Ironically, it was Pascoli, the least celebrated of this triumvirate, whose understated rhythms and clean diction had the most lasting influence.

The twentieth century has proved to be the greatest period of Italian poetry since the Renaissance, as well as the most dynamic and controversial. Three groups dominated early twentieth century Italian poetry—the *crepuscolari* or "twilight poets," the futurists, and the hermetics. Rejecting the hyper-romanticism of D'Annunzio, the *crepuscolari* used understatement and irony to describe the lonely monotony of modern life. The work of Guido Gozzano (1883-1916), the chief poet of the movement, bears a striking resemblance to the early poetry of T. S. Eliot. The era of *crepuscolarismo* was influential but short-lived. Suddenly in 1909, futurism stole the scene when Filippo Tommaso Marinetti (1876-1944) published his exuberant Futurist Manifesto on the front page of the Parisian *Le Figaro*. This vastly influential manifesto remains one of the key documents of modern art, and it immediately catapulted Marinetti into international fame. Demanding a violent rejection of the past (including conventional grammar and typography), futurism praised speed, energy, change, and technology. For most Italian poets, futurism was an exciting experimental phase when all innovations seemed possible. Completing the work of *crepuscolarismo* in bringing new life to Italy's literary tradition, futurism ultimately also declined, and by the mid-twenties Marinetti was the only important writer left in the movement.

Hermeticism exercised less international influence than futurism, but it produced greater poetry. Indeed of Italy's four most highly regarded modern poets—Umberto Saba, Guiseppe Ungaretti, Salvatore Quasimodo, and Eugenio Montale—only Saba stands outside the hermetic tradition. Hermeticism (*poesia ermetica*) was never a unified school of poetry like futurism. Instead it may be seen as a particularly Italian adaptation and perfection of the symbolist aesthetic. Hermeticism tried to give lyric poetry the intense purity and suggestiveness of music. In his poems Ungaretti, the central figure of the movement, tried to bring every work "to an extreme state of tension" that would reveal its purest meaning. Focused inwardly on its own task of self-discovery, hermetic poetry can occasionally become so compressed and allusive as to be difficult, but this tradition has created some of the best European poetry of the century, an achievement internationally recognized by the Nobel Prizes for Quasimodo in 1959 and Montale in 1975. Though no longer a dominant force in Italian letters, hermeticism left a legacy of precision, honesty, and intensity.

In this anthology we have tried to include no translations that do not stand on their own as poems in English. However closely it may translate the literal sense of an original text, bad verse in one language is never faithful to a good poem in another. Finding good poetic translations has been difficult because there is much truth in the famous Italian phrase, *traduttore-traditore* (translator-traitor), and too many Italian poets have been hopelessly betrayed by their well-meaning translators. Few European literatures have suffered so many wretched English translations. And yet there is no better testimony to the attraction of Italian poetry than the number of prominent English and American poets who have translated it over the centuries. But even this heritage has not sufficed to represent the full range of Italian poetry. Although a number of new translations have been made especially for this anthology, we have still had to omit certain poems we should have wished to include because no satisfactory translations could be found. Likewise, for reasons of space, we have limited our selection from important longer poems such as Ariosto's *Orlando Furioso* and Tasso's *La Gerusalemme Liberata* to key passages.

Our anthology also tries to reflect the rich influence Italian poetry has had on English verse, for no modern literature has played a more important role in its development. Louise Bogan once said that it took a civilization to conceive the sonnet's shape and discover its uses, and the impact of just this one form on English poetry has been immense. The introduction of new forms into a literature can have an energizing, liberating effect. They allow poets to say new things or approach old truths in a new way. When Sir Thomas Wyatt introduced the sonnet into English in the early sixteenth century with his imitations of Petrarch, he provided the language with its most versatile and enduring lyric form. Wyatt also introduced *ottava rima*, the measure perfected by Ariosto and Tasso, which became one of the most important stanzas in English. Used by Spenser, Sidney, Milton, Keats, and others, it has proved a stanza versatile enough for poems as dissimilar as Byron's *Don Juan* and Yeats' "Among School Children." *Terza rima*, the stanza invented by Dante for his *Divine Comedy* and introduced into English by Chaucer, has provided the form for major poems by

21

Sidney, Byron, Shelley and Auden. Petrarch was a dominant influence on Tudor poetry just as four centuries later Dante proved to be one of the guiding spirits of modernist British and American poetry. Even less important poets like Giambattista Marino exercised enormous influence at certain times. His extravagant use of conceit and startling metaphors created the vogue of "Marinism" among the English metaphysicals, Crashaw, Carew, Drummond, Lord Herbert, Sherburne, and Stanley. In our selection we attempted to portray the extent and richness of this heritage by showing how many of the best poets in the language since Chaucer have turned to Italy for inspiration. Alongside the better-known examples like the Earl of Surrey's Petrarch or Pound's Cavalcanti there are many less famous conjunctions like Wordsworth's Michelangelo or Byron's Pulci that sometimes shed almost as much light on the English translator as on the Italian original. Indeed the study of these translations may lead to radical reassessments. No one who has read through Dante Gabriel Rossetti's extensive collection, *The Early Italian Poets* (1861), will ever again underestimate his importance to Victorian poetry. He emerges as a Pound-like figure of his era expanding its poetic resources through translation. Without his work it would be impossible to represent Italian Renaissance poetry adequately in English. His best translations are fine English poems in their own right, and his splendid version of Niccolo delgi Albizzi's only known poem, "Prolonged Sonnet: When the Troops Were Returning to Milan," stands as one of the most powerful anti-war poems in the language.

No book of this size can represent the full range of Italian poetry, especially in the modern period where dozens of accomplished poets vie for the reader's attention. In presenting the twentieth century, we have concentrated on established writers of permanent merit, especially the great early modernists. And rather than provide a superficial scattering of younger contemporary poets, we have presented fewer poets with multiple selections of their work. Our anthology concludes with the poems of two neo-realists both of whose lives were tragically short, Rocco Scotellaro (1923-1953) and Pier Paolo Pasolini (1922-1975). To provide an adequate exploration of Italian poets born later would require another whole anthology.

Dana Gioia
William Jay Smith

POEMS

SAN FRANCESCO D'ASSISI

c.1182–1226

IL CANTICO DELLE CREATURE

Altissimu, omnipotente, bon Signore,
    tue son le laude, la gloria e l'onore et onne benedictione.
    Ad te solo Altissimo, se konfano
    et nullu omu ene dignu Te mentovare.
Laudato si, mi Signore, cum tucte le tue creature,
    spetialmente messor lo frate sole,
    lo quale jorna, et illumini per lui;
    et ellu è bellu e radiante cum grande splendore;
    de Te, Altissimo, porta significatione.
Laudato si, mi Signore, per sora luna e le stelle;
    in celu l'ài formate clarite et pretiose et belle.
Laudato si, mi Signore, per frate vento
    et per aere et nubilo et sereno et onne tempo,
    per le quale a le tue creature dai sustentamento.
Laudato si, mi Signore, per sor' acqua,
    la quale è multo utile, et humele, et pretiosa et casta.
Laudato si, mi Signore, per frate focu,
    per lo quale ennallumini la nocte,
    et ello è bellu, et jucundo, et robustoso et forte.
Laudato si, mi Signore, per sora nostra matre terra,
    la quale ne sustenta e governa,
    e produce diversi fructi, con coloriti fiori et herba.

ST. FRANCIS OF ASSISI

※

CANTICLE OF CREATED THINGS

Thine be the praise, good Lord
omnipotent, most high, Thine
the honor, the glory, and every blessing.
To Thee alone, most high, do these belong;
to speak Thy name no living man is worthy.

Be praised, my Lord, with all that Thou hast made;
above all else the sun, our master and our brother,
whence Thy gift of daylight comes.
He is most fair, and radiant with great splendor,
and from Thee, most high, his meaning comes.

Be praised, my Lord, for our sister the moon,
    and for the stars;
Thou hast placed in the heavens their clear
    and precious beauty.

Be praised, my Lord, for our brother the wind
and for the air in all weathers, cloudy and clear,
whence comes sustenance for all
    which Thou hast made.

Be praised, my Lord, for our sister water,
who is most useful, precious, humble and pure.
Be praised, my Lord, for our brother fire,
for Thine is the power by which he lights the dark;
Thine are his beauty and joy, his vigor and strength.

Be praised, my Lord, for earth, our mother
    and our sister;
by Thy power she sustains and governs us,
and puts forth fruit in great variety, with grass
    and colorful flowers.

Laudato si, mi Signore, per quilli, che perdonano per lo tuo
amore
e sostengo infirmitate et tribulatione.
Beati quilli, che sosterrano in pace,
ka de Te, Altissìmo, sirano incoronati.
Laudato si, mi Signore, per sora nostra morte corporale,
da la quale nullu homo vivente po skappare.
Guai a quilli, ke morrano ne le peccata mortali.
Beati quilli, che se trovarà ne le tue sanctissime voluntati;
ka la morte secunda nol farrà male.
Laudate et benedicete mi Signore, e rengratiate,
e serviteli cum grande humilitate.

St. Francis of Assisi

Be praised, my Lord, for those who forgive
    by the power of Thy love within them,
for those who bear infirmities and trials;
blessed are they who endure in peace,
For Thou at last shalt crown them, O most high.

Be praised, my Lord, for our sister bodily death,
from whom no living man escapes;
woe unto those who die in mortal sin,
but blessed be those whom death shall find
    living by thy most sacred wishes,
for through the second death no harm
    shall come to them.

Praise my Lord and give thanks unto Him;
bless my Lord and humbly serve Him.

(HENRY TAYLOR)

JACOPO DA LENTINI

fl. c. 1200–1250

SONETTO
LO VISO MI FA ANDARE ALEGRAMENTE

Lo viso mi fa andare alegramente,
  lo bello viso mi fa rinegare,
  lo viso me conforta ispesamente,
  l'adorno viso che mi fa penare.
  Lo chiaro viso de la più avenente,
  l'adorno viso riso me fa fare.
  Di quello viso parlane la gente,
  che nullo viso contra li pò stare.
Chi vide mai così begli ochi in viso?
  nè sì amorosi fare li senbianti?
  nè boca con cotanto dolce riso?
  Quand'eo li parlo, moroli davanti,
  e paremi ch' i vada in paradiso,
  e tegnomi sovrano d' ogn' amanti.

JACOPO DA LENTINI

SONNET
OF HIS LADY'S FACE

Her face has made my life most proud and glad;
　Her face has made my life quite wearisome;
　It comforts me when other troubles come,
And amid other joys it strikes me sad.
Truly I think her face can drive me mad;
　For now I am too loud, and anon dumb.
　There is no second face in Christendom
Has a like power, nor shall have, nor has had.

What man in living face has seen such eyes,
　Or such a lovely bending of the head,
　　Or mouth that opens to so sweet a smile?
In speech, my heart before her faints and dies,
　And into Heaven seems to be spirited;
　　So that I count me blest a certain while.

(D. G. ROSSETTI)

JACOPO DA LENTINI

𝔷

SONETTO
MADONNA E IL PARADISO

Io m'aggio posto in core a Dio servire
  Com' io potesse gire in Paradiso,
  Al santo loco, ch'aggio audito dire,
  O' si mantien sollazzo, gioco e riso.
Sanza Madonna non vi vorría gire,
  Quella ch' ha bionda testa e chiaro viso,
  Che sanza lei non potería gaudire,
  Istando da la mia donna diviso.
Ma non lo dico a tale intendimento
  Perch' io peccato ci volesse fare;
  Se non veder lo suo bel portamento,
  E lo bel viso e 'l morbido sguardare:
  Chè 'l mi terría in gran consolamento
  Veggendo la mia donna in gioia stare.

JACOPO DA LENTINI

SONNET
OF HIS LADY IN HEAVEN

I have it in my heart to serve God so
  That into Paradise I shall repair,
  The holy place through the which everywhere
  I have heard say that joy and solace flow.
Without my lady I were loath to go,—
  She who has the bright face and the bright hair;
  Because if she were absent, I being there
  My pleasure would be less than nought, I know.
Look you, I say not this to such intent
  As that I there would deal in any sin:
  I only would behold her gracious mien
And beautiful soft eyes, and lovely face,
  That so it should be my complete content
  To see my lady joyful in her place.

(D. G. ROSSETTI)

RUSTICO DI FILIPPO
1200?–1270

SONETTO
MESSERINO DE' CAPONSACCHI

Quando Dio messer Messerin fece
  Ben si credette far gran maraviglia,
  Ch' uccello e bestia ed uom ne soddisfece
  Chè a ciascheduna natura s'appiglia:
Chè nel gozzo anitrocol contraffece,
  Nelle reni giraffa m'assomiglia,
  Ed uom saría, secondo che si dice,
  Nella piacente sua cera vermiglia.
Ancor, risembra corvo nel cantare,
  Ed è diritta bestia nel savere,
  Ed uomo è somigliato al vestimento.
Quando Dio il fece, poco avea che fare,
  Ma volle dimostrar lo suo potere,
  Sì strana cera fare ebbe in talento.

RUSTICO DI FILIPPO

SONNET
OF THE MAKING OF MASTER MESSERIN

When God had finished Master Messerin,
  He really thought it something to have done:
  Bird, man, and beast had got a chance in one,
And each felt flattered, it was hoped, therein.
For he is like a goose i' the windpipe thin,
  And like a cameleopard high i' the loins;
  To which, for manhood, you'll be told, he joins
Some kinds of flesh-hues and a callow chin.
As to his singing, he affects the crow;
  As to his learning, beasts in general;
  And sets all square by dressing like a man.
God made him, having nothing else to do;
  And proved there is not anything at all
  He cannot make, if that's a thing He can.

(D. G. ROSSETTI)

JACOPONE DA TODI

1230?–1306

❧

LAUDA DELLE MALATTIE

O Signor, per cortesia,
Mandame la malsania!

A me la freve quartana,
La contina e la terzana,
La doppia cotidiana
Colla grande idropesia.

A me venga mal de dente,
Mal de capo e mal de ventre,
A lo stomaco dolor pungente,
En canna la squinantia.

Mal de occhi e doglia de fianco
E l'apostema al lato manco;
Tiseco me ionga en anco
Ed omne tempo la frenesia.

Agia el fegato rescaldato,
La milza grossa, el ventre enfiato,
Lo polmone sia piagato
Con gran tossa e parlasia.

A me vengan le fistelli
Con migliaia de carboncelli,
E li granchi sian quelli
Che tutto pieno ne sia.

A me venga la podagra;
Mal de ciglia si m'agrava,
La disinteria sia piaga
E l'emoroide a me se dia.

JACOPONE DA TODI

PRAISE OF DISEASES

O Lord, in your courtesy
Send me each infirmity!

Send the quartan fever to me,
Send the constant, tertiary,
Send me fever, double, daily,
And great dropsy's misery.

Send me every kind of toothache,
Headache and the stomach ache,
Make my belly sharply ache,
For my throat a malady.

Trouble in eyes and pain for side,
Imposthume within left side,
Let consumption gnaw me inside,
And all the time insanity.

Let my liver burn with fire,
My spleen grow large, my paunch swell higher,
Lungs go ulcered, and a dire
Cough seize on me, and a palsy.

Let my flesh grow fistular,
And my body carbuncular,
And my cancers such as are
Enough to fill me thoroughly.

Let the gout descend to torment,
Sore eyes bring cause for new lament,
Dysentery keep me bent
And hemorrhoids perpetually.

A me venga el mal de l'asmo
   E iongasece quel del pasmo
   Como al can venga rasmo
   Ed en bocca la grancia.

A me lo morbo caduco
   De cadere en acqua e 'n foco,
   E giamai non trovi loco
   Ch'io afflitto non ce sia.

A me venga cechitate,
   Muteza e sorditate,
   La miseria e povertate
   Ed onne tempo in trapperia.

Tanto sia el fetor fetente,
   Che non sia nul om vivente
   Che non fuga da me dolente,
   Posto en tanta enfermaria.

En terribile fossato,
   Che Regoverci e nominato,
   Loco sia abandonato
   Da onne bona compagnia.

Gelo, grandine, tempestate,
   Fulguri, troni, oscuritate,
   Non sia nulla aversitate
   Che me non agia en sua balia.

Glie demonia enfernali
   Essi sian mei ministrali,
   Che m'exerciten li mali
   C'ho guadagnati a mia follia.

Enfin del mondo a la finita,
   Si me duri questa vita,
   E poi, a la sceverita,
   Dura morte me se dia.

Let the asthma make me strain,
Let its spasm bring me pain;
Like a dog's make mad my brain,
My mouth with cankers tortured be.

Let the falling sickness maim,
Let me fall in water and flame,
And never find a spot where came
No hurt, but pain me utterly.

Let me go sightless, strike me blind;
Deafness, muteness let me find,
Wretched poverty unkind,
Always ensnared in misery.

Let my fetor stink to heaven
So great that not one person even
Will be who from me is not driven,
Placed in so much agony.

Let this terrible ditch, a site
Regoverci called aright,
Be a place abandoned quite
By every goodly company.

Let ice and hail and tempest rise,
Lightning, thunder, blackest skies,
Let there be no adversities
Which do not hold me at their mercy.

Let the demons out of hell
Be my ministers as well,
Let them try me with evil spell:
This I have earned with my folly.

Until this world of ours is done,
If that long my life shall run,
Till final dissolution
Let harsh death be given me.

Elegome en sepultura
Ventre de lupo en voratura,
E le reliquie en cacatura
En spineta e rogaria.

Gli miracol po' la morte,
Chi ce vien agia le scorte,
E le vessazion forte
Con terribel fantasia.

Onom che m'ode mentovare
Si se degia stupefare,
Colla croce se signare
Che mal contro non sia en via.

Signor mio, non è vendetta
Tutta la pena c'ho detta,
Che me creasti en tua diletta
Ed io t'ho morto a villania.

Give me when at last I'm dead
To a wolf's belly famishéd;
My bones? Be they in ordure laid,
The wilderness my cemetery.

Let dreadful spirits torment my ghost,
Let them escort me, be my host,
And strong vexations trouble most
With their frightful fantasy.

Let every man who hears my shame,
If he's aghast at my ill-fame,
Cross himself in Jesus' name
Lest he meet ill on his journey.

My Lord, not for revenge or spite
Is all this pain that I indite,
But that You made me in love's delight,
And I have slain You for villainy.

(L. R. LIND)

JACOPONE DA TODI

CANTICA

Ordena questo amore, tu che m'ami:
  Non è virtute senza ordene trovata;
  Poiche trovare tanto tu m'abrami
  Ca mente con virtute è renovata,
  A me amare voglio che tu chiami
  La caritate, qual sia ordenata:
  Arbore si è provata—per l'ordene del frutto,
  El quale demostra tutto—de onne cosa el valore.—

Tutte le cose qual aggio ordenate,
  Si so fatte con numero e mesura,
  Ed al lor fine son tutte ordenate,
  Conservanse per orden tal valura:
  È molto più ancora caritate
  Si è ordenata nella sua natura.
  Donqua co per calura,—alma, tu se' empazita?
  For d'orden tu se' uscita,—non·t'è freno el fervore.—

JACOPONE DA TODI

❧

CANTICA
OUR LORD CHRIST: OF ORDER

Set Love in order, thou that lovest Me.
  Never was virtue out of order found;
And though I fill thy heart desirously,
  By thine own virtue I must keep My ground:
When to My love thou dost bring charity,
  Even she must come with order girt and gown'd.
    Look how the trees are bound
    To order, bearing fruit;
    And by one thing compute,
In all things earthly, order's grace or gain.

All earthly things I had the making of
  Were numbered and were measured then by Me;
And each was ordered to its end by Love,
  Each kept, through order, clean for ministry.
Charity most of all, when known enough,
  Is of her very nature orderly.
    Lo, now! what heat in thee,
    Soul, can have bred this rout?
    Thou putt'st all order out.
Even this love's heat must be its curb and rein.

(D. G. ROSSETTI)

ANONIMO

STRAMBOTTI SICILIANI
Secolo XIII

I

Non mi mandar messaggi, ché son falsi;
Non mi mandar messaggi, ché son rei.
Messaggio sieno gli occhi quando gli alsi,
Messaggio sieno gli occhi tuoi a' miei.
Riguardami le labbra mie rosse,
Ch' aggio marito che non le conosce.

II

Più che lo mele hai dolce la parola,
Saggia e onesta, nobile e insegnata,
Hai le bellezze della Camiola,
Isotta la bionda e Morgana la fata.
Se Biancifiori ci fossi ancora,
Delle bellezze la giunta è passata.
Sotto le ciglia porti cinque cuose:
Amore e foco e fiamma e giglio e rose.

ANONYMOUS

༞

POPULAR SICILIAN LOVE SONGS
Thirteenth Century

I

Send me no messages, for they are lies;
Send me no messages, for they are sin;
No message save the uplifting of the eyes;
No message save your glance that comes to win
The knowledge of my lips how red they be.
Ah, men are bats, fair hues no husbands see!

(CECIL CLIFFORD PALMER)

II

More than honey the words you speak are sweet,
Honest and wise, nobly and wittily said,
Yours are the beauties of Camiola complete,
Of Iseult the blonde and Morgana the fairy maid.
If Blanchefleur should be added to the group,
Your loveliness would tower above each head.
Beneath your brows five beautiful things repose:
Love and a fire and flame, the lily, the rose.

(L. R. LIND)

43

ANONIMO

FOR DE LA BELLA CAIBA
Secolo XIII

For del la bella caiba · fugge lo lusignolo.
Piange lo fantino ; però che non trova
lo so usilino · ne la gaiba nova,
e dice con duolo: · chi gli avrì l'usolo?
e dice con duolo: · chi gli avrì l'usolo?
E in un boschetto · se mise ad andare
sentì l'osoletto · sì dolce cantare.
—Oi bel lusignolo · torne nel mio brolo
oi bel lusignolo · torna nel mio brolo.

ANONYMOUS

‰

OUT FROM ITS FINE CAGE
Thirteenth Century

Out from its fine cage flies the nightingale.
The little boy cries when he finds no more
His little bird in its bright new cage;
And in tears he says: "Who opened its door?"
And in tears he says: "Who opened its door?"
Then out in a wood he goes walking
And hears the sweet song of that fledgling.
"Come back to my garden, oh, sweet nightingale!
Come back to my garden, oh, sweet nightingale!"

(WILLIAM JAY SMITH)

ANONIMO

ॐ

TAPINA AHIMÈ, CH'AMAVA UNO SPARVERO
Secolo XIII

Tapina ahimè, ch'amava uno sparvero:
amaval tanto ch'io me ne moria;
a lo richiamo ben m'era manero,
e dunque troppo pascer no'l dovia.

Or è montato e salito sì altero,
assai più alto che far non solia,
ed è assiso dentro uno verzero:
un'altra donna lo tene in balía.

Isparvier mio, ch'io t'avea nodrito,
sonaglio d'oro ti facea portare
perché dell'uccellar fosse più ardito:

or se' salito sí come lo mare,
ed ha' rotti li geti e se' fuggito,
quando eri fermo nel tuo uccellare.

ANONYMOUS

❦

ALAS, ALL FOR A SPARROWHAWK I SIGH
Thirteenth Century

Alas, all for a sparrowhawk I sigh,
so much that I am nearly dead of love,
for once he used to answer to my cry,
and he was tame and gentle as a dove.
　　But lately he has risen up so high
that I have seen him vanish far above,
and to a garden he is wont to fly,
and perches on another lady's glove.
　　My sparrowhawk, that I might win your grace,
about your neck a golden bell I tied,
so you could be more ardent in the chase,
　　but now you have arisen like the tide,
and torn your bonds and fled without a trace,
when once you were contented at my side.

(MARION SHORE)

47

ANONIMO

INDOVINELLI TOSCANI

L'OLIVA

Son la bella del palazzo;
Casco in terra e non mi ammazzo;
Faccio lume al gran Signore,
Son servita con amore.

IL GRANO

Io son preso e son legato:
Son battuto e flagellato,
E di spine incoronato.
Non son uomo, non son Dio:
Ma se giungo all'esser mio,
Sarò uomo e sarò Dio.

ANONYMOUS

❦

TUSCAN RIDDLES

THE OLIVE

I am the fair one of the palace field:
I fall to earth, and yet I am not killed;
For that High Lord I go to make a light,
And I am served with love, both day and night.

(GRACE WARRACK)

THE WHEAT
(*of the briar-crowned stack*)

I have been taken, have been bound;
I have been beaten all around,
And with thorns I have been crowned.
Not as man, nor God, I grew:
But if I reach my Being True,
I shall be Man, and God, for you.

(GRACE WARRACK)

RINALDO D'AQUINO

fl. 1240–1250

❦

LAMENTO PER LA PARTENZA DEL CROCIATO

Giammai non mi conforto,
　Nè mi vo' rallegrare;
　Le navi sono al porto,
　E vogliono collare.
　Vassene la più gente
　In terra d'oltremare,
　Ed io, lassa dolente!
　Come degg'io fare?

Vassene 'n altra contrata,
　E no 'l mi manda a dire,
　Ed io rimagno ingannata,
　Tanti son li sospire,
　Che mi fanno gran guerra
　La notte co la dia;
　Nè'n cielo nè in terra
　Non mi pare ch'io sia!

O santus santus Deo,
　Che'n la Vergin venisti,
　Tu salva l'amor meo,
　Poi da me 'l dipartisti.
　Oi alta potestate,
　Temuta e dottata,
　La dolze mi' amore
　Ti sia raccomandata!

RINALDO D'AQUINO

LAMENT FOR THE
SAILING OF THE CRUSADE

Past comfort, all despairing,
My heart can find no ease;
Eastward the ships are faring,
Sails set to catch the breeze.
The bravest folk are leaving
For lands across the sea,
Here must I linger grieving
Alone in misery.

He sails the mighty ocean
And leaves to me no sign
In earnest of devotion,
O faithless love of mine.
By day and night tormented
What bitter tears I shed;
I am well nigh demented,
Neither alive nor dead.

O God, Who livest ever,
And Whom a maiden bore,
Since Thou from me didst sever
My love, I Thee implore:
Protect him from all dangers,
God of awesome power,
Stand with him amongst strangers,
Be near him every hour.

La crux salva la gente,
   E me fa disviare;
   La crux mi fa dolente,
   Nè mi val Dio pregare.
   Oimè, crux pellegrina,
   Perchè m'hai si distrutta?
   Oimè, lassa tapina!
   Ch'io ardo e incendo tutta!

Lo 'mperador con pace
   Tutto 'l mondo mantene,
   Ed a me guerra face;
   M'ha tolta la mia speme.
   Oi alta potestate,
   Temuta e dottata,
   La mia dolze amore
   Ti sia raccomandata!

Quando la crux pigliò,
   Certo no 'l mi pensai,
   Quello che tanto m'amò,
   Ed io lui tanto amai:
   Ch'io ne fui battuta,
   E messa in prigionia,
   E in celata tenuta
   Per la vita mia.

Le navi so' a le celle,
   In buon' or possan andare,
   E lo mio amor con elle,
   E la gente c'ha andare.
   O padre criatore,
   A san' porto le adduce,
   Che vanno a servidore
   De la tua santa Cruce.

Rinaldo d'Aquino

O cross that means salvation
To Christians, must you go
Leaving me in desperation?
O cross, you are my foe—
As with a fever burning
I shake and turn and toss;
O bitter is the learning
How cruel can be the cross.

The Emperor restoring
The world to peaceful sway
With me alone is warring
And takes my hope away.
O Lord of might and glory,
Standing all kings above,
Give ear to my sad story,
Watch over my true love.

He took the cross, uncaring
For love we two had known,
Love we had joyed in sharing
And now I bear alone.
For love of him they beat me
And locked me fast away
Behind cell bars that cheat me
Of blessed light of day.

The ships with anchors weighing
Stand ready to depart,
The host brooks no delaying
And carries off my heart.
O Father of all living,
They go to serve Thy cross;
O keep them, All-forgiving,
Safe from hurt and loss.

Però ti prego, Dolcetto,
  Che sai la pena mia,
  Che me n' facci un sonetto
  E mandilo in Soria,
  Ch'io non posso abentare
  La notte nè la dia.
  In terra d'oltremare
  Istà la vita mia.

Dolcetto mine, what say you?
You know what grief is mine,
Make me a song, I pray you,
To send to Palestine.
All day and night unending
I weep in misery;
My life and heart are wending
To lands across the sea.

(T. G. BERGIN)

CECCO ANGIOLIERI
1258?–?1320

SONETTO
S'I' FOSSI FOCO

S'i' fossi foco, arderei lo mondo;
  S'i' fossi vento, lo tempesterei;
  S'i' fossi acqua, io l' annegherei;
  S'i' fossi Dio, mandereil' n profondo;
S'i' fossi papa, sare' allor giocondo
  Che tutt' i cristian tribolerei;
  S'i' fossi 'mperator, sai che farei?
  A tutti mozzarei lo capo a tondo.
S'i' fossi morte, andarei da mio padre;
  S'i' fossi vita, fuggirei da lui:
  Similemente faria di mi' madre.
S'i' fossi Cecco, com' i' sono e fui,
  Torrei le donne giovani e leggiadre,
  E vecchie e laide lasserei altrui.

CECCO ANGIOLIERI

SONNET
OF ALL HE WOULD DO

If I were fire, I'd burn the world away;
   If I were wind, I'd turn my storms thereon;
   If I were water, I'd soon let it drown;
   If I were God, I'd sink it from the day;
If I were Pope, I'd never feel quite gay
   Until there was no peace beneath the sun;
   If I were Emperor, what would I have done?—
   I'd lop men's heads all round in my own way.
If I were Death, I'd look my father up;
   If I were Life, I'd run away from him;
   And I'd treat my mother to like calls and runs.
If I were Cecco (and that's all my hope),
   I'd pick the nicest girls to suit my whim,
   And other folk should get the ugly ones.

(D. G. ROSSETTI)

CECCO ANGIOLIERI

SONETTO
ATTENDE VANAMENTE, PER USCIR
DI POVERTÀ, LA MORTE DEL PADRE

Qual è senza danar innamorato
faccia le forch' e 'mpicchis' elli stesso,
ch' e' non muor una volta, ma più spesso,
che non fa que', che del ciel fu cacciato.
  E io, tapin! che, per lo mi' peccato,
s' egli è al mondo Amor, cert' i' son esso,
non ho di che pagar potesse un messo,
se d' alcun uom mi fossi richiamato.
  Dunque, perchè riman ch' i' non m' impicco?
Chè tragg' un mi' pensèr, ch' è molto vano:
c' ho un mi' padre vecchissimo e ricco,
  ch' aspetto ched e' muoi' a mano a mano;
ed e' morrà quando 'l mar sarà sicco,
sì l' ha Dio fatto, per mio strazio, sano!

CECCO ANGIOLIERI

SONNET
OF WHY HE IS UNHANGED

Whoever without money is in love
  Had better build a gallows and go hang;
  He dies not once, but oftener feels the pang
Than he who was cast down from Heaven above.
And certes, for my sins it's plain enough,
  If Love's alive on earth, that he's myself,
  Who would not be so cursed with want of pelf
If others paid my proper dues thereof.
Then why am I not hanged by my own hands?
  I answer: for this empty narrow chink
    Of hope;—that I've a father old and rich,
And that if once he dies I'll get his lands;
    And die he must, when the sea's dry, I think.
    Meanwhile God keeps him whole and me i' the
    ditch.

(D. G. ROSSETTI)

CECCO ANGIOLIERI

SONETTO
DEI BRUTTI SCHERZI,
CHE GLI GIOCA LA POVERTÀ

La povertà m'ha sì disamorato,
che, s' i' scontro mie donn'entro la via,
a pena la conosco, 'n fede mia,
e 'l nome ho già quasi dimenticato.
 Da l' altra parte m'ha 'l cuor sì agghiacciato,
che, se mi fosse fatta villania
dal più agevol villanel, che sia,
di me non avrebb' altro, che 'l peccato.
 Ancor m'ha fatto vie più sozzo gioco:
chè tal solev'usar meco a diletto,
che, s'i' 'l pur miro, sì li paio un foco.
 Ond'i' vo' questo motto aver per detto:
che, s'uom dovesse stare con un cuoco,
sì 'l dovria far per non vivarci bretto.

CECCO ANGIOLIERI

SONNET
OF WHY HE WOULD BE A SCULLION

I am so out of love through poverty
  That if I see my mistress in the street
  I hardly can be certain whom I meet,
And of her name do scarce remember me.
Also my courage it has made to be
  So cold, that if I suffered some foul cheat
  Even from the meanest wretch that one could beat,
Save for the sin I think he should go free.
Ay, and it plays me a still nastier trick:
  For, meeting some who erewhile with me took
    Delight, I seem to them a roaring fire.
So here's a truth whereat I need not stick;—
  That if one could turn scullion to a cook,
    It were a thing to which one might aspire.

(D. G. ROSSETTI)

CECCO ANGIOLIERI

SONETTO
I' SONO INNAMORATO, MA NON TANTO

I' sono innamorato, ma non tanto
che non men passi ben leggeramente;
di ciò mi lodo e tègnomi valente,
ch'a l'Amor non so dato tutto quanto.

E' basta ben se per lui gioco e canto
e amo e serverìa chi gli è servente:
ogni soperchio val quanto nïente,
e ciò non regna en me, ben mi dò vanto.

Però non pensi donna che sia nata,
che l'ami ligio com'i' veggio molti,
sia quanto voglia bella e delicata,

ché troppo amare fa gli òmini stolti;
però non vo' tener cotal usata,
che cangia 'l cor e divisa gli volti.

CECCO ANGIOLIERI

SONNET
I AM IN LOVE, BUT AM NOT SO IN LOVE

I am in love, but am not so in love
I cannot quit the feeling without smart;
I'm proud of this, it puts me in good heart
that unto Love's not pledged my every move.
To play for him and praise him, that's enough,
to love and serve who serve him with like art:
but overplaying is not worthy sport;
such is not master here, these proud words prove.

Therefore no woman underneath the sun
may think me liege, though others bend the knee,
and she be sweet and pretty beyond name.
By too much love are imbeciles undone,
and I've no flair for fashionable misery
that blights the heart, and twists the face in shame.

(FELIX STEFANILE)

NICCOLÒ DEGLI ALBIZZI

fl. 1300

SONETTO PROLUNGATO
QUANDO LA GENTE
TORNAVA DA MILANO

Fratel, se tu vedessi questa gente
   Passar per Roma tutti isgominati,
   Con visi neri gialli e affumicati,
   Diresti: dell' andata ognun si pente.
Le panche suonan sì terribilmente
   Quando son giù dal ponte in qua passati,
   Volgendo gli occhi a guisa d' impiccati,
   Nè 'n dosso, in capo, in piè hanno niente.
Le coste anco vedresti, e tutto ossame
   De' loro cavalli, e le lor selle rotte
   Hanno ripiene di paglia e di strame.
E si vergognan, che passan di notte;
   Vannosi inginocchiando per la fame,
   Trottando e saltellando come botte.
         E le loro armi tutte
   Anno lasciate per fino alle spade;
   E stan cheti com' uom quando si rade.

NICCOLÒ DEGLI ALBIZZI

PROLONGED SONNET
WHEN THE TROOPS
WERE RETURNING FROM MILAN

If you could see, fair brother, how dead beat
   The fellows look who come through Rome to-day,—
   Black-yellow smoke-dried visages,—you'd say
   They thought their haste at going all too fleet.
Their empty victual-wagons up the street
   Over the bridge dreadfully sound and sway;
   Their eyes, as hanged men's, turning the wrong way;
   And nothing on their backs, or heads, or feet.
One sees the ribs and all the skeletons
   Of their gaunt horses; and a sorry sight
   Are the torn saddles, crammed with straw and stones.
They are ashamed, and march throughout the night,
   Stumbling, for hunger, on their marrowbones;
   Like barrels rolling, jolting, in this plight.
   Their arms all gone, not even their swords are saved;
   And each as silent as a man being shaved.

(D. G. ROSSETTI)

GUIDO GUINIZELLI

c.1235-1276

❦

CANZONE
ORIGINE E NATURA D'AMORE

Al cor gentil ripara sempre Amore
   Come a la selva augello in la verdura:
   Nè fe Amore avanti gentil core,
   Nè gentil core avanti Amore, Natura;
   Ch'adesso che fo il Sole
   Sì tosto lo splendore fo lucente,
   Nè fo avanti il Sole.
   E prende Amore in gentilezza loco
   Così propiamente
   Come clarore in clarità di foco.

Foco d'amore in gentil cor s'apprende,
   Come vertute in pietra preziosa;
   Chè dalla stella valor non discende,
   Avanti 'l Sol la faccia gentil cosa:
   Poi che n'ha tratto fore
   Per sua forza, lo Sol ciò che li è vile,
   La stella 'i da valore.
   Così lo cor, ch' è fatto da Natura
   Schietto, puro e gentile,
   Donna, a guisa di stella, lo inamura.

Amor per tal ragion sta in cor gentile,
   Per qual lo fuoco in cima del doppiero
   Splende allo so diletto, chiar, sottile:
   Non li starìa altrimenti, tant' è fero!
   Però prava natura
   Incontr' Amor fa come l'acqua al foco
   Caldo, per la freddura.
   Amore in gentil cor prende rivera
   Per so consimil loco,
   Com' adamàs del ferro in la minera.

GUIDO GUINIZELLI

CANZONE
OF THE GENTLE HEART

Within the gentle heart Love shelters him
As birds within the green shade of the grove.
Before the gentle heart, in nature's scheme,
Love was not, nor the gentle heart ere Love.
For with the sun, at once,
So sprang the light immediately; nor was
Its birth before the sun's.
And Love hath his effect in gentleness
Of very self; even as
Within the middle fire the heat's excess.

The fire of Love comes to the gentle heart
Like as its virtue to a precious stone;
To which no star its influence can impart
Till it is made a pure thing by the sun:
For when the sun hath smit
From out its essence that which there was vile
The star endoweth it.
And so the heart created by God's breath
Pure, true, and clean from guile
A woman, like a star, enamoureth

In gentle heart Love for like reason is
For which the lamp's flame is fanned and bowed:
Clear, piercing bright, it shines for its own bliss;
Nor would it burn there else, it is so proud.
For evil natures meet
With Love as it were water met with fire,
As cold abhorring heat.
Through gentle heart Love doth a track divine,—
Like knowing like; the same
As diamond runs through iron in the mine.

Fere lo Sole il fango tutto 'l giorno:
    Vile riman, nè il Sol perde calore.
    Dice uom altier:—Gentil per schiatta torno;—
    Lui sembro 'l fango, e 'l Sol gentil valore.
    Chè non de' dare uom fede
    Che gentilezza sia, fuor di corraggio,
    In degnità di rede,
    Se da vertute non ha gentil core:
    Com' acqua porta raggio,
    E'l ciel ritien la stella e lo splendore.

Splende in la Intelligenza dello cielo
    Dio creator, più ch' a' nostri occhi il Sole:
    Quella 'ntende 'l so Fattor oltra 'l velo;
    Lo ciel volgendo, a lui ubidir tòle,
    E consegue al primiero
    Del giusto Dio beato compimento.
    Così dar dovrìa il vero
    La bella donna, che negli occhi splende,
    Del suo gentil talento,
    Chi mai lei ubidir non si disprende.

Donna, Dio mi dirà:—Che presumisti?—
    Sendo l'anima mia a lui davanti;
    —Lo ciel passasti, e fino a me venisti,
    E desti in vano amor, me per sembianti:
    Ch' a me convien la laude,
    E alla Reina del reame degno,
    Per cui cessa ogni fraude.—
    Dir li potrò:—Tenea d'Angel sembianza
    Che fosse del tuo regno:
    Non mi sie fallo, s' io le posi amanza.—

The sun strikes full upon the mud all day:
It remains vile, nor the sun's worth is less.
"By race I am gentle," the proud man doth say:
He is the mud, the sun is gentleness.
Let no man predicate
That aught the name of gentleness should have,
Even in a king's estate,
Except the heart there be a gentle man's.
The star-beam lights the wave,—
Heaven holds the star and the star's radiance.

God, in the understanding of high Heaven,
Burns more than in our sight the living sun:
There to behold His Face unveiled is given;
And Heaven, whose will is homage paid to One,
Fulfills the things which live
In God, from the beginning excellent.
So should my lady give
That truth which in her eyes is glorified,
On which her heart is bent,
To me whose service waiteth at her side.

My lady, God shall ask, "What daredst thou?"
(When my soul stands with all her acts reviewed;)
"Thou passedst Heaven, into My sight, as now,
To make Me of vain love similitude.
To Me doth praise belong,
And to the Queen of all the realm of grace
Who slayeth fraud and wrong."
Then may I plead: "As though from Thee he came,
Love wore an angel's face:
Lord, if I loved her, count it not my shame."

(D. G. ROSSETTI)

GUIDO GUINIZELLI

č

SONETTO
VOGLIO DEL VER LA MIA DONNA LAUDARE

Voglio del ver la mia donna laudare,
et assembrargli la rosa e lo giglio:
come la stella Diana splende e pare,
e ciò ch' è lassù bello, a lei somiglio.
Verde rivera a lei rassembro e l' a' re,
tutti colori e fior, giallo e vermiglio,
oro e argento e ricche gio' preclare;
medesmo Amor per lei raffina miglio.
 Passa per via sì adorna e sì gentile,
ch' abassa orgoglio a cui dona salute:
e fal di nostro fè se non la crede.
E non le può appressar om che sia vile:
ancor ve ne dirò maggior virtute:
null' om può mal pensar fin che la vede.

GUIDO GUINIZELLI

✾

SONNET
HE WILL PRAISE HIS LADY

Yea, let me praise my lady whom I love:
  Likening her unto the lily and rose:
  Brighter than morning star her visage glows;
She is beneath even as her Saint above;
She is as the air in summer which God wove
  Of purple and of vermilion glorious;
  As gold and jewels richer than man knows.
Love's self, being love for her, must holier prove.
Ever as she walks she hath a sober grace,
  Making bold men abashed and good men glad;
  If she delight thee not, thy heart must err.
No man dare look on her, his thoughts being base:
  Nay, let me say even more than I have said;—
  No man could think base thoughts who looked on
    her.

(D. G. ROSSETTI)

FOLGORE DA SAN GIMIGNANO
1250?–?1317

SONETTI DEI MESI

GENNAIO

I' doto voi, nel mese di Gennaio,
   Corte con fochi di salette accese,
   Camere, letti, ed ogni bello arnese,
   Lenzuol di seta e copertoi di vaio,
Tregèa, confetti, e mescere arazaio,
   Vestiti di doasio e di rascese,
   E'n questo modo star a le difese,
   Mova scirocco, garbino e rovaio.
Uscir di for' alcuna volta il giorno,
   Gittando della neve bella e bianca
   A le donzelle, che staran dattorno:
E, quando fosse la compagna stanca,
   A questa corte facciasi ritorno,
   E si riposi la brigata franca.

APRILE

D'April vi dono la gentil campagna,
   Tutta fiorita de bell'erba fresca;
   Fontane d'acqua che non vi rincresca;
   Donne e donzelle per vostra compagna:
Ambianti palafren, destrier di Spagna,
   E gente costumata a la francesca,
   Cantar, danzar a la provenzalesca
   Con istormenti novi della Magna.

FOLGORE DA SAN GIMIGNANO

SONNETS OF THE MONTHS
Addressed to a
Fellowship of Sienese Nobles

JANUARY

For January I give you vests of skin,
    And mighty fires in hall, and torches lit;
    Chambers and happy beds with all things fit;
    Smooth silken sheets, rough furry counterpanes;
And sweetmeats baked; and one that deftly spins
    Warm arras; and Douay cloth, and store of it;
    And on this merry manner still to twit
    The wind, when most his mastery the wind wins.
Or issuing forth at seasons in the day,
    Ye'll fling soft handfuls of the fair white snow
    Among the damsels standing round, in play:
And when you all are tired and all aglow,
    Indoors again the court shall hold its sway,
    And the free Fellowship continue so.

APRIL

I give you meadow-lands in April, fair
    With over-growth of beautiful green grass;
    There among fountains the glad hours shall pass,
And pleasant ladies bring you solace there.
With steeds of Spain and ambling palfreys rare;
    Provençal songs and dances that surpass;
    And quaint French mummings; and through hollow
        brass
A sound of German music on the air.

E dintorno vi sian molti giardini,
  E giachita vi sia ogni persona:
  Ciascun con reverenza adori e 'nchini
A quel gentil, ch'ho dato la corona
  Di pietre preziose, le più fini
  Ch'a 'l Presto Gianni o 'l re di Babilona.

MAGGIO

Di Maggio sì vi dò molti cavagli
  E tutti quanti siano affrenatori,
  Portanti tutti, dritti corridori,
  Pettorali e testiere con sonagli,
E bandiere e coverte a molti intagli
  E zendadi di tutti li colori;
  Le targhe a modo degli armeggiatori,
  Viole, rose e fior ch'ogni uom abbagli.
E rompere e fiaccar bigordi e lance,
  E piover da finestre e da balconi
  In giù ghirlande, e in sù melarance.
E pulzellette giovani e garzoni
  Baciarsi ne la bocca e ne le guance:
  D'amor e di goder vi si ragioni.

And gardens ye shall have, that every one
   May lie at ease about the fragrant place;
     And each with fitting reverence shall bow down
     Unto that youth to whom I gave a crown
   Of precious jewels like to those that grace
The Babylonian Kaiser, Prester John.

MAY

I give you horses for your games in May,
   And all of them well trained unto the course,—
   Each docile, swift, erect, a goodly horse;
   With armor on their chests, and bells at play
Between their brows, and pennons fair and gay;
   Fine nets, and housings meet for warriors,
   Emblazoned with the shields ye claim for yours;
   Gules, argent, or, all dizzy at noonday.

And spears shall split, and fruit go flying up
   In merry counterchange for wreaths that drop
   From balconies and casements far above;
And tender damsels with young men and youths
   Shall kiss together on the cheeks and mouths;
   And every day be glad with joyful love.

DE OTTOBRE

D'ottobre nel conta' c'ha bono stallo
  Pregovi, figloli, che voi n'andate,
  Traetevi bon tempo e uccellate
  Come vi piace a piè et a cavallo;
La sera per la sala andate a ballo,
  E bevete del mosto e v'enibriate,
  Che non ci ha miglor vita en veritate,
  E questo è ver come 'l fiorino e giallo.
E poscia vi levate la matina,
  E lavatevi 'l viso con le mani;
  Lo rosto e 'l vino è bona medicina,
A le guangnele! starete più sani
  Che pesce in lago o 'n fiume o in marina,
  Avendo meglor vita di cristiani.

DI DECEMBRE

E di decembre una città en piano,
  Sale terrene, grandissimi fochi,
  Tappedi tesi, tavolieri e giochi,
  Torticci accesi, e star co' dati en mano;
E l'oste enbriaco è catellano,
  E porci morti e fenissimi cochi,
  Ghiotti morselli, ciascun bea e mandochi,
  Le botte sian maggior che san Galgano.
E siate ben vestiti e foderati
  Di guarnacche, tabarri e di mantelli,
  E di cappucci fini e smisurati;
E beffe far dei tristi cattivelli,
  De' miseri dolenti sciagurati;
  Avari, non voglate usar con elli.

Folgore da San Gimignano

OCTOBER

Next, for October, to some sheltered coign
   Flouting the winds, I'll hope to find you slunk;
   Though in bird-shooting (lest all sport be sunk),
   Your foot still press the turf, the horse your groin,
At night with sweethearts in the dance you'll join,
   And drink the blessed must, and get quite drunk,
   There's no such life for any human trunk;
   And that's a truth that rings like golden coin!
Then, out of bed again when morning's come,
   Let your hands drench your face refreshingly,
   And take your physic roast, with flask and knife,
Sounder and snugger you shall feel at home
   Than lake-fish, river-fish, or fish at sea,
   Inheriting the cream of Christian life.

DECEMBER

Last, for December, houses on the plain,
   Ground-floors to live in, logs heaped mountain-high,
   And carpets stretched, and newest games to try,
   And torches lit, and gifts from man to man:
(Your host, a drunkard and a Catalan;)
   And whole dead pigs, and cunning cooks to ply
   Each throat with tit-bits that shall satisfy;
   And wine-butts of Saint Galganus' brave span.
And be your coats well-lined and tightly bound,
   And wrap yourselves in cloaks of strength and weight,
   With gallant hoods to put your faces through.
And make your game of abject vagabond
   Abandoned miserable reprobate
   Misers; don't let them have a chance with you.

(D. G. ROSSETTI)

GUIDO CAVALCANTI

c. 1255–1300

℮

SONETTO
AVETE IN VOI LI FIORI E LA VERDURA

Avete in voi li fiori e la verdura
  E ciò che luce ed è bello a vedere;
  Risplende più che sol vostra figura,
  Chi vo' non vede ma' non può valere.
In questo mondo non ha creatura
  Sì piena di beltà, nè di piacere:
  E chi d'amor si teme, l'assicura
  Vostro bel viso, e non può più temere.
Le donne chi vi fanno compagnia
  Assa'mi piaccion per lo vostro amore,
  Ed i' le prego, per lor cortesia,
Che, qual più puote, più vi faccia onore,
  Ed aggia cara vostra segnoria,
  Perchè di tutte siete la migliore.

GUIDO CAVALCANTI

SONNET
YOU HAVE IN YOU
THE FLOWERS AND THE GREEN GRASS

You have in you the flowers and the green grass:
  And what is shining or is fair to see:
  Light of the sun your own light doth surpass:
  Who has not seen you, worthless wight must be!
And in this world of ours, no creature is
  So full of pleasure and delightfulness:
  If any man fear love, new courage his,
  Seeing your face, so much himself to bless!
The ladies all, that bear you company,
  For your dear sake, are pleasing to my sight,
  And I would beg them of their courtesy,
To do you honor, each to strive her best,
  And in your sovereignty to have delight
  Since of them all you are the loveliest.

(G. S. FRASER)

GUIDO CAVALCANTI

SONETTO
BELTÀ DI DONNA DI PIACENTE CORE

Beltà di donna di piacente core,
    E cavalieri armati che sien genti,
    Cantar d'augelli e ragionar d'amore,
    Adorni legni 'n mar forte correnti,
Aria serena quand' appar l'albore,
    E bianca neve scender senza venti,
    Rivera d'acqua e prato d'ogni fiore,
    Oro, argento, azzurro 'n ornamenti,
Passa la gran beltate e la piacenza
    De la mia donna e il suo gentil coraggio
    Sì che rassembra vile a chi ciò guarda.
E tanto è più d'ogn'altra conoscenza,
    Quanto lo cielo de la terra è maggio:
    A simil di natura ben non tarda.

GUIDO CAVALCANTI

❦

SONNET
BEAUTY OF LADIES
OF COMPASSIONATE HEART

Beauty of ladies of compassionate heart
　　And cavaliers, in arms, and high in pride,
　　And singing birds, and lovers' rhetoric art,
　　And painted ships which on the strong seas ride,
And air serene at the first peep of dawn,
　　And blanchèd snow descending with no wind,
　　And watery bank, and flower-adornèd lawn,
　　And ornaments with azure and gold refined,
So much her beauty and her nobleness
　　Surpass, and such a courage do they carry,
　　Those seem but stale in the beholder's eye:
So much more knowledge in her looks doth lie
　　As the low earth than the high heaven is less:
　　To such a one good luck will never tarry.

(G. S. FRASER)

GUIDO CAVALCANTI

BALLATA 11
ULTIMO CANTO: DALL'ESILIO

Perch'i' non spero di tornar giammai,
    Ballatetta, in Toscana,
    Va' tu, leggera e piana
    Dritta alla donna mia,
    Che per su cortesia,
    Ti farà molto onore.

Tu porterai novelle di sospiri,
    Piene di doglia e di molta paura;
    Ma guarda che persona non ti miri
    Che sia nimica di gentil natura:
    Chè certo per la mia disavventura
    Tu saresti contesa,
    Tanto da lei ripresa
    Che mi sarebbe angoscia:
    Dopo la morte poscia
    Pianto e novel dolore.

Tu senti, ballatetta, che la morte
    Mi stringe sì che vita m'abbandona,
    E senti come 'l cor si sbatte forte
    Per quel che ciascun spirito ragiona.
    Tanto è distrutta già la mia persona
    Ch'i' non posso soffrire;

GUIDO CAVALCANTI

ℰ

BALLATA 11
LAST SONG: FROM EXILE

Since I do not hope to return ever,
Little ballad, to Tuscany,
Go thou, swift and sleight,
Unto my lady straight
Who, of her courtesy,
Will give thee gentle cheer.

Thou shalt bring news of sighs,
Of deep grief, of much fear:
But guard that none thy journey spies
Who's enemy to gentleness:
Or, sure, for my unhappiness,
Thou'lt be delayed
And so assayed
'Twill be my pain,
Past death, to plain
New grief and many a tear.

Thou feel'st how death, O little song,
Clippeth me close in whom life endeth:
Thou feel'st this heart to beat too strong
So fierce each vital sprite contendeth.
So much consumèd is this body now
Its suffering is done, I trow:

Se tu mi vuo' servire,
Mena l'anima teco,
Molto di ciò ti preco,
Quando uscirà del core.

Deh! ballatetta, alla tua amistate
Quest' anima che trema raccomando:
Menala teco ne la sua pietate
A quella bella donna a cui ti mando.
Deh! ballatetta, dille sospirando,
Quando le se' presente:
"Questa vostra servente
Vien per istar con vui,
Partita da colui
Che fu servo d'amore."

Tu, voce sbigottita e deboletta,
Ch' esci piangendo de lo cor dolente,
Coll' anima e con questa ballatetta
Va ragionando de la strutta mente.
Voi troverete una Donna piacente
Di sì dolce intelletto,
Che vi sarà diletto
Davanti starle ognora.
Anima, e tu l'adora
Sempre nel su' valore.

Thou, for thy part,
Thou then, prithee,
Take thou this soul with thee
Whenever forth it issueth from my heart.

'Las little ballad! for thy amity
This trembling soul I recommend thee:
Bear it with thee, with all its pity,
To that sweet fair to whom I send thee.
'Las! little ballad! say with a sigh
When thou stand'st her before:
"Here doth your servant lie
Come to make stay with you
Parted from him who
Was Love's servitor."

And thou, bewilderèd and enfeeblèd voice,
Now from this sore heart weeping issue find,
And with this soul and with this little song
Go reasoning of this exhausted mind.
There thou wilt find a lady pleasurable
And of a mind so choice
'Twere thy delight if able
To go her ways before,
My soul: and her adore
For her true worth, for ever.

(G. S. FRASER)

GUIDO CAVALCANTI

CANZONE
DONNA MI PREGA

Donna mi prega, perchè voglio dire
  D'un accidente che sovente è fero,
  Ed è si altero ch' è chiamato amore,
  Sì che chi 'l nega possa il ver sentire.
  Ed al presente conoscente chero,
  Perch' io non spero ch' om di basso core
  A tal ragione porti conoscenza;
  Chè senza natural dimostramento
  Non ho talento di voler provare
  Là dov' ei posa e chi lo fa criare,
  E qual è sua vertute e sua potenza,
  L' essenza, e poi ciascun suo movimento,
  E 'l piacimento che 'l fa dir amare,
  E s' omo per veder lo può mostrare.

In quella parte dove stà memora
  Prende suo stato, sì formato come
  Diafan dal lume, d'una oscuritate
  La qual da Marte viene e fa dimora.
  Egli è creato ed à sensato nome,
  D' alma costume, è di cor volontate;
  Vien da veduta forma che s'intende
  Che prende nel possibile intelletto
  Come in suggetto loco e dimoranza;
  In quella parte mai non à posanza,
  Perchè da qualitate non discende;

GUIDO CAVALCANTI

CANZONE
A LADY ASKS ME

Because a lady asks me, I would tell
Of an affect that comes often and is fell
And is so overweening: Love, by name.
E'en its deniers can now hear the truth,
I for the nonce to them that know it call,
Having no hope at all
              that man who is base in heart
Can bear his part of wit
              into the light of it,
And save they know't aright from nature's source
I have no will to prove Love's course
                    or say
Where he takes rest; who maketh him to be;
Or what his active *virtù* is, or what his force;
Nay, nor his very essence or his mode;
What his placation; why he is in verb,
Or if a man have might
              To show him visible to men's sight.

In memory's locus taketh he his state
Formed there in manner as a mist of light
Upon a dusk that is come from Mars and stays.
Love is created, hath a sensate name,
His modus takes from soul, from heart his will;
From form seen doth he start, that, understood,
Taketh in latent intellect—
As in a subject ready—
              place and abode,
Yet in that place it ever is unstill,
Spreading its rays, it tendeth never down

Risplende in sè perpetuale affetto;
Non à diletto, ma consideranza,
Sì che non pote largir simiglianza.

Non è vertute, ma da quella viene,
    Ch' è perfezione che si pone tale;
    Non razionale, ma che sente dico;
    Fuor di salute guidicar mantiene,
    E l' intenzione per ragione vale;
    Discerne male in cui è vizio amico;
    Di sua potenza segue spesso morte,
    Se forte la virtù fosse impedita,
    La quale aita la contraria via;
    Non perchè opposto naturale sia,
    Ma quanto che da buon perfetto tort' è
    Per sorte, non può dir om c' aggia vita,
    Che stabilita non à signoria;
    A simil può valor quand' om l' oblia.

L' esser è, quando lo volere è tanto
    C' oltra misura di natura torna;
    Poi non s' adorna di riposo mai,
    Move, cangiando core, riso e pianto,
    E la figura con pietate [paura L] storna;
    Poco soggiorna; ancor di lui vedrai
    Ch 'n gente di valor lo più si trova;
    La nuova qualità move i sospiri,
    E vuol c' om miri non fermato [in un formato L] loco,
    Destandosi ira la qual manda foco;

By quality, but is its own effect unendingly
Not to delight, but in an ardour of thought
That the base likeness of it kindleth not.

It is not *virtù*, but perfection's source
Lying within perfection postulate
Not by the reason, but 'tis felt, I say.
Beyond salvation, holdeth its judging force,
Maintains intention reason's peer and mate;
Poor in discernment, being thus weakness' friend,
Often his power meeteth with death in the end
Be he withstayed
                or from true course
                                bewrayed
E'en though he meet not with hate
                           or villeiny
Save that perfection fails, be it but a little;
Nor can man say he hath his life by chance
Or that he hath not stablished seigniory
Or loseth power, e'en lost to memory.

He comes to be and is when will's so great
It twists itself from out all natural measure;
Leisure's adornment puts he then never on,
Never thereafter, but moves changing state,
Moves changing colour, or to laugh or weep
Or wries the face with fear and little stays,
Yea, resteth little
                    yet is found the most
Where folk of worth be host.
And his strange property sets sighs to move
And wills man look into unformèd space
Rousing there thirst
                    that breaketh into flame.

Imaginar non pot' om che nol prova;
E non si mova perch' a lui si tiri,
E non si giri per trovarvi gioco,
Nè certamente gran saver nè poco.

Di simil tragge complessione sguardo,
Che fa parere lo piacere certo;
Non può coperto star quando è sorgiunto,
Non già selvagge le biltà son dardo,
Chè tal volere per temere è sperto;
Consegue merto spirito ch'è punto;
E non si può conoscer per lo viso,
C' om priso bianco in tal obietto cade,
E chi ben vade forma non lì vede,
Perchè lo mena chi da lei procede
Fuor di colore, d' essere diviso,
Assiso in mezzo oscuro, luci rade;
Fuor d' ogni fraude dice degno in fede,
Chè solo di costui nasce mercede.

Tu puoi sicuramente gir, canzone,
Dove ti piace; ch' i' ò si t' adornata
C' assai lodata sarà tua ragione
Dalle persone c' ànno intendimento;
Di star con l' altre tu non ài talento.

None can imagine love
                    that knows not love;
Love doth not move, but draweth all to him;
Nor doth he turn
          for a whim
                    to find delight
Nor to seek out, surely,
                    great knowledge or slight.
Look drawn from like,
               delight maketh certain in seeming,
Nor can in covert cower,
                beauty so near,
Not yet wild-cruel as darts,
So hath man craft from fear
                    in such his desire
To follow a noble spirit,
                    edge, that is, and point to the dart,
Though from her face indiscernible;
He, caught, falleth
                    plumb onto the spike of the targe.
Who well proceedeth, form not seeth,
                    following his own emanation.
There, beyond colour, essence set apart,
In midst of darkness light light giveth forth
Beyond all falsity, worthy of faith, alone
That in him solely is compassion born.

Safe may'st thou go, my canzon, whither thee pleaseth
Thou art so fair attired that every man and each
Shall praise thy speech
So he have sense or glow with reason's fire,
To stand with other
               hast thou no desire.

                                        (EZRA POUND)

GUIDO CAVALCANTI

č

SONETTO
CHI È QUESTA CHE VIEN,
CH' OGNI UOM LA MIRA

Chi è questa che vien, ch' ogni uom la mira,
  Che fa di clarità l'aer tremare?
  E mena seco Amor, sicchè parlare
  Null' uom ne puote, ma ciascun sospira?
Ahi Dio, che sembra quando gli occhi gira?
  Dicalo Amor, ch' io nol saprei contare;
  Cotanto d'umiltà donna mi pare,
  Che ciascun' altra inver di lei chiam' ira.
Non si poria contar la sua piacenza,
  Che a lei s'inchina ogni gentil virtute,
  E la Beltade per sua Dea la mostra.
Non fu sì alta già la mente nostra,
  E non s'è posta in noi tanta salute
  Che propiamente n'abbiam conoscenza.

GUIDO CAVALCANTI

SONNET
A RAPTURE CONCERNING HIS LADY

Who is she coming, whom all gaze upon,
  Who makes the air all tremulous with light,
And at whose side is Love himself? that none
  Dare speak, but each man's sighs are infinite.
  Ah me! how she looks round from left to right,
Let Love discourse: I may not speak thereon.
Lady she seems of such high benison
  As makes all others graceless in men's sight.
The honour which is hers cannot be said;
  To whom are subject all things virtuous,
    While all things beauteous own her deity.
Ne'er was the mind of man so nobly led,
  Nor yet was such redemption granted us
    That we should ever know her perfectly.

(D. G. ROSSETTI)

GUIDO CAVALCANTI

SONETTO IV

S' io priego questa donna, che pietate
Non sia nemica del suo cor gentile,
Tu dí ch' io sono sconoscente e vile,
E disperato e pien di vanitate.

Onde ti vien sì nova crudeltate?
Gia rassomigli a chi ti vede umile,
Seggia, adorna, ed accorta, e sottile,
E facta a modo di soavitate.

L'anima mia dolente e paurosa
Piange nel sospirar che nel cor trova,
Sì che bagnati di pianto escon fore.

Allhor mi par che ne la mente piova
Una figura di donna pensosa,
Che vegna per veder morir lo core.

GUIDO CAVALCANTI

SONNET IV

If I should pray this lady pitiless
That Mercy to her heart be no more foeman,
You'd call me clownish, vile, and say that no man
Was so past hope and filled with vanities.

Where find you now these novel cruelties?
For still you seem humility's true leaven,
Wise and adorned, alert and subtle even,
And fashioned out in ways of gentleness.

My soul weeps through her sighs for grievous fear
And all those sighs, which in the heart were found,
Deep drenched with tears do sobbing thence depart,

Then seems that on my mind there rains a clear
Image of a lady, thoughtful, bound
Hither to keep death-watch upon that heart.

(EZRA POUND)

GUIDO CAVALCANTI

BALLATA II

Io vidi donne con la donna mia:
Non che niuna mi sembrasse donna;
Ma simigliavan sol la sua ombria.

Già non la lodo, se non perch' è 'l vero,
E non biasimo altrui, se m'intendete:
Ma ragionando muovesi un pensiero
A dir: Tosto, miei spiriti, morrete.
Crudei, se me veggendo non piagete;
Che stando nel pensier gli occhi fan via
A lagrime del cor, che non la oblia.

GUIDO CAVALCANTI

❦

BALLATA II

Fair women I saw passing where she passed;
And none among them women, to my vision;
But were like nothing save her shadow cast.

I praise her in no cause save verity's
None other dispraise, if ye comprehend me.
A spirit moveth speaking prophecies
Foretelling: Spirits mine, swift death shall end ye,
Cruel! if seeing me no tears forelend ye,
Sith but the being in thought sets wide mine eyes
For sobbing out my heart's full memories.

(EZRA POUND)

GUIDO CAVALCANTI

❧

BALLATA V

Veggio ne gli occhi de la donna mia
Un lume pien di spiriti d'Amore,
Che portano un piacer novo nel core,
Si che vi desta d' allegrezza vita.

    Cosa m'avvien, quand'io le son presente,
Ch' i' i' non la posso a lo 'ntelletto dire:
Veder mi par de le sue labbia uscire
Una sì bella donna, che la mente
Comprender non la può che 'nmantenente
Ne nasce un' altra di bellezza nova.
Da la qual par, ch' una stella si mova,
E dica: Tua salute è dipartita.

    Là dove questa bella donna appare
S'ode una voce, che la vien davanti,
E par, che d'umiltà 'l suo nome canti
Sì dolcemente, che s'io 'l vo' contare,
Sento che 'l suo valor mi fa tremare;
E movonsi ne l' anima sospiri,
Che dicon: Guarda, se tu costei miri,
Vedrai la sua virtù nel ciel salita.

GUIDO CAVALCANTI

BALLATA V

Light do I see within my Lady's eyes
And loving spirits in its plenisphere
Which bear in strange delight on my heart's care
Till Joy's awakened from that sepulchre.

That which befalls me in my Lady's presence
Bars explanations intellectual,
I seem to see a lady wonderful
Spring forth between her lips, one whom no sense
Can fully tell the mind of, and one whence
Another, in beauty, springeth marvellous,
From whom a star goes forth and speaketh thus:
'Now thy salvation is gone forth from thee."

There where this Lady's loveliness appeareth,
Is heard a voice which goes before her ways
And seems to sing her name with such sweet praise
That my mouth fears to speak what name she beareth,
And my heart trembles for the grace she weareth,
While far in my soul's deep the sighs astir
Speak thus: 'Look well! For if thou look on her,
Then shalt thou see her virtue risen in heaven."

(EZRA POUND)

FRANCESCO DA BARBERINI
1264–1348

❧

DAGLI DOCUMENTI D'AMORE

Vuo guardar tuo figliolo
Siche non aggia duolo
Vanne ala parte prima
Che lui da vici lima
Vuo guardar magion tua
Fagli un uscio et non piua
Vuo guardar li tuoi fructi
Siene cortese a tutti.

FRANCESCO DA BARBERINI

OF CAUTION

Say, wouldst thou guard thy son,
That sorrow he may shun?
Begin at the beginning
And let him keep from sinning.
Wouldst guard thy house? One door
Make to it, and no more.
Wouldst guard thine orchard-wall?
Be free of fruit to all.

(D. G. ROSSETTI)

DANTE ALIGHIERI
1265–1321

❧

SONETTO
A GUIDO CAVALCANTI

Guido, vorrei che tu e Lapo ed io
    Fossimo presi per incantamento,
    E messi ad un vascel, ch' ad ogni vento
    Per mare andasse a voler vostro e mio;
Sicchè fortuna, od altro tempo rio
    Non ci potesse dare impedimento,
    Anzi, vivendo sempre in un talento,
    Di stare insieme crescesse il disio.
E monna Vanna e monna Bice poi,
    Con quella ch' è sul numero del trenta,
    Con noi ponesse il buono incantatore:
E quivi ragionar sempre d'amore:
    E ciascuna di lor fosse contenta,
Siccome io credo che sariamo noi.

DANTE ALIGHIERI

SONNET
TO GUIDO CAVALCANTI

Guido, I would that Lapo, thou, and I,
  Led by some strong enchantment, might ascend
  A magic ship, whose charmèd sails should fly
  With winds at will, where'er our thoughts might wend,
And that no change, nor any evil chance,
  Should mar our joyous voyage; but it might be
  That even satiety should still enhance
  Between our hearts their strict community:
And that the bounteous wizard then would place
  Vanna and Bice and my gentle love,
  Companions of our wandering, and would grace
With passionate talk, wherever we might rove,
  Our time, and each were as content and free
  As I believe that thou and I should be.

(PERCY BYSSHE SHELLEY)

DANTE ALIGHIERI

❦

SONETTO
SPESSE FIATE VEGNONMI A LA MENTE

Spesse fiate vegnonmi a la mente
　le oscure qualità ch'Amor mi dona,
　e vènmene pietà, sì che sovente
　io dico: "Lasso !, avviene elli a persona?";
　ch'Amor m'assale subitanamente,
　sì che la vita quasi m'abbandona:
　campami un spirto vivo solamente,
　e que' riman, perchè di voi ragiona.
Poscia mi sforzo, chè mi voglio atare;
　e così smorto, d'onne valor voto,
　vegno a vedervi, credendo guerire:
　e se io levo gli occhi per guardare,
　nel cor mi si comincia uno tremoto,
　che fa de' polsi l'anima partire.

DANTE ALIGHIERI

❧

SONNET
COMES OFTEN TO MY MEMORY

Comes often to my memory
the darkness Love has fixed in me
so that I cry, self-pityingly,
"What other man has lived this through?"

For Love attacks me suddenly,
life's energies abandon me,
one spirit only lives and moves
within, because it speaks of you.

Then I, to save myself, must force
my steps: a pallid, empty thing
I come to you to be made whole,

but when I raise my eyes to yours
my heart is seized with shuddering
that from the bloodstream drives my soul.

(FREDERICK MORGAN)

DANTE ALIGHIERI

SONETTO
TANTO GENTILE
E TANTA ONESTA PARE

Tanto gentile e tanta onesta pare
  La donna mia, quand' ella altrui saluta,
  Ch' ogni lingua divien tremando muta,
  E gli occhi non l' ardiscon di guardare.
Ella sen va, sentendosi laudare,
  Benignamente d'umiltà vestuta;
  E par che sia una cosa venuta
  Di cielo in terra a miracol mostrare.
Mostrasi si piacente a chi la mira,
  Che dà per gli occhi una dolcezza al core,
  Che intender non la può chi non la prova.
E par che della sua labbia si muova
  Un spirito soave e pien d' amore,
  Che va dicendo all' anima: sospira.

DANTE ALIGHIERI

SONNET
MY LADY LOOKS
SO GENTLE AND SO PURE

My lady looks so gentle and so pure
  When yielding salutation by the way,
  That the tongue trembles and has nought to say,
  And the eyes, which fain would see, may not endure.
And still, amid the praise she hears secure,
  She walks with humbleness for her array;
  Seeming a creature sent from Heaven to stay
  On earth, and show a miracle made sure.
She is so pleasant in the eyes of men
  That through the sight the inmost heart doth gain
  A sweetness which needs proof to know it by:
And from between her lips there seems to move
  A soothing spirit that is full of love,
  Saying for ever to the soul, "O sigh!"

(D. G. ROSSETTI)

DANTE ALIGHIERI

SESTINA 1

Al poco giorno, ed al gran cerchio d'ombra
   Son giunto, lasso! ed al bianchir de' colli,
   Quando si perde lo color nell'erba,
   E 'l mio disio però non cangia il verde;
   Si è barbato nella dura pietra,
   Che parla e sente come fosse donna.

Similemente questa nuova donna
   Si sta gelata, come neve all'ombra,
   Che non la muove, se non come pietra,
   Il dolce tempo, che riscalda i colli,
   E che gli fa tornar di bianco in verde,
   Perchè gli copre di fioretti e d'erba.

Quand' ella ha in testa una ghirlanda d'erba
   Trae della mente nostra ogni altra donna;
   Perchè si mischia il crespo giallo e 'l verde
   Sì bel, ch'Amor vi viene a stare all'ombra:
   Che m' ha serrato tra piccoli colli
   Più forte assai che la calcina pietra.

Le sue bellezze han più virtù che pietra,
   E 'l colpo suo non può sanar per erba;
   Ch' io son fuggito per piani e per colli,
   Per potere scampar da cotal donna;
   Ed al suo viso non mi può far ombra
   Poggio, nè muro mai, nè fronda verde.

DANTE ALIGHIERI

SESTINA 1
OF THE LADY PIETRA DEGLI SCROVIGNI

To the dim light and the large circle of shade
I have clomb, and to the whitening of the hills,
There where we see no color in the grass.
Natheless my longing loses not its green,
It has so taken root in the hard stone
Which talks and hears as though it were a lady.

Utterly frozen is this youthful lady,
Even as the snow that lies within the shade;
For she is no more moved than is the stone
By the sweet season which makes warm the hills
And alters them afresh from white to green
Covering their sides again with flowers and grass.

When on her hair she sets a crown of grass
The thought has no more room for other lady,
Because she weaves the yellow with the green
So well that Love sits down there in the shade,—
Love who has shut me in among low hills
Faster than between walls of granite-stone.

She is more bright than is a precious stone;
The wound she gives may not be healed with grass:
I therefore have fled far over plains and hills
For refuge from so dangerous a lady;
But from her sunshine nothing can give shade,—
Not any hill, nor wall, nor summer-green.

Io l' ho veduta già vestita a verde
  Sì fatta, ch'ella avrebbe messo in pietra
  L'Amor ch'io porto pure alla sua ombra:
  Ond' io l' ho chiesta in un bel prato d' erba
  Innamorata, com'anco fu donna,
  E chiuso intorno d' altissimi colli.

Ma ben ritorneranno i fiumi a' colli
  Prima che questo legno molle e verde
  S'infiammi (come suol far bella donna)
  Di me, che mi torrei dormir su pietra
  Tutto il mio tempo, e gir pascendo l' erba,
  Sol per vedere de' suoi panni l' ombra.

Quandunque i colli fanno più nera ombra,
  Sotto il bel verde la giovane donna
  Gli fa sparir, come pietra sott' erba.

Dante Alighieri

A while ago, I saw her dressed in green,—
So fair, she might have wakened in a stone
This love which I do feel even for her shade;
And therefore, as one woos a graceful lady,
I wooed her in a field that was all grass
Girdled about with very lofty hills.

Yet shall the streams turn back and climb the hills
Before Love's flame in this damp wood and green
Burn, as it burns within a youthful lady,
For my sake, who would sleep away in stone
My life, or feed like beasts upon the grass,
Only to see her garments cast a shade.

How dark soever the hills throw out their shade,
Under her summer-green the beautiful lady
Covers it, like a stone covered in grass.

(D. G. ROSSETTI)

DANTE ALIGHIERI

❦

LA DIVINA COMMEDIA
Inferno—Canto iii

PER ME SI VA NELLA CITTÀ DOLENTE,
  PER ME SI VA NELL'ETERNO DOLORE,
  PER ME SI VA TRA LA PERDUTA GENTE.
GIUSTIZIA MOSSE IL MIO ALTO FATTORE:
  FECEMI LA DIVINA POTESTATE,
  LA SOMMA SAPIENZA E IL PRIMO AMORE.
DINANZI A ME, NON FUR COSE CREATE
  SE NON ETERNE, ED IO ETERNO DURO:
  LASCIATE OGNI SPERANZA, VOI CH'ENTRATE.
Queste parole di colore oscuro
  vid'io scritte al sommo d'una porta;
  perch'io: « Maestro, il senso lor m'è duro ».
Ed egli a me, come persona accorta:
  « Qui si convien lasciare ogni sospetto;
  ogni viltà convien che qui sia morta.
Noi siam venuti al luogo ov'io t'ho detto
  che tu vedrai le genti dolorose
  ch'hanno perduto il ben dell'intelletto ».
E poichè la sua mano all mia pose
  con lieto volto, ond'io mi confortai,
  mi mise dentro alle segrete cose.
Quivi sospiri, pianti ed alti guai
  risonavan per l'aer sanza stelle,
  perch'io al cominciar ne lagrimai.
Diverse lingue, orribili favelle,
  parole di dolore, accenti d'ira,
  voci alte e fioche, e suon di man con elle,
facevano un tumulto, il qual s'aggira
  sempre, in quell'aria sanza tempo tinta,
  come la rena quando a turbo spira.

DANTE ALIGHIERI

❧

THE GATES OF HELL
(Inferno—Canto iii)

THROUGH ME THE WAY IS TO THE CITY OF WOE:
  THROUGH ME THE WAY INTO THE ETERNAL PAIN;
  THROUGH ME THE WAY AMONG THE LOST BELOW.
RIGHTEOUSNESS DID MY MAKER ON HIGH CONSTRAIN.
  ME DID DIVINE AUTHORITY UPREAR;
  ME SUPREME WISDOM AND PRIMAL LOVE SUSTAIN.
BEFORE I WAS, NO THINGS CREATED WERE
  SAVE THE ETERNAL, AND I ETERNAL ABIDE.
  RELINQUISH ALL HOPE, YE WHO ENTER HERE.
These words, of a dim color, I espied
  Written above the lintel of a door.
  Whereat: "Master, the sense is hard," I cried.
And he, as one experienced in that lore:
  "Here all misgiving must thy mind reject.
  Here cowardice must die and be no more.
We are come to the place I told thee to expect,
  Where thou shouldst see the people whom pain stings
  And who have last the good of the intellect."
His hand on mine, to uphold my falterings,
  With looks of cheer that bade me comfort keep,
  He led me on into the secret things.
Here lamentation, groans, and wailings deep
  Reverberated through the starless air,
  So that it made me at the beginning weep.
Uncouth tongues, horrible shriekings of despair,
  Shrill and faint voices, cries of pain and rage,
  And, with it all, smiting of hands, were there,
Making a tumult, nothing could assuage,
  To swirl in the air that knows not day or night,
  Like sand within the whirlwind's eddying cage.

(LAURENCE BINYON)

DANTE ALIGHIERI

Inferno—Canto v

Siede la terra dove nata fui
  su la marina dove 'l Po discende
  per aver pace co' seguaci sui.
Amor, ch'al cor gentil ratto s'apprende,
  prese costui della bella persona
  che mi fu tolta; e 'l modo ancor m'offende.
Amor, ch'a nullo amato amar perdona,
  mi prese del costui piacer sì forte,
  che, come vedi, ancor non m'abbandona.
Amor condusse noi ad una morte:
  Caina attende chi vita ci spense.'
  Queste parole da lor ci fur porte.
Quand' io intesi quell'anime offense,
  china' il viso, e tanto il tenni basso,
  fin che 'l poeta mi disse: 'Che pense?'
Quando rispuosi, cominciai: 'Oh lasso,
  quanti dolci pensier, quanto disio
  menò costoro al doloroso passo!'
Poi mi rivolsi a loro e parla' io,
  e cominciai: 'Francesca, i tuoi martiri
  a lacrimar mi fanno tristo e pio.
Ma dimmi: al tempo de' dolci sospiri,
  a che e come concedette amore
  che conosceste i dubbiosi disiri?'
E quella a me: 'Nessun maggior dolore
  che ricordarsi del tempo felice
  nella miseria; e ciò sa 'l tuo dottore.
Ma s' a conoscer la prima radice
  del nostro amor tu hai cotanto affetto,
  dirò come colui che piange e dice.
Noi leggiavamo un giorno per diletto
  di Lancialotto come amor lo strinse:
  soli eravamo e sanza alcun sospetto.

DANTE ALIGHIERI

※

FRANCESCA OF RIMINI
(Inferno—Canto v)

"The land where I was born sits by the seas,
  Upon that shore to which the Po descends,
  With all his followers, in search of peace.
Love, which the gentle heart soon apprehends,
  Seized him for the fair person which was ta'en
  From me, and me even yet the mode offends.
Love, who to none beloved to love again
  Remits, seized me with wish to please so strong,
  That, as thou seest, yet, yet it doth remain.
Love to one death conducted us along,
  But Caina waits for him our life who ended:"
  These were the accents utter'd by her tongue.—
Since I first listen'd to these souls offended,
  I bow'd my visage, and so kept it till—
  "What think'st thou," said the bard; when I unbended,
And recommenced: "Alas! unto such ill
  How many sweet thoughts, what strong ecstasies
  Led these their evil fortune to fulfil!"
And then I turn'd unto their side my eyes,
  And said, "Francesca, thy sad destinies
  Have made me sorrow till the tears arise.
But tell me, in the season of sweet sighs,
  By what and how thy love to passion rose,
  So as his dim desires to recognise?"
Then she to me: "The greatest of all woes
  Is to remind us of our happy days
  In misery, and that thy teacher knows.
But if to learn our passion's first root preys
  Upon thy spirit with such sympathy,
  I will do even as he who weeps and says.
We read one day for pastime, seated nigh,
  Of Lancilot, how love enchain'd him too.
  We were alone, quite unsuspiciously.

Per più fïate li occhi ci sospinse
   quella lettura, e scolorocci il viso;
   ma solo un punto fu quel che ci vinse.
Quando leggemmo il disïato riso
   esser baciato da cotanto amante,
   questi, che mai da me non fia diviso,
la bocca mi baciò tutto tremante.
   Galeotto fu il libro e chi lo scrisse:
   quel giorno più non vi leggemmo avante.'
Mentre che l'uno spirto questo disse,
   l'altro piangea, sì che di pietade
   io venni men così com' io morisse;
e caddi come corpo morto cade.

But oft our eyes met, and our cheeks in hue
  All o'er discolour'd by that reading were;
  But one point only wholly us o'erthrew;
When we read the long-sigh'd-for smile of her,
  To be thus kiss'd by such devoted lover,
  He who from me can be divided ne'er
Kiss'd my mouth, trembling in the act all over:
  Accursed was the book and he who wrote!
  That day no further leaf we did uncover."
While thus one spirit told us of their lot,
  The other wept, so that with pity's thralls
  I swoon'd, as if by death I had been smote
And fell down even as a dead body falls.

(LORD BYRON)

DANTE ALIGHIERI

ℰ

Inferno—Canto xxxiii

"Quando fui desto innanzi la dimane,
   pianger senti' fra 'l sonno i miei figliuoli
   ch' eran con meco, e domandar del pane.
Ben se' crudel, se tu già non ti duoli,
   pensando ciò che 'l mio cor s' annunziava;
   e se non piangi, di che pianger suoli?
Già eran desti, e l' ora s' appressava
   che 'l cibo ne solea esser addotto,
   e per suo sogno ciascun dubitava;
e io senti' chiavar l' uscio di sotto
   all' orribile torre; ond' io guardai
   nel viso a' mie' figliuoi sanza far motto.
Io non piangea, sì dentro impetrai
   piangevan elli; e Anselmuccio mio
   disse: 'Tu guardi sì, padre! che hai?
Perciò non lacrimai nè rispuos' io
   tutto quel giorno nè la notte appresso,
   infin che l' altro sol nel mondo uscio.
Come un poco di raggio si fu messo
   nel doloroso carcere, e io scorsi
   per quattro visi il mio aspetto stesso,
ambo le man per lo dolor mi morsi;
   ed ei, pensando ch' i' 'l fessi per voglia
   di manicar, di subito levorsi,
e disser: 'Padre, assai ci fia men doglia,
   se tu mangi di noi: tu ne vestisti
   queste misere carni, e tu le spoglia.'
Queta' mi allor per non farli più tristi;
   lo dì e l' altro stemmo tutti muti:
   ahi dura terra, perché non t'apristi?
Poscia che fummo al quarto dì venuti,
   Gaddo mi si gettò disteso a' piedi,
   dicendo: 'Padre mio, ché non m'aiuti?'

DANTE ALIGHIERI

UGOLINO
(Inferno—Canto xxxiii)

When I awoke before the dawn, my head
Swam with cries of my sons who slept in tears
Beside me there, crying out for bread.
(If your sympathy has not already started
At all that my heart was foresuffering
And if you are not crying, you are hardhearted.)
They were awake now, it was near the time
For food to be brought in as usual,
Each one of them disturbed after his dream,
When I heard the door being nailed and hammered
Shut, far down in the nightmare tower.
I stared in my sons' faces and spoke no word.
My eyes were dry and my heart was stony.
They cried and my little Anselm said,
"What's wrong? Why are you staring, daddy?"
But I shed no tears, I made no reply
All through that day, all through the night that followed
Until another sun blushed in the sky
And sent a small beam probing the distress
Inside those prison walls. Then when I saw
The image of my face in their four faces
I bit on my two hands in desperation
And they, since they thought hunger drove me to it,
Rose up suddenly in agitation
Saying, "Father, it will greatly ease our pain
If you eat us instead, and you who dressed us
In this sad flesh undress us here again."
So then I calmed myself to keep them calm.
We hushed. That day and the next stole past us
And earth seemed hardened against me and them.
For four days we let the silence gather.
Then, throwning himself flat in front of me,
Gaddo said, "Why don't you help me, father?"
He died like that, and surely as you see

Quivi morì; e come tu mi vedi,
   vid'io cascar li tre ad uno ad uno
   tra 'l quinto dì e 'l sesto; ond'io mi diedi,
già cieco, a brancolar sovra ciascuno,
   e due dì li chiamai, poi che fur morti.
   Poscia, più che 'l dolor, poté 'l digiuno.''

Quand'ebbe detto ciò, con gli occhi torti
   riprese 'l teschio misero co' denti,
   che furo all'osso, come d'un can, forti.

Me here, one by one I saw my three
Drop dead during the fifth day and the sixth day
Until I saw no more. Searching, blinded,
For two days I groped over them and called them.
Then hunger killed where grief had only wounded.'
When he had said all this, his eyes rolled
And his teeth, like a dog's teeth clamping round a bone,
Bit into the skull and again took hold.

(SEAMUS HEANEY)

DANTE ALIGHIERI

Purgatorio—Canto xi

"O vana gloria dell' umane posse,
  com' poco verde in su la cima dura,
  se non è giunta dall' etati grosse!
Credette Cimabue nella pittura
  tener lo campo, ed ora ha Giotto il grido,
  sì che la fama di colui è oscura.
Così ha tolto l' uno all' altro Guido
  la gloria della lingua; e forse è nato
  chi l' uno e l' altro caccerà di nido.
Non é il mondan romore altro che un fiato
  di vento, che or vien quinci ed or vien quindi,
  e muta nome, perchè muta lato.
Che fama avrai tu più, se vecchia scindi
  da te la carne, che se fossi morto
  innanzi che lasciassi il pappo e il dindi,
pria che passin mill' anni? ch' è più corto
  spazio all' eterno, che un mover di ciglia
  al cerchio che più tardi in cielo è torto.
Colui, che del cammin sì poco piglia
  dinanzi a me, Toscana sonò tutta,
  ed ora a pena in Siena sen pispiglia,
ond' era sire, quando fu distrutta
  la rabbia fiorentina, che superba
  fu a quel tempo, sì com' ora è putta.
La vostra nominanza è color d' erba,
  che viene e va, e quei la discolora,
  per cui ell' esce della terra acerba."

DANTE ALIGHIERI

꙳

ODERISI D'AGOBBIO ON PRIDE
(Purgatorio—Canto xi)

"O gifted men, vainglorious for first place,
　　how short a time the laurel crown stays green
　　unless the age that follows lacks all grace!

Once Cimabue thought to hold the field
　　in painting, and now Giotto has the cry
　　so that the other's fame, grown dim, must yield.

So from one Guido has another shorn
　　poetic glory, and perhaps the man
　　who will un-nest both is already born.

A breath of wind is all there is to fame
　　here upon earth: it blows this way and that,
　　and when it changes quarter it changes name.

Though loosed from flesh in old age, will you have
　　in, say, a thousand years, more reputation
　　than if you went from child's play to the grave?

What, to eternity, is a thousand years?
　　Not so much as the blinking of an eye
　　to the turning of the slowest of the spheres.

All Tuscany once sounded with the fame
　　of this one who goes hobbling on before me;
　　now, one hears scarce a whisper of his name,

even in Siena, where he was in power
　　when he destroyed the rage of Florence (then,
　　as much a shrew as she is, now, a whore).

The fame of man is like the green of grass:
　　it comes, it goes; and He by whom it springs
　　bright from earth's plenty makes it fade and pass."

(JOHN CIARDI)

DANTE ALIGHIERI

Purgatorio—Canto xxx

Io vidi già nel cominciar del giorno
   la parte oriental tutta rosata,
   e l'altro ciel di bel sereno adorno;
e la faccia del sol nascere ombrata,
   sí che, per temperanza di vapori,
   l'occhio la sostenea lunga fiata:
cosí dentro una nuvola di fiori
   che dalle mani angeliche saliva
   e ricadeva in giú dentro e di fuori,
sopra candido vel, cinta d'oliva,
   donna m'apparve, sotto verde manto,
   vestita di color di fiamma viva.
E lo spirito mio, che già cotanto
   tempo era stato che alla sua presenza
   non era, di stupor, tremando, affranto,
sanza degli occhi aver piú conoscenza,
   per occulta virtú che da lei mosse,
   d'antico amor sentí la gran potenza.
Tosto che nella vista mi percosse
   l'alta virtú che già m'avea trafitto
   prima ch'io fuor di puerizia fosse,
volsimi alla sinistra col rispitto
   col quale il fantolin corre alla mamma
   quando ha paura o quando egli è afflitto,
per dicere a Virgilio: « Men che dramma
   di sangue m'è rimasa che non tremi;
conosco i segni dell'antica fiamma!»

DANTE ALIGHIERI

THE LADY CLOTHED IN FLAME
(Purgatorio—Canto xxx)

I have seen, at the beginning of day,
The eastern part of the sky all roseate
And the rest of it dressed in tranquillity;

And the face of the sun appear shadowy,
And such that it was so tempered by mist
That the eye could bear to look for a long time:

So, inside a great cloud of flowers
Which leapt out of the angelic hands
And fell inside the chariot and all around it,

Over a white veil, crowned with olive,
A lady came to me, under her green cloak
Clothed in the color of flame.

And my spirit, which for so long a time
Had not been in her presence,
Trembled with wonder, crushed,

Without knowing her any more, with my eyes,
But through the secret virtue which went out from her,
Felt the great power of the ancient love.

The moment that, as I looked, I was struck
By the high virtue which had already stabbed me
Before I was out of my boyhood,

I turned round to my left, with that trust
With which a child runs to his mother,
When he is afraid or in trouble,

To say to Virgil: "Less than a drop of blood
Is left in me, that is not trembling:
I know the signs of the ancient flame."

(C. H. SISSON)

125

DANTE ALIGHIERI

Paradiso — Canto xxxiii

Vergine madre, figlia del tuo figlio
  umile e alta più che creatura,
  termine fisso d'eterno consiglio,
tu se' colei che l'umana natura
  nobilitasti sì che 'l suo fattore
  non disdegnò di farsi sua creatura.
Nel ventre tuo si raccese l'amore
  per lo cui caldo nell' eterna pace
  così è germinato questo fiore.
Qui se' a noi meridiana face
  di caritate, e giuso, infra i mortali
  se' di speranza fontana vivace.
Donna, se' tanto grande e tanto vali,
  che qual vuol grazia ed a te non ricorre,
  sua disianza vuol volar senz'ali.
La tua benignità non pur soccorre
  a chi domanda, ma molte fiate
  liberamente al dimandar precorre.
In te misericordia, in te pietate,
  in te magnificenza, in te s'aduna
  quantunque in creatura è di bontate.

DANTE ALIGHIERI

❧

SAINT BERNARD'S HYMN OF PRAISE TO THE VIRGIN MARY
(Paradiso—Canto xxxiii)

Virgin mother, daughter of your son,
  More humble and more high than other creatures,
  The constant goal of the eternal plan,
You are the one who so raised human nature
  That your Creator did not hesitate
  To be created in your mortal flesh,
And in your womb was gathered all the love
  The warmth of which fills our eternal peace
  And nourishes this flower as it grows.
For us in heaven you are the bright sun
  Of charity at noon and to the living
  You are the running fountain of their faith.
Lady, you are so powerful and great
  That he who would seek grace and not seek you
  Gains less than if he tried flying without wings.
Your blessings do not fall only on those
  Who ask for them, but many times they come
  Freely to those who do not know their need.
In you is mercy, in you is pity,
  In you is power, in you is gathered
  All the good of all created things.

(DANA GIOIA)

CINO DA PISTOIA
1270-1336

ใช้

SONETTO
TUTTO CIÒ CH'ALTRI AGRADA,
A ME DISGRADA

Tutto ciò ch'altri agrada, a me disgrada;
    Et èmmi a noia e spiace tutto 'l mondo.
    'Or dunque che ti piace?' I' ti rispondo:
    Quando l' un l' altro spessamente agghiada.
E piacemi veder colpi di spada
    Altrui nel volto, e navi andare a fondo;
    E piacerebbemi un Neron secondo,
    E ch' ogni bella donna fosse lada.
Molto mi spiace allegrezza e sollazzo,
    E sol malenconia m' aggrada forte,
    E tutto 'l dì vorrei seguire un pazzo;
E far mi piaceria di pianto corte,
    E tutti quelli ammazzar ch' io ammazzo
    Nel fero pensier dove io trovo morte.

CINO DA PISTOIA

SONNET
ALL THAT'S TO OTHERS PLEASING,
I DISLIKE

All that's to others pleasing, I dislike;
   The whole world brings me ennui and grief.
   —Then, what do you enjoy?—I answer, brief:
   —When each opponent makes the fatal strike:

I like to watch blows of a sword fully
   On another's face, and vessels foundering:
   To be a second Nero would be pleasing,
   And that each lovely woman should be ugly.

Amusement and good cheer I cannot breathe:
   And melancholy's what I relish most:
   All day I'd gladly follow some tomfool,
   And pay my court to sorrow for a while,
   And slaughter all whom in my cruel thoughts
   I do slaughter, there where I find death.

(BARBARA HOWES)

CINO DA PISTOIA

MADRIGALE V

Io mi son dato tutto a tragger oro
   A poco a poco del fiume, che 'l mena,
Pensandone arricchire,
   E credone ammassar più che 'l re Poro,
Traendol sottilmente fra l'arena;
   Ond'io potrei gioire,
   E penso tanto a questo mio lavoro,
Che s'io trovassi d'ariento vena,
   Non mi potria gradire;
   Però che non è mai maggior tesoro,
Che quel, che lo cor tragge fuor di pena,
   E contenta il disire.
   Però contento son pure ad amare
   Voi, gentil Donna, da cui mi convene
Più sottilmente la speranza trare,
   Che l'oro di quel fiume.

CINO DA PISTOIA

MADRIGAL

To his Lady Selvaggia Vergiolesi; likening his Love to
a search for Gold

I am all bent to glean the golden ore
　　Little by little from the river-bed;
　　　　Hoping the day to see
When Croesus shall be conquered in my store.
　　Therefore, still sifting where the sands are spread,
　　　　I labor patiently:
Till, thus intent on this thing and no more,—
　　If to a vein of silver I were led,
　　　　It scarce could gladden me.
And, seeing that no joy's so warm i' the core
　　As this whereby the heart is comforted
　　　　And the desire set free,—
Therefore thy bitter love is still my scope,
　　Lady, from whom it is my life's sore theme
More painfully to sift the grains of hope
　　Than gold out of that stream.

(D. G. ROSSETTI)

FRANCESCO PETRARCA

1304–1374

S'AMOR NON E, CHE DUNQUE E QUEL CH'IO SENTO

S'amor non è, che dunque è quel ch' io sento?
ma s'egli è amor, per Dio, che cosa e quale?
se bona, ond' è l'effetto aspro mortale?
se ria, ond' è sí dolce ogni tormento?
    S' a mia voglia ardo ond' è 'l pianto e lamento?
s' a mal mio grado, il lamentar che vale?
O viva morte, o dilettoso male,
come puoi tanto in me, s' io nol consento?
    E s' io 'l consento, a gran torto mi doglio.
Fra sí contrari venti in frale barca
mi trovo in alto mar senza governo,
    sí lieve di saver, d'error sí carca,
ch'i' medesmo non so quel ch' io mi voglio,
e tremo a mezza state, ardendo il verno.

FRANCESCO PETRARCH

THE SONG OF TROYLUS

If no love is, O God, what fele I so?
And if love is, what thinge and whiche is he?
If love be gode, from whennes comth my wo?
If it be wykke, a wonder thynketh me,
Whenne every torment and adversite,
That cometh of him, may to me savory thynke;
For ay thirst I the more that Iche it drynke.

And if that in myn owne lust I brenne,
From whennes cometh my wailynge and my pleynte?
If harme agree me, whereto pleyne I thenne?
I noot, ne why, unwery, that I feynte.
O quyke deth! O swete harm so queynte!
How may I se in me swiche quantite,
But if that I consente that it so be?

And if that I consente, I wrongfully
Compleyne ywis; thus possed to and fro,
Al sterelees withinne a boot am I
Amyd the see, betwexen windes two,
That in contrarie standen ever mo.
Allas! what is this wonder maladye?
For hete of cold, for cold of hete I dye.

(GEOFFREY CHAUCER)

133

FRANCESCO PETRARCA

SONETTO
MILLE FIATE, O DOLCE MIA GUERRERA

Mille fiate, o dolce mia guerrera,
per aver co' begli occhi vostri pace
v'aggio proferto il cor, m'a voi non piace
mirar sì basso colla mente altera;

e se di lui fors'altra donna spera,
vive in speranza debile e fallace:
mio, perchè sdegno ciò ch'a voi dispiace,
esser non può già mai così com'era.

Or s'io lo scaccio, et e' non trova in voi
ne l'esilio infelice alcun soccorso,
né sa star sol, né gire ov'altri il chiama,

poria smarrire il suo natural corso:
che grave colpa fia d'ambeduo noi,
e tanto più de voi, quanto più v'ama.

FRANCESCO PETRARCH

SONNET
HOW OFT HAVE I,
MY DERE AND CRUELL FOO

How oft have I, my dere and cruell foo,
With those your Iyes for to get peace and truyse,
Profferd you myn hert, but you do not use
Emong so high thinges to cast your mynde so lowe.
Yf any othre loke for it, as ye trowe,
There vayn weke hope doeth greately theim abuse;
And thus I disdain that that ye refuse;
It was ones myn: it can no more be so.
Yf I then it chase, nor it in you can fynde
In this exile no manner of comfort,
Nor lyve allone, nor where he is called resort,
He may wander from his naturall kynd.
So shall it be great hurt unto us twayn,
And yours the losse and myn the dedly pain.

(SIR THOMAS WYATT)

FRANCESCO PETRARCA

SONETTO
ROTTA E L'ALTA COLONNA
E 'L VERDE LAURO

Rotta è l'alta colonna e 'l verde lauro
che facean ombra al mio stanco pensero:
perduto ò quel che ritrovar non spero
dal borrea a l' austro, o dal mar indo al mauro.

Tolto m'ài, morte, il mio doppio tesauro
che mi fea viver lieto e gire altero,
e ristorar nol pò terra né impero,
né gemma oriental né forza d'auro.

Ma se consentimento è di destino,
che posso io piú se no aver l' alma trista,
umidi gli occhi sempre, e 'l viso chino?

O nostra vita ch' è sí bella in vista,
com' perde agevolmente in un matino
quel che 'n molti anni a gran pena s' acquista!

FRANCESCO PETRARCH

❧

SONNET
THE PILLER PEARISHT IS
WHEARTO I LENT

The piller pearisht is whearto I lent,
The strongest staye of myne unquyet mynde;
The lyke of it no man agayne can fynde,
From East to West, still seking thoughe he went.
To myne unhappe! for happe away hath rent
Of all my joye the vearye bark and rynde;
And I (alas) by chaunce am thus assynde
Dearlye to moorne till death do it relent.
But syns that thus it is by destenye,
What can I more but have a wofull hart,
My penne in playnt, my voyce in wofull crye,
My mynde in woe, my bodye full of smart,
And I my self my self alwayes to hate,
Till dreadfull death do ease my dolefull state?

(SIR THOMAS WYATT)

FRANCESCO PETRARCA

SONETTO
UNA CANDIDA CERVA SOPRA L'ERBA

Una candida cerva sopra l' erba
verde m' apparve, con duo corna d' oro,
fra due riviere, all' ombra d' un alloro,
levando 'l sole a la stagione acerba.

Era sua vista sí dolce superba
ch' i' lasciai per seguirla ogni lavoro,
come l'avaro che 'n cercar tesoro
con diletto l' aflanno disacerba.

« Nessun mi tocchi » al bel collo d' intorno
scritto avea di diamanti e di topazi,
« libera farmi al mio Cesare parve ».

Ed era 'l sol già volto al mezzo giorno;
gli occhi miei stanchi di mirar, non sazi,
quand' io caddi ne l'acqua, ed ella sparve.

FRANCESCO PETRARCH

SONNET
WHO SO LIST TO HOUNT

Who so list to hount, I knowe where is an hynde,
But as for me, helas, I may no more:
The vayne travaill hath weried me so sore.
I ame of theim that farthest cometh behinde.
Yet may I by no meanes my weried mynde
Drawe from the Diere: but as she fleeth afore,
Faynting I folowe. I leve of therefore,
Sins in a nett I seke to hold the wynde.
Who list her hount I put him owte of dowbte,
As well as I may spend his tyme in vain:
And, graven with Diamonds, in letters plain
There is written her faier neck rounde abowte:
Noli me tangere, for Cesars I ame,
And wylde for to hold though I seme tame.

(SIR THOMAS WYATT)

FRANCESCO PETRARCA

𝔢

SONETTO
PASSA LA NAVE MIA COLMA D'OBLIO

Passa la nave mia colma d'oblio
per aspro mare, a mezza notte, il verno,
enfra Scilla e Cariddi; ed al governo
siede 'l signore, anzi 'l nimico mio;

a ciascun remo un penser pronto e rio
che la tempesta e 'l fin par ch' abbi a scherno;
la vela rompe un vento umido, eterno
di sospir', di speranze e di desio;

pioggia di lagrimar, nebbia di sdegni
bagna e rallenta le già stanche sarte,
che son d'error con ignoranzia attorto.

Celansi i duo mei dolci usati segni;
morta fra l'onde è la ragion e l'arte:
tal ch' incomincio a desperar del porto.

FRANCESCO PETRARCH

❦

SONNET
MY GALY CHARGED WITH FORGETFULNES

My galy charged with forgetfulnes
Thorrough sharpe sees in wynter nyghtes doeth pas
Twene Rock and Rock; and eke myn ennemy, Alas,
That is my lorde, sterith with cruelnes;
And every owre a thought in redines,
As tho that deth were light in suche a case.
An endles wynd doeth tere the sayll a pase
Of forced sightes and trusty ferefulnes.
A rayn of teris, a clowde of derk disdain
Hath done the wered cordes great hinderaunce,
Wrethed with errour and eke with ignoraunce.
The starres be hid that led me to this pain,
Drowned is reason that should me confort,
And I remain dispering of the port.

(SIR THOMAS WYATT)

FRANCESCO PETRARCA

CANZONE

Standomi un giorno solo a la fenestra
onde cose vedea tante, e sí nove,
ch' era sol di mirar quasi già stanco,
una fera m' apparve da man destra
con fronte umana da far arder Giove,
cacciata da duo veltri, un nero, un bianco,
che l' un e l' altro fianco
de la fera gentil mordean sí forte
che 'n poco tempo la menaro al passo,
ove, chiusa in un sasso,
vinse molta bellezza acerba morte:
e mi fe' sospirar sua dura sorte.

Indi per alto mar vidi una nave
con le sarte di seta, e d' or la vela,
tutta d' avorio e d' ebeno contesta;
e 'l mar tranquillo, e l' aura era soave,
e 'l ciel qual è se nulla nube il vela;
ella carca di ricca merce onesta;
poi repente tempesta
oriental turbò sí l' aere e l' onde
che la nave percosse ad uno scoglio.
O che grave cordoglio!
Breve ora oppresse, e poco spazio asconde
l' alte ricchezze a nul' altre seconde.

FRANCESCO PETRARCH

❦

VISIONS

I

Being one day at my window all alone,
  So manie strange things happened me to see,
As much it grieveth me to thinke thereon.
  At my right hand a hynde appear'd to mee,
So faire as mote the greatest god delite;
  Two eager dogs did her pursue in chace,
Of which the one was blacke, the other white:
  With deadly force so in their cruell race
They pincht the haunches of that gentle beast,
  That at the last, and in short time, I spide,
Under a rocke, where she alas, opprest,
  Fell to the ground, and there untimely dide.
Cruell death vanquishing so noble beautie
Oft makes me wayle so hard a destenie.

II

After, at sea a tall ship did appeare,
  Made all of heben and white yvorie;
The sailes of golde, of silke the tackle were:
  Milde was the winde, calme seem'd the sea to bee.
The skie eachwhere did show full bright and faire
  With rich treasures this gay ship fraighted was:
But sudden storme did so turmoyle the aire,
  And tumbled up the sea, that she (alas)
Strake on a rock, that under water lay,
  And perished past all recoverie.
O! how great ruth, and sorrowfull assay,
  Doth vex my spirite with perplexitie,
Thus in a moment to see lost, and drown'd,
So great riches, as like cannot be found.

In un boschetto novo, i rami santi
fiorian d' un lauro giovenetto e schietto,
ch' un delli arbor' parea di paradiso,
e di sua ombra uscían sí dolci canti
di vari augelli e tant' altro diletto,
che dal mondo m' avean tutto diviso;
e mirandol io fiso,
cangiossi 'l cielo intorno, e tinto in vista
folgorando 'l percosse, e da radice
quella pianta felice
subito svelse: onde mia vita è trista,
ché simile ombra mai non si racquista.

Chiara fontana in quel medesmo bosco
sorgea d' un sasso, ed acque fresche e dolci
spargea, soavemente mormorando;
al bel seggio, riposto, ombroso e fosco,
né pastori appressavan né bifolci,
ma ninfe e muse, a quel tenor cantando;
ivi m' assisi, e quando
più dolcezza prendea di tal concento
e di tal vista, aprir vidi uno speco,
e portarsene seco
la fonte e 'l loco: ond' ancor doglia sento
e sol de la memoria mi sgomento.

Una strania fenice, ambedue l' ale
di porpora vestita, e 'l capo d' oro,
vedendo per la selva, altera e sola,
veder forma celeste ed immortale
prima pensai, fin ch' a lo svelto alloro
giunse ed al fonte che la terra invola.

III

The heavenly branches did I see arise
  Out of the fresh and lustie lawrell tree,
Amidst the young greene wood of paradise;
  Some noble plant I thought my selfe to see:
Such store of birds therein yshrowded were,
  Chaunting in shade their sundrie melodie,
That with their sweetnes I was ravisht nere.
  While on this lawrell fixed was mine eie.
The skie gan everie where to overcast,
  And darkened was the welkin all about,
When sudden flash of heavens fire out brast,
  And rent this royall tree quite by the roote;
Which makes me much and ever to complaine;
For no such shadow shal be had againe.

IV

Within this wood, out of a rocke did rise
  A spring of water, mildly rumbling downe,
Whereto approched not in anie wise
  The homely shepheard, nor the ruder clown;
But manie muses, and the nymphes withall,
  That sweetly in accord did tune their voyce
To the soft sounding of the waters fall;
  That my glad heart thereat did much rejoyce.
But, while herein I tooke my chiefe delight,
  I saw (alas) the gaping earth devoure
The spring, the place, and all cleane out of sight;
  Which yet aggreeves my hart even to this houre,
And wounds my soule with rufull memorie,
To see such pleasures go so suddenly.

V

I saw a phoenix in the wood alone,
  With purple wings, and crest of golden hewe;
Strange bird he was, whereby I thought anone,
  That of some heavenly wight I have the vewe;
Untill he came unto the broken tree,
  And to the spring, that late devoured was.
What say I more? each thing at last we see

Ogni cosa al fin vola:
ché, mirando le frondi a terra sparse
e 'l troncon rotto e quel vivo umor secco,
volse in sé stessa il becco
quasi sdegnando, e 'n un punto disparse:
onde 'l cor di pietate e d' amor m'arse.

Alfin vid' io per entro i fiori e l'erba
pensosa ir sí leggiadra e bella Donna,
che mai no 'l penso ch' i' non arda e treme:
umile in sé, ma 'ncontra Amor superba;
ed avea in dosso sí candida gonna,
sí testa ch' or e neve parea inseme,
ma le parti supreme
eran avolte d' una nebbia oscura;
punta poi nel tallon d'un picciol angue,
come fior colto langue,
lieta si dipartío, nonché secura.
Ai, nulla, altro che pianto, al mondo dura!

Canzon, tu puoi ben dire:
Queste sei visioni al signor mio
àn fatto un dolce di morir desio.

Doth passe away: the phoenix there alas,
Spying the tree destroid, the water dride,
   Himselfe smote with his beake, as in disdain,
And so foorthwith in great despight he dide;
   That yet my heart burnes, in exceeding paine,
For ruth and pitie of so hapless plight:
O! let mine eyes no more see such a sight.

VI

At last so faire a ladie did I spie,
   That thinking yet on her I burne and quake;
On hearbs and flowres she walked pensively,
   Milde, but yet love she proudly did forsake:
White seem'd her robes, yet woven so they were,
   As snow and golde together had been wrought:
Above the wast a darke clowde shrouded her,
   A stinging serpent by the heele her caught;
Wherewith she languisht as the gathered floure;
   And, well assur'd, she mounted up to ioy.
Alas, on earth so nothing doth endure,
   But bitter griefe and sorrowfull annoy:
Which makes their life wretched and miserable,
Tossed with stormes of fortune variable.

VII

When I beheld this fickle trustles state
   Of vaine worlds glorie, flitting too and fro,
And mortall men tossed by troublous fate
   In restles seas of wretchedness and woe;
I wish I might this wearie life forgoe,
   And shortly turne unto my happie rest,
Where my free spirite might not anie moe
   Be vext with sights, that doo her peace molest.
And ye, faire ladie, in whose bounteous brest
   All heavenly grace and vertue shrined is,
When ye these rythmes doo read, and vew the rest,
   Loath this base world, and thinke of heavens blis:
And though ye be the fairest of Gods creatures,
Yet thinke, that Death shall spoyle your godly features.

(EDMUND SPENSER)

FRANCESCO PETRARCA

❧

SONETTO
OR CHE 'L CIEL A LA TERRA
E 'L VENTO TACE

CLXIV

Or che ' l ciel e la terra e 'l vento tace,
e le fere e gli augelli il sonno affrena,
notte il carro stellato in giro mena
e nel suo letto il mar senz' onda giace,

vegghio, penso, ardo, piango, e chi mi sface
sempre m' è inanzi per mia dolce pena:
guerra è 'l mio stato, d' ira e di duol piena,
e sol di lei pensando ò qualche pace.

Cosí sol d'una chiara fonte viva
move 'l dolce e l'amaro ond' io mi pasco;
una man sola mi risana e punge;

e perché 'l mio martir non giunga a riva,
mille volte il dí moro e mille nasco:
tanto da la salute mia son lunge.

FRANCESCO PETRARCH

SONNET:
ALAS SO ALL THINGES
NOWE DOE HOLD THEIR PEACE

Alas so all thinges nowe doe holde their peace.
Heaven and earth disturbed in nothing:
The beastes, the ayer, the birdes their song doe cease:
The nightes chare the starres aboute dothe bring:
Calme is the Sea, the waves worke lesse and lesse:
So am not I, whom love alas doth wring,
Bringing before my face the great encrease
Of my desires, whereat I wepe and syng
In joye and wo as in a doubtful ease.
For my swete thoughtes sometyme doe pleasure bring:
But by and by the cause of my disease
Geves me a pang, that inwardly dothe sting,
When that I thinke what griefe it is againe,
To live and lacke the thing should ridde my paine.

(HENRY HOWARD, EARL OF SURREY)

FRANCESCO PETRARCA

SONETTO
AMOR, CHE NEL PENSER
MIO VIVE E REGNA

Amor, che nel penser mio vive e regna
e 'l suo seggio maggior nel mio cor tene,
talor armato ne la fronte vene;
ivi si loca et ivi pon sua insegna.

Quella ch'amare e sofferir ne 'nsegna,
e vol che 'l gran desio, l'accesa spene,
ragion, vergogna e reverenza affrene,
di nostro ardir fra se stessa si sdegna.

Onde Amor paventoso fugge al core,
lasciando ogni sua impresa, e piange e trema;
ivi s' asconde e non appar più fore.

Che poss' io far, temendo il mio signore,
se non star seco infin a l' ora estrema?
ché bel fin fa chi ben amando more.

FRANCESCO PETRARCH

SONNET
COMPLAINT OF A LOVER REBUKED

Love, that liveth, and raigneth in my thought,
That built his seat within my captive brest,
Clad in the armes, wherin with me he fought,
Oft in my face he doth his banner rest.
She, that me taught to love, and suffer payne,
My doutfull hope, and eke my hot desire,
With shamefast cloke to shadow and restraine,
Her smiling grace converteth straight to yre.
And coward love then to the hart apace
Taketh his flight, wheras he lurkes and plaines
His purpose lost, and dare not shew his face.
For my lordes gilt thus faultlesse bide I paines,
Yet from my lorde shall not my foote remove.
Swete is his death, that takes his end by love.

(HENRY HOWARD, EARL OF SURREY)

FRANCESCO PETRARCA

❦

SONETTO
NON DA L'ISPANO IBERO
A L'INDO IDASPE

Non da l' ispano Ibero a l' indo Idaspe
ricercando del mar ogni pendice,
né dal lito vermiglio a l'onde caspe,
né 'n ciel né 'n terra è piú d' una fenice.

Qual destro corvo o qual manca cornice
canti 'l mio fato, o qual Parca l' innaspe?
ché sol trovo Pietà sorda com'aspe,
misero, onde sperava esser felice!

Ch' i' non vo' dir di lei; ma chi la scorge,
tutto 'l cor di dolcezza e d' amor gl' empie:
tanto n' à seco, e tant' altrui ne porge;

e, per far mie dolcezze amare ed empie,
o s' infinge o non cura o non s' accorge
del fiorir queste inanzi tempo tempie.

FRANCESCO PETRARCH

SONNET
THE SOOTE SEASON
THAT BUD AND BLOME FURTH BRINGES

The soote season, that bud and blome furth bringes,
With grene hath clad the hill and eke the vale;
The nightingale with fethers new she singes;
The turtle to her make hath tolde her tale.
Somer is come, for every spray nowe springes;
The hart hath hong his olde hed on the pale;
The buck in brake his winter cote he flings;
The fishes flote with newe repaired scale;
The adder all her sloughe awaye she slinges;
The swift swalow pursueth the flyes smale;
The busy bee her honye now she minges.
Winter is worne, that was the flowers bale.
And thus I see among these pleasant thinges
Eche care decayes, and yet my sorrow springes.

(HENRY HOWARD, EARL OF SURREY)

153

FRANCESCO PETRARCA

SONETTO
PACE NON TROVO,
E NON HO DA FAR GUERRA

Pace non trovo, e non ho da far guerra;
   E temo, e spero; et ardo, e son un ghiaccio;
   E volo sopra 'l cielo, e giaccio in terra;
   E nulla stringo, e tutto 'l mondo abbraccio.
Tal m' ha in pregion, che non m' apre nè serra,
   Nè per suo mi riten nè scioglie il laccio;
   E non m' ancide Amore, e non mi sferra,
   Nè mi vuol vivo nè mi trae d' impaccio.
Veggio senza occhi, e non ho lingua, e grido;
   E bramo di perir, e cheggio aita;
   Et ho in odio me stesso, et amo altrui.
Pascomi di dolor, piangendo rido;
   Egualmente mi spiace morte e vita:
   In questo stato son, donna, per vui.

MADRIGALE 52

Non al suo amante più Diana piacque,
Quando per tal ventura tutto ignuda
La vide in mezzo de le gelide acque,
Ch' a me la pastorella alpestra e cruda
Posta a bagnar un leggiadretto velo,
Ch' a l' aura il vago e biondo capel chiuda,
Tal che mi fece, or quand' egli arde 'l cielo,
Tutto tremar d'un amoroso gielo.

FRANCESCO PETRARCH

SONNET
I FIND NO PEACE
AND BEAR NO ARMS FOR WAR

I find no peace and bear no arms for war,
  I fear, I hope; I burn yet shake with chill;
  I fly the Heavens, huddle to earth's floor,
  Embrace the world yet all I grasp is nil.
Love will not close nor shut my prison's door
  Nor claim me his nor leave me to my will;
  He slays me not yet holds me evermore;
  Would have me lifeless yet bound to my ill.
Eyeless I see and tongueless I protest,
  And long to perish while I succor seek;
  Myself I hate and would another woo.
I feed on grief, I laugh with sob-racked breast,
  And death and life alike to me are bleak:
  My lady, thus I am because of you.

(T. G. BERGIN)

MADRIGAL 52

Diana, naked in the shadowy pool,
Brought no more rapture to the greedy eyes
Of him who watched her splashing in the cool
Than did my glimpse of a maiden unaware
Washing a snood, the gossamer garment of
My lady's wild and lovely golden hair;
Wherefore, although the sky burn hot above,
I shake and shiver with a chill of love.

(MORRIS BISHOP)

FRANCESCO PETRARCA

❧

SONETTO
LIETI FIORI E FELICI E BEN NATE ERBE

Lieti fiori e felici e ben nate erbe
Che Madonna pensando premer sòle;
Piaggia ch'ascolti sue dolci parole,
E del bel piede alcun vestigio serbe;

Schietti arboscelli e verdi frondi acerbe;
Amorosette e pallide vïole;
Ombrose selve, ove percote il sole
Che vi fa co' suoi raggi alte e superbe;

O soave contrada, o puro fiume
Che bagni il suo bel viso e gli occhi chiari
E prendi qualità dal vivo lume:

Quanto v'invidio gli atti onesti e cari!
Non fia in voi scoglio omai che per costume
D'arder co la mia fiamma non impari.

MADRIGALE 121
OR VEDI, AMOR,
CHE GIOVENETTA DONNA

Or vedi, Amor, che giovenetta donna
tuo regno sprezza e del mio mal non cura,
e tra duo ta' nemici è sí secura.

Tu se' armato, ed ella in treccie e 'n gonna
si siede e scalza in mezzo i fiori e l'erba,
ver me spietata e 'ncontr' a te superba.

I' son pregion; ma se pietà ancor serba
l'arco tuo saldo e qualcuna saetta,
fa di te e di me, Signor, vendetta.

FRANCESCO PETRARCH

❦

SONNET
WHEN SHE WALKS BY HERE

When she walks by here
The grass bends down, the gentle flowers.
The mark of her foot remains in the damp ground beside water.

You have known her, the slenderness of trees,
Young green branches: making a shadowy wood
The sun breaks with its narrow shafts of gold smoke.

River, that has become her face, takes fire
Looking at me; fire from the sun has washed her.

The stones themselves are burning in my shadow.

(NICHOLAS KILMER)

MADRIGAL 121

Now Love, see how this lady, young and fair,
disdains your might, and grants my ills no cure;
with two such foes, so heedless and secure.
    You travel armed, while she, with braided hair,
goes roaming barefoot through the fields in flower,
so cold to me, so scornful of your power.
    A prisoner now, I wait upon the hour
when you, my lord, with one unfailing dart
avenge at last your honor and my heart.

(MARION SHORE)

GIOVANNI BOCCACCIO

1313–1375

SONETTO
VETRO SON FATTI I FIUMI

Vetro son fatti i fiumi, ed i ruscelli
gli serra di fuor ora la freddura;
vestiti son i monti e la pianura
di bianca neve e nudi gli arbuscelli,
l'erbette morte, e non cantan gli uccelli
per la stagion contraria a lor natura;
borea soffia, ed ogni creatura
sta chiusa per lo freddo ne' sua ostelli.

Ed io, dolente, solo ardo ed incendo
in tanto foco, che quel di Vulcano
a rispetto non è una favilla;

e giorno e notte chiero, a giunta mano,
alquanto d'acqua il mio signor, piangendo,
nè ne posso impetrar sol una stilla.

GIOVANNI BOCCACCIO

SONNET
RIVERS HAVE TURNED TO GLASS

Rivers have turned to glass, and brooks, because
Of the fierce cold, are locked in from without;
Mountains and plains are hooded all in white
Snow, barren the underbrush, young trees,
The grass is dead; not a bird sings or caws
During a season gone against their nature;
The north wind blows, and each and every creature,
To escape the chill, stays shut within his house.

I alone, grieving, take fire and burn
With so intense a flame that even Vulcan,
Compared to me, produced merely a spark;

Hands joined together, day and night I turn
To my lord begging for water, only to learn,
Weeping, I cannot obtain a single drop.

(BARBARA HOWES)

GIOVANNI BOCCACCIO

❦

SONETTO
OR SEI SALITO, CARO SIGNOR MIO

Or sei salito, caro signor mio,
   Nel regno al qual salir ancor aspetta
   Ogn' anima da Dio a quello eletta,
   Nel suo partir di questo mondo rio;
Or sei colà, dove spesso il desio
   Ti tirò già per veder Lauretta;
   Or sei dove la mia bella Fiammetta
   Siede con lei nel cospetto di Dio.
Or con Sennuccio, e con Cino, e con Dante
   Vivi sicuro d' eterno riposo,
   Mirando cose da noi non intese.
Deh! s' a grado ti fui nel mondo errante,
   Tirami dietro a te, dove gioioso
   Veggia colei che pria d' amor m' accese.

GIOVANNI BOCCACCIO

SONNET
TO THAT FAIR KINGDOM,
O MY GENTLE LORD

To that fair kingdom, o my gentle lord,
  Whither all souls aspire in God's grace,
  Leaving behind this sinful world and base
  You have ascended and have your reward
(Which here you oft and ardently implored)
  And may look now upon your Laura's face,
  There my Fiammetta also has her place
  In His sight Whom the angels have adored.
Sennuccio, Cino, Dante—these for aye
  Are of your company, and in peace untold
  You penetrate to depths we may not chart.
If in this erring world you loved me, pray
  Raise me up with you where I may behold
  Her who first kindled love within my heart.

(T. G. BERGIN)

GIOVANNI BOCCACCIO

da *IL NINFALE FIESOLANO*

Ed avvisossi di prima lasciarle
tutte spogliar, e poi egli spogliarsi,
acciò che le lor armi adoperarle
contra lui non potessono; ed a trarsi
cominciò lento il vestir, per poi farle,
quando nell'acqua entrasse per bagnarsi,
per vergogna fuggir pe' boschi via:
e Mensola per forza riterria.

E 'nnanzi che spogliato tutto fosse,
le ninfe eran nell'acqua tutte quante;
e poi spogliato verso lor si mosse,
mostrando tutto ciò ch'avea davante.
Ciascuna delle ninfe si riscosse,
e, con boce paurosa e tremante,
cominciarono urlando: "Oh me, oh me,
or non vedete voi chi costui è?"

Non altrimenti lo lupo affamato
percuote alla gran turba degli agnelli,
ed un ne piglia, e quel se n'ha portato,
lasciando tutti gli altri tapinelli:
ciascun belando fugge spaventato,
pur procacciando di campar le pelli;
così correndo Africo per quell'acque,
sola prese colei che più gli piacque.

162

GIOVANNI BOCCACCIO

THE RAPE OF MENSOLA
(from *Nymphs of Fiesole*)

He deemed it best to let them all disrobe
before he, too, decided to undress:
this way they would not wield their darts against
   him.
Slowly, he started stripping off his dress,
thinking that, once he stepped into the pool
to bathe like them, they all would scatter fast,
in terror and in shame, while, brave and bold,
Mensola he at last would seize and hold.

Slowly he was disrobing, very slowly,
while now the nymphs were splashing in the waves.
All naked, suddenly he turned to them,
thus baring everything he had in front.
Suddenly startled, all the nymphs at once
uttered a sigh of helplessness and fear.
"Good heavens! Oh, good heavens!" they began
to scream, most frantic. "She's a man—a man!"

The same thing happens when a hungry wolf
suddenly breaks into a flock of lambs:
he seizes one of them and steals away,
leaving the others fleeing and afraid:
bleating and bleating in confusion, lost,
the little creatures try to save their lives;
thus Africo, now running through those waters,
grabbed the one nymph he liked more than the
   others.

E tutte l'altre ninfe molto in fretta
uscir dell'acqua, a' lor vestir correndo;
né però niuna fu, che lì sel metta,
ma coperte con essi, via fuggendo,
ché punto l'una l'altra non aspetta,
né mai indietro si givan volgendo;
ma chi qua e chi là si dileguoe,
e ciascuna le sue armi lascioe.

Africo tenea stretta con braccia
Mensola sua nell'acqua, che piangea,
e baciandole la vergine faccia,
cota' parole verso lei dicea:
"O dolce la mia vita, non ti spiaccia
se io t'ho presa, ché Venere iddea
me t'ha promessa, cuor del corpo mio;
deh, più non pianger, per l'amor di Dio!"

Mensola le parole non intende,
ch'Africo le dicea, ma quanto puote,
con quella forza ch'ell'ha si difende,
e fortemente in qua e 'n là si scuote
dalle braccia di colui che l'offende,
bagnandosi di lagrime le gote;
ma nulla le valea forza o difesa,
ch'Africo la tenea pur forte presa.

Per la contesa che facean, si desta
tal, che prima dormia malinconoso,
e, con superbia rizzando la cresta,
cominciò a picchiar l'uscio, furioso;
e tanto dentro vi diè della testa,
ch'egli entrò dentro, non già con riposo,
ma con battaglia grande ed urlamento,
e forse che di sangue spargimento.

Dismayed, the others from the water sped,
frantically looking for their scattered gowns;
but none of them was given time to dress.
Shielding as best they could their nakedness,
and with no thought of waiting for each other,
they fled and fled, and never turned to look:
some went this way and some the other way,
and on the bank all of their weapons lay.

But in the water Africo was clasping
Mensola in his arms, despite her tears.
With kisses, kisses on her virgin face
he kept repeating such sweet words to her,
"Life of my life, my darling, do not cry
if I have seized you. Goddess Venus herself
has promised you to me, my life, my love:
oh, weep no more, for all the gods above!"

Mensola did not listen to his plea,
but with her strength, with all her strength she
    fought
to free herself and run from his embrace:
now this way and now that, most violently
she shook, in vain, in his relentless arms
while tears of wrath, not love, streamed down her
    cheeks.
But futile was her fight, for Africo,
holding her in his grip, did not let go.

Throughout this lively struggle in the pool,
someone who until now had sadly slept
lifted his head with soon-awakened pride,
and started knocking, wrathful, on the door.
With such a rage he pushed his head inside
that not with peace he entered but with war:
indeed, a roaring battle, fierce and loud,
with even, perhaps, the shedding of some blood.

Ma poi che messer Mazzone ebbe avuto
Monteficalli, e nel castello entrato,
fu lietamente dentro ricevuto
da que' che prima l'avean contrastato;
ma poi che molto si fu dibattuto,
per la terra lasciare in buono stato,
per pietà lagrimò, e del castello
uscì poi fuor, umil più ch'un agnello.

Poi che Mensola vide esserle tolta
la sua verginità contro a sua voglia,
forte piangendo ad Africo fu volta
e disse: "Poi c'hai fatto la tua voglia
ed hai 'ngannata me, fanciulla stolta,
usciàn dell'acqua almen, ch'i' muo' di doglia.
però ch'i' vo' del mondo far partita,
togliendomi. con le mie man, la vita".

But when at last Sir Stock had won Black Hill
and stepped into the castle joyously,
the foe that had resisted his advance
welcomed and greeted him with great content.
Finally, having labored long and hard
to leave the conquered post in perfect peace,
he shed a pitying tear, and left the castle
meek as a lamb, and wholly dumb and docile.

Mensola, seeing that her maidenhood
had now against her will been snatched away,
turning to Africo with bitter tears,
said, "Now that you've fulfilled your every wish,
deceiving thus a foolish girl like me,
let us at least get off the stream: my grief
is such that to this world I'll say goodbye:
right now, of my own hand I want to die."

(JOSEPH TUSIANI)

GIOVANNI BOCCACCIO

❧

SONETTO
INTORN' AD UNA FONTE, IN UN PRATELLO

Intorn' ad una fonte, in un pratello
di verdi erbette pieno e di bei fiori,
sedean tre angiolette, i loro amori
forse narrando, ed a ciascuna 'l bello
viso adombrava un verde ramicello
ch'i capei d'or cingea, al qual di fuori
e dentro insieme i dua vaghi colori
avvolgeva un suave venticello.

    E dopo alquanto l'una alle due disse
(com'io udi'):—Deh, se per avventura
di ciascuna l'amante or qui venisse,
fuggiremo noi quinci per paura?—
A cui le due risposer:—Chi fuggisse,
poco savia saria, con tal ventura!

GIOVANNI BOCCACCIO

SONNET
OF THREE GIRLS AND OF THEIR TALK

By a clear well, within a little field
  Full of green grass and flowers of every hue,
  Sat three young girls, relating (as I knew)
Their loves. And each had twined a bough to shield
Her lovely face; and the green leaves did yield
  The golden hair their shadow; while the two
  Sweet colours mingled, both blown lightly through
With a soft wind for ever stirred and still'd.
After a little while one of them said,
  (I heard her,) "Think! If, ere the next hour struck,
  Each of our lovers should come here to-day,
Think you that we should fly or feel afraid?"
  To whom the others answered, "From such luck
  A girl would be a fool to run away."

(D. G. ROSSETTI)

ANONIMO
Secolo XIV

ꝭ

PIACESSE A DIO CHE E'
NON FOSSI MAI NATA

Piacesse a Dio che e' non fossi mai nata!
   O lassa dolorosa,
   Fresca son più che rosa,
   E veggome in un vecchio maritata!

Oi me dolente! son vaga e gioconda
   E d' Amor sento sua dolce saetta,
   Guardandomi nel specchio bianca e bionda
   Me veggo tutta quanta amorosetta,
   Ond' io prego Jesù che gran vendetta
   Faccia a queí che marito
   Me diè, che è già fiorito
   E la sua barba bianca è diventata.

Piacesse a Dio che e' non fossi mai nata!
   Mei mi sarebbe ancora essere in casa,
   Parvola poveretta como m' era,
   Ch' a esser così d'ogni allegrezza rasa,
   Chè mai veder non posso primavera!
   Piacesse a Dio che e' non fossi mai nata!

ANONYMOUS
Fourteenth Century

૮

WOULD IT HAD PLEASED THE LORD
THAT I NEVER WAS BORN

Would it had pleased the Lord that I never was born!
O wretched, dolorous,
Fresh am I more than a rose,
And here I'm married to an old man, forlorn!

Ah, grief is mine! I'm lively, without a care,
I feel Love's tender arrow whizz my way.
Seeing myself in the mirror blonde and fair,
I look on a lovable girl;
And I pray that Jesus may hurl
His wrath upon those who gave me
My husband; he's old as can be,
And his beard is white and worn.

Would it had pleased the Lord that I never was born!
I might have stayed home alone,
Poor little girl I was then,
Than to live deprived of every joy that's known,
For I'll never be able to see the Springtime again!
Would it had pleased the Lord that I never was born!

(L. R. LIND)

LUIGI PULCI
1432-1484

❦

MORGANTE E I CINGHIALI

Ecco apparir una gran gregge, al passo,
Di porci, e vanno con molta tempesta,
Ed arrivorno alla fontana appunto,
Donde il gigante è da lor sopraggiunto.

Morgante alla ventura a un saetta:
Appunto nell'orecchio lo 'ncartava;
Dall'altro lato passò la verretta,
Onde 'l cinghial giù morto gambettava;
Un altro, quasi per farne vendetta,
Addosso al gran gigante irato andava;
E perchè e' giunse troppo tosto al varco,
Non fu Morgante a tempo a trar coll'arco.

Vedendosi venuto il porco addosso,
Gli dette in sulla testa un gran punzone,
Per modo che gl' infranse insino all'osso,
E morto allato a quell'altro lo pone;
Gli altri porci, veggendo quel percosso
Si misson tutti in fuga pel vallone;
Morgante si levò il tinello in collo
Ch'era pien d'acqua, e non si muove un crollo . . .

Orlando, che 'l vedea tornar sì tosto
Co' porci morti e con quel vaso pieno,
Maravigliossi che sia tanto forte;
Così l'abate; e spalancan le porte.

LUIGI PULCI

MORGANTE AND THE BOARS

And lo! a monstrous herd of swine appears
And onward rushes with tempestuous tread,
And to the fountain's brink precisely pours;
So that the Giant's joined by all the boars.

Morgante at a venture shot an arrow,
Which pierced a pig precisely in the ear,
And passed unto the other side quite through;
So that the boar, defunct, lay tripped up near.
Another, to revenge his fellow farrow,
Against the Giant rushed in fierce career,
And reached the passage with so swift a foot,
Morgante was not now in time to shoot.

Perceiving that the pig was on him close,
He gave him such a punch upon the head,
As floored him so that he no more arose,
Smashing the very bone; and he fell dead
Next to the other. Having seen such blows,
The other pigs along the valley fled;
Morgante on his neck the bucket took,
Full from the spring, which neither swerved nor shook . . .

Orlando, seeing him so soon appear
With the dead boars, and with that brimful vase,
Marvelled to see his strength so very great;
So did the abbot, and set wide the gate.

(LORD BYRON)

MATTEO MARIA BOIARDO

1441-1494

❦

SONETTO
FIOR SCOLORITI E PALIDE VIOLE

Fior scoloriti e palide viole,
   Che sì suavemente il vento move,
   Vostra Madonna dove è gita? e dove
   È gito il sol che aluminar vi sòle?
Nostra Madonna se ne gì col sole,
   Che ognor ce apriva di belleze nove,
   E, poichè tanto bene è gito altrove,
   Mostramo aperto quanto ce ne dole.
Fior sfortunati e viole infelici,
   Abandonati dal divino ardore,
   Che vi infondeva vista sì serena!
Tu dici il vero: e nui ne le radici
   Sentiamo il danno; e tu senti nel core
   La perdita che nosco al fin ti mena.

MATTEO MARIA BOIARDO

SONNET
POOR DROOPING FLOWERS
AND PALLID VIOLETS

Poor drooping flowers and pallid violets
  On whom the gentle breezes softly play—
  Say where your Mistress is, and, flowers, say
  Where is the Sun that warmed your flowerets.
Our Mistress' presence to the Sun submits
  Which each hour decked us out in new array;
  Now that such loveliness has past away
  Opening we show how grief our station fits.
O flowers misfortunate and violets forlorn
  Abandoned by the Sun-God's wondrous art
  That kindled colors of so lovely blend!
You speak the truth. We too great harm have borne;
  Feel in our roots as you feel in your heart
  The loss that leads you with us to our end.

(PETER RUSSELL)

LORENZO DE' MEDICI
1449–1492

TRIONFO DI BACCO ED ARIANNA

Quant' è bella giovinezza
che si fugge tuttavia!
chi vuol esser lieto, sia:
di doman non c' è certezza.
Quest' è Bacco e Arianna,
belli, e l' un dell' altro ardenti;
perchè 'l tempo fugge e 'nganna,
sempre insieme stan contenti.
Queste ninfe e altre genti
sono allegre tuttavia:
chi vuol esser lieto, sia:
di doman non c' è certezza.
Questi lieti satiretti
delle ninfe innamorati,
per caverne e per boschetti
han lor posto cento aguati:
or, da Bacco riscaldati,
ballan, saltan tuttavia;
chi vuol esser lieto, sia:
di doman non c' è certezza.
Queste ninfe hanno ancor caro
da loro essere ingannate:
non puon far a Amor riparo
se non genti rozze e 'ngrate:
ora insieme mescolate
fanno festa tuttavia:

LORENZO DE' MEDICI

TRIUMPH OF BACCHUS AND ARIADNE

Youth is sweet and well
But doth speed away!
Let who will be gay,
To-morrow, none can tell.
  Bacchus and his Fair,
Contented with their fate,
Chase both time and care,
Loving soon and late;
High and low estate
With the nymphs at play;
Let who will be gay,
To-morrow, none can tell.
  Laughing satyrs all
Set a hundred snares,
Lovelorn dryads fall
In them unawares:
Glad with wine, in pairs
They dance the hours away:
Let who will be gay,
To-morrow, none can tell.
  Not unwillingly
Were these nymphs deceived:
From Love do but flee
Graceless hearts aggrieved:
Deceivers and deceived
Together wend their way.

chi vuol esser lieto, sia:
di doman non c' è certezza.
    Questa soma, che vien dreto
sopra l' asino, è Sileno:
così vecchio è ebbro e lieto,
già di carne e d' anni pieno:
se non può star ritto, almeno
ride e gode tuttavia:
chi vuol esser lieto, sia:
di doman non c' è certezza.
    Mida vien dopo costoro:
ciò che tocca, oro diventa:
e che giova aver tesoro,
poichè l' uom non si contenta?
che dolcezza vuoi che senta
chi ha sete tuttavia?
chi vuol esser lieto, sia:
di doman non c' è certezza.
    Ciascun apra ben gli orecchi,
di doman nessun si paschi;
oggi siam, giovani e vecchi,
lieti ognun, femmine e maschi;
ogni tristo pensier caschi;
facciam festa tuttavia:
chi vuol esser lieto, sia:
di doman non c' è certezza.
    Donne e giovanetti amanti,
viva Bacco e viva Amore!
ciascun suoni, balli e canti!
arda di dolcezza il core!
non fatica, non dolore!
quel c' ha esser, convien sia:
chi vuol esser lieto, sia:
di doman non c' è certezza.
    Quant' è bella giovinezza
che si fugge tuttavia.

Let who will be gay,
To-morrow, none can tell.
  Fat Silenus nears
On an ass astride:
Full of wine and years,
Come and see him ride:
He lolls from side to side
But gleefully alway:
Let who will be gay,
To-morrow, none can tell.
  Midas following,
Turneth all to gold:
What can treasure bring
To a heart that's cold?
And what joy unfold
For who thirsteth, pray?
Let who will be gay,
To-morrow, none can tell.
  Ears be very bold,
Count not on to-morrow:
Let both young and old,
Lads and lassies, borrow
Joy and banish sorrow,
Doleful thoughts and grey:
Let who will be gay,
To-morrow, none can tell.
  Lads and lassies all,
Love and Bacchus hail!
Dance and song befall!
Pain and sadness fail!
Tender hearts prevail,
Happen then what may!
Let who will be gay,
To-morrow, none can tell.
  Youth is sweet and well
But doth speed away.

(LORNA DE' LUCCHI)

LORENZO DE' MEDICI

LASCIA L'ISOLA TUA TANTO DILETTA

Lascia l' isola tua tanto diletta,
lascia il tuo regno delicato e bello,
Ciprigna dea, e vien sopra il ruscello
che bagna la minuta e verde erbetta.
Vieni a quest' ombra ed alla dolce auretta
che fa mormoreggiar ogni arbuscello,
a' canti dolci d' amoroso augello;
questa da te per patria sia eletta.
   E se tu vien tra queste chiare linfe,
sia teco il tuo amato e caro figlio;
chè qui non si conosce il suo valore.
Togli a Diana le sue caste ninfe,
che sciolte or vanno e senz' alcun periglio,
poco prezzando la virtù d' Amore.

LORENZO DE' MEDICI

❦

LEAVE, CYTHEREA,
YOUR ENCHANTED ISLE

Leave, Cytherea, your enchanted isle,
Remote, green-shaded is that Paradise:
Its crisp-cool waters, its rain-jeweled showers,
Its fountains rising to the ravished eyes. . . .
Rest, white-limbed Goddess, while the magic waters
Multiply into fountains, sky-drawn springs,
Bathe in the rose-faint heavens while the clouds sail,
Move with the sun and hear the Sirens sing,
The fountains answer, and the streams prolong
That song of air, of water-wavering clouds.

Swan-guarded, close-locked world, O Cytherea,
Eternity at peace is mortal here,
Lured by the silver breath of purest song—
See how the love-lost seek your land and long
To claim the vistas of delight, they bring
The Sun-Seeker, he who leads them all,
Your laughing son, young Eros, winged and tall.

(MARYA ZATURENSKA)

ANGELO POLIZIANO
1454–1494

č

CANZONE A BALLO

I' mi trovai, fanciulle, un bel mattino
Di mezzo maggio, in un verde giardino.

Eran d'intorno violette e gigli
 Fra l'erba verde, e vaghi fior novelli
 Azurri gialli candidi e vermigli:
 Ond' io pòrsi la mano a côr di quelli
 Per adornar e' mie' biondi capelli
 E cinger di grillanda il vago crino.
 I' mi trovai, fanciulle, un bel mattino
 Di mezzo maggio, in un verde giardino.

Ma poi ch' i' ebbi pien di fiori un lembo,
 Vidi le rose e non pur d'un colore.
 Io corsi allor per empier tutto el grembo,
 Perch' era sì soave il loro odore
 Che tutto mi senti' destar el core
 Di dolce voglia e d'un piacer divino.
 I' mi trovai, fanciulle, un bel mattino
 Di mezzo maggio, in un verde giardino.

I' posi mente: quelle rose allora
 Mai non vi potre' dir quant' eran belle.
 Quale scoppiava dalla boccia ancora,
 Qual' erano un po' passe e qual novelle.

ANGELO POLIZIANO

DANCE SONG

I found myself, young girls, while it was May,
In a green garden, at the break of day.

Lillies and violets blossomed all around
On the green turf, and flowers new-sprung and fair—
Yellow, and blue, and red, and white—were found;
Then I reached out my hand to pluck them there,
To decorate with them my own brown hair,
And with a wreath confine its disarray.
   I found myself, young girls, while it was May,
   In a green garden, at the break of day.

But when I'd plucked a border-full of blossom,
I saw with various hues the roses bloom,
And so I ran to fill my lap and bosom,
So soft and fragrantly they breathed perfume;
For thence I felt a sweet desire consume
My heart, where heavenly pleasure made its way.
   I found myself, young girls, while it was May,
   In a green garden, at the break of day.

I pondered to myself, "Of all these roses,
How can I tell among them which are fairest,
Which of them lately now its bud discloses,
Which are still fresh, and which to fading nearest?"

Amor mi disse allor:—Va', cò di quelle
Che più vedi fiorite in sullo spino.—
I' mi trovai, fanciulle, un bel mattino
Di mezzo maggio, in un verde giardino.

Quando la rosa ogni suo' foglia spande,
　Quando è più bella, quando è più gradita,
　Allora è buona a mettere in ghirlande,
　Prima che sua bellezza sia fuggita:
　Sicchè, fanciulle, mentre è più fiorita,
　Coglian la bella rosa del giardino.
　I' mi trovai, fanciulle, un bel mattino
　Di mezzo maggio, in un verde giardino.

Then Love said, "Gather those which seem in rarest
And fullest blossom on the thorny spray—"
   I found myself, young girls, while it was May,
   In a green garden, at the break of day.

"When first the rose's petals are outspread,
Most lovely and most welcome it appears;
Then weave it in a garland for your head,
In time, before its beauty disappears:
Even so, young girls, while its pride still it wears,
Gather the rose that makes your garden gay."
   I found myself, young girls, while it was May,
   In a green garden, at the break of day.

(JOHN HEATH-STUBBS)

NICCOLÒ MACHIAVELLI
1469–1527

CANZONE

Chi giammai donna offende
a torto o a ragion, folle è se crede
trovar per prieghi o pianti in lei merzede.
Come la scende in questa mortal vita,
con l'alma insieme porta
superbia, sdegno e di perdono oblio:
inganno e crudeltà le sono scorta,
e tal le dànno aita
che d'ogni impresa appaga el suo desio;
e se sdegno aspro e rio
la muove o gelosia, adopra e vede;
e la sua forza, mortal forza eccede.

NICCOLÒ MACHIAVELLI

SONG

He who offends a woman,
Justly or no, in vain
Can hope by prayer or pleading
Her charity to gain.
At the birth of every woman,
Her soul brings in its train
Pride, deceit and hardness,
Cruelty and disdain.
With these to guide and help her
She wins in every fight;
And if she is inspired
By jealousy or spite
She plans and executes her will
With superhuman might.

(J. R. HALE)

NICCOLÒ MACHIAVELLI

L'OCCASIONE

Chi sei tu, che non par donna mortale,
   Di tanta grazia il ciel t'adorna e dota?
   Perchè non posi? e perchè a' piedi hai l'ale?—
"Io son l'Occasïon, a pochi nota;
   E la cagion che sempre mi travagli
   È perchè io tengo un piè sopra una ruota.
Volar non è ch'al mio correr s'agguagli;
   E però l'ale a' piedi mi mantengo,
   Acciò nel corso mio ciascuno abbagli.
Gli sparsi miei capei dinanzi io tengo;
   Con essi mi ricopro il petto e 'l volto,
   Perch' un non mi conosca quando io vengo.
Dietro dal capo ogni capel m'è tolto,
   Onde in van si affatica un, se gli avviene
   Ch'io l'abbia trapassato, o s'io mi volto."
"Dimmi: chi è colei che teco viene?"
   "È Penitenza; e però nota e intendi:
   Chi non sa prender me, costei ritiene.
E tu, mentre parlando il tempo spendi,
   Occupato da molti pensier vani,
   Già non t'avvedi, lasso, e non comprendi
Com' io ti son fuggita tra le mani!"

NICCOLÒ MACHIAVELLI

❦

OPPORTUNITY

"But who are thou, with curious beauty graced,
O woman, stamped with some bright heavenly seal?
Why go thy feet on wings, and in such haste?"

"I am that maid whose secret few may steal,
Called Opportunity. I hasten by
Because my feet are treading on a wheel,

"Being more swift to run than birds to fly.
And rightly on my feet my wings I wear,
To blind the sight of those who track and spy;

"Rightly in front I hold my scattered hair
To veil my face, and down my breast to fall,
Lest men should know my name when I am there;

"And leave behind my back no wisp at all
For eager folk to clutch, what time I glide
So near, and turn, and pass beyond recall."

"Tell me; who is that Figure at thy side?"
"Penitence. Mark this well that by degrees
Who lets me go must keep her for his bride.

"And thou hast spent much time in talk with me
Busied with thoughts and fancies vainly grand,
Nor hast remarked, O fool, neither dost see
How lightly I have fled beneath thy hand."

(JAMES ELROY FLECKER)

LODOVICO ARIOSTO
1474-1533

da *ORLANDO FURIOSO*
(Canto xxxiv)

Non stette il duca a ricercare il tutto;
che là non era asceso a quello effetto.
Da l'apostolo santo fu condutto
in un vallon fra due montagne istretto,
ove mirabilmente era ridutto
ciò che si perde o per nostro diffetto,
o per colpa di tempo o di Fortuna:
ciò che si perde qui, là si raguna.

Non pur di regni o di ricchezze parlo,
in che la ruota instabile lavora;
ma di quel ch'in poter di tor, di darlo
non ha Fortuna, intender voglio ancora.
Molta fama è là su, che come tarlo
il tempo al lungo andar qua giù divora:
là su infiniti prieghi e voti stanno,
che da noi peccatori a Dio si fanno.

Le lacrime e i sospiri degli amanti,
l'inutil tempo che si perde a giuoco,
e l'ozio lungo d'uomini ignoranti,
vani disegni che non han mai loco,
i vani desidèri sono tanti,
che la più parte ingombran di quel loco:
ciò che in somma qua giù perdesti mai,
là su salendo ritrovar potrai.

LODOVICO ARIOSTO

☙

ASTOLFO VISITS THE MOON
(Orlando Furioso, Canto xxxiv)

Twere infinit to tell what wondrous things
He saw that passed ours not few degrees.
What towns, what hills, what rivers, and what
    springs,
What dales, what pallaces, what goodly trees,
But to be short, at last his guide him brings
Unto a goodlie vallie where he sees
A mightsie masse of things straugnely confused,
Things that on earth were lost or were abused.

A store house straunge, that what on earth is lost
By fault, by time, by fortune, there is found,
And like a merchandize is there engrost
In straunger sort then I can well expound,
Nor speake I sole of wealth or things of cost
In which blind fortunes powre doth most abound,
But ev'n of things quite out of fortunes powre
Which wilfullie we wast each day and houre.

The precious time that fools mispend in play,
The vaine attempts that never take effect,
The vows that sinners make and never pay,
The counsells wise that carelesse men neglect,
The fond desires that lead us oft astray,
The prayses that with pride the heart infect,
And all we loose with follie and mispending
May there be found unto this place ascending.

Passando il paladin per quelle biche,
or di questo or di quel chiede alla guida.
Vide un monte di tumide vesiche,
che dentro parea aver tumulti e grida;
e seppe ch'eran le corone antiche
e degli Assirii e de la terra lida,
e de' Persi e de' Greci, che già furo
incliti, et or n'è quasi il nome oscuro.

Ami d'oro e d'argento appresso vede
in una massa, ch'erano quei doni
che si fan con speranza di mercede
ai re, agli avari principi, ai patroni.
Vede in ghirlande ascosi lacci; e chiede,
et ode che son tutte adulazioni.
Di cicale scoppiate imagine hanno
versi ch'in laude dei signor si fanno.

Di nodi d'oro e gemmati ceppi
vede c'han forma i mal seguiti amori.
V'eran d'aquile artigli; e che fur, seppi,
l'autorità ch'ai suoi danno i signori.
I mantici ch'intorno han pieni i greppi,
sono i fumi dei principi e i favori
che danno un tempo ai ganimedi suoi,
che se ne van col fior degli anni poi.

Ruine di cittadi e di castella
stavan con gran tesor quivi sozzopra.
Domanda, e sa che son trattati, e quella
congiura che sì mal par che si cuopra.
Vide serpi con faccia di donzella,
di monetieri e di ladroni l'opra:
poi vide boccie rotte di più sorti,
ch'era il servir de le misere corti.

Now as *Astolfo* by those regions past
He asked many questions of his guide
And as he on t'one side his eye did cast,
A wondrous hill of bladders he espyde,
And he was told they had been in time past
The pompous crowns and scepters full of pride
Of monarks of Assiria and of Greece
Of which now scantlie their is left a peece.

He saw great store of baited hookes with gold,
And those were gifts that foolish men prepard
To give to Princes covetous and old
With fondest hope of future vaine reward.
Then were there ropes all in sweet garlands rold,
And those were all false flatteries he hard.
Then heard he crickets songs like to the verses
The servant in his masters prayses reherses.

There did he fond loves that men pursew
To looke like golden gives with stones all set;
Then things like Eagles talents he did vew,
Those offices that favorites do get;
Then saw he bellows large that much winde
    blew,
Large promises that Lords make and forget
Unto their Ganimeds in flowre of youth
But after nought but beggerie insewth.

He saw great Cities seated in fayre places
That overthrown quite topsie turvie stood;
He askt and learnd the cause of their defaces
Was treason that doth never turne to good.
He saw fowle serpents with fayre womens faces,
Of coyners and of thieves the cursed brood.
He saw fine glasses all in peeces broken
Of service lost in court, a wofull token.

Vide gran copia di panie con visco,
ch'erano, o donne, le bellezze vostre.
Lungo sara², se tutte in verso ordisco
le cose che gli fur quivi dimostre;
che dopo mille e mille io non finisco,
e vi son tutte l'occurrenzie nostre:
sol la pazzia non v'è poca né assai;
che sta qua giù, né se ne parte mai.

Quivi ad alcuni giorni e fatti sui,
ch'egli già avea perduti, si converse;
che se non era interprete con lui,
non discernea le forme lor divirse.
Poi giunse a quel che par sì averlo a nui,
che mai per esso a Dio voti non ferse;
io dico il senno: e n'era quivi un monte,
solo assai più che l'atre cose conte.

Of birdlymd rodds he saw no litle store,
And these (O Ladies fayre) your bewties be.
I do omit ten thousand things and more
Like unto these that there the Duke did see,
For all that here is lost, there evermore
Is kept and thither in a trise doth flee.
Howbeit more nor lesse there was no folly,
For still that here with us remaineth wholly.

He saw some of his own lot time and deeds,
But yet he knew them not to be his own,
They seemd to him disguisd in so straunge weeds
Till is instructer made them better known,
But last the thing which no man thinks he needs,
Yet each man needeth most, to him was shown
By name mans wit which here we leese so fast
As that one substance all the other past.

(SIR JOHN HARINGTON)

LODOVICO ARIOSTO

❦

da *ORLANDO FURIOSO*
(Canto xxxv. 23-25)

Son, come i cigni, anco i poeti rari,
    Poeti che non sian del nome indegni,
    Sì perchè il ciel degli uomini preclari
    Non pate mai che troppa copia regni.
    Sì per gran colpa dei Signori avari
    Che lascian mendicare i sacri ingegni;
    Che le virtù premendo et esaltando
    I vizii, caccian le buone arti in bando.

Credi che Dio questi ignoranti ha privi
    De lo 'ntelletto, e loro offusca i lumi;
    Che de la poesia gli ha fatto schivi,
    Acciò che morte il tutto ne consumi.
    Oltre che del sepolcro uscirìan vivi,
    Ancor ch'avesser tutti i rei costumi,
    Pur che sapesson farsi amica Cirra,
    Più grato odore avrian che nardo o mirra.

Non sì pietoso Enea, nè forte Achille
    Fu, come è fama, nè sì fiero Ettorre;
    E nè son stati e mille e mille e mille
    Che lor si puon con verità anteporre;
    Ma i donati palazzi e le gran ville
    Da i descendenti lor, gli ha fatto porre
    In questi senza fin sublimi onori
    Da l'onorate man de gli scrittori.

LODOVICO ARIOSTO

❦

ON POETS
(Orlando Furioso, Canto xxxv. 23-25)

Just as those swans are, poets must be rare
(Poets whose practice does not shame the art),
Not only because heaven will tolerate
No crowding in humanity's vanguard,
But also because noble patronage
Has scandalously let great genius starve,
Promoting viscious lives, but to the good
Proscriptive, and to art fetters and doom.

Believe me, these fools are in God's hands!
Such senseless absence of enlightenment,
Shunning poet and poetry, unwittingly plans
Oblivion for them, unbroken, after death.
And yet, they might make shrouds mere swaddling-bands,
Though in their lives the guiltiest and worst men,
If they befriended some Parnassian singer:
Then, they might still smell sweet as nard or myrrh!

"The good Aeneas" was less good, "the strong
Achilles" or "dauntless Hector" less heroic
Living than sung; it would do truth no wrong
If we throned thousand upon thousand before them;
But palaces and country-seats that fall
Like rain of presents and bequests afforded
A theme to honor the givers, without end:
High honor, from the already honored pen!

(EDWIN MORGAN)

197

MICHELANGELO BUONARROTI
1475–1564

❧

A GIOVANNI DA PISTOIA QUANDO L'AUTORE DIPENGEVA LA VOLTA DELLA SISTINA, *1509*

I' ho già fatto un gozzo in questo stento,
Come fa l'acqua a' gatti in Lombardia,
O ver d'altro paese che si sia,
Ch' a forza 'l ventre appicca sotto 'l mento.
La barba al cielo, e la memoria sento
In sullo scrigno, e'l petto fo d'arpia;
E 'l pennel sopra 'l viso tuttavia
Mel fa, gocciando, un ricco pavimento.
E lombi entrati mi son nella peccia,
E fo del cul per contrappeso groppa,
E' passi senza gli occhi muovo invano.
Dinanzi mi s'allunga la corteccia,
E per piegarsi addietro si ragroppa,
E tendomi com' arco soriano.
   Però fallace e strano
Surge il iudizio che la mente porta;
Chè mal si tra' per cerbottana torta.
   La mia pittura morta
Difendi orma', Giovanni, e'l mio onore,
Non sendo in loco bon, nè io pittore.

MICHELANGELO BUONARROTI

TO GIOVANNI DA PISTOIA ON THE PAINTING OF THE SISTINE CHAPEL, *1509*

I've grown a goitre by dwelling in this den—
As cats from stagnant streams in Lombardy,
Or in what other land they hap to be—
Which drives the belly close beneath the chin:
My beard turns up to heaven; my nape falls in,
Fixed on my spine: my breast-bone visibly
Grows like a harp: a rich embroidery
Bedews my face from brush-drops thick and thin.
My loins into my paunch like levers grind:
My buttock like a crupper bears my weight;
My feet unguided wander to and fro;
In front my skin grows loose and long; behind,
By bending it becomes more taut and strait;
Crosswise I strain me like a Syrian bow:
Whence false and quaint, I know,
Must be the fruit of squinting brain and eye;
For ill can aim the gun that bends awry.
Come then, Giovanni, try
To succor my dead pictures and my fame;
Since foul I fare and painting is my shame.

(JOHN ADDINGTON SYMONDS)

MICHELANGELO BUONARROTI

AL COR DI ZOLFO, ALLA CARNE DI STOPPA

Al cor di zolfo, alla carne di stoppa,
  All' ossa che di secco legno sieno
  All' alma senza guida e senza freno,
  Al desir pronto, alla vaghezza troppa,
Alla cieca ragion debile e zoppa,
  Al visco, a' lacci di che 'l mondo è pieno,
  Non è gran maraviglia, in un baleno
  Arder nel primo foco che s'intoppa.
Alla bell' Arte che, se dal ciel seco
  Ciascun la porta, vince la natura,
  Quantunque sè ben prema in ogni loco;
S'io nacqui a quella nè sordo nè cieco,
  Proporzionato a chi'l cor m' arde e fura,
  Colpa è di chi m' ha destinato al foco.

MICHELANGELO BUONARROTI

❧

WITH HEART AND BREAST OF BRIMSTONE, FLESH OF FLAX

With heart and breast of brimstone, flesh of flax,
  Bones of inflammable-brittle fuel-timber,
  Soul unguided by hand or hampered by bridle,
  Quick-whipped desire, will-fever's superflux,
Mind blind and maimed and disendowed of force;
  With the world's fill of bait and trap and pitfall—
  Little indeed is the wonder of the igniting
  Lightning-like at the very first-launched fires!
Art, beauty: which in the divinity shown
  Through him who owns them can still vanquish nature
  As far as he truly speaks and shapes each scene:
If I to them was born neither stock nor stone
  But heart-harmonied to whoever plucks me into blazing,
  Blame to nature for this doom of fire I assign.

(EDWIN MORGAN)

MICHELANGELO BUONARROTI

BEN PUÒ TALOR
COL MIO ARDENTE DESIO

Ben può talor col mio ardente desio
    Salir la speme, e non esser fallace;
    Chè s' ogni nostro affetto al ciel dispiace,
    A che fin fatto avrebbe il mondo Dio?
Qual più giusta cagion dell' amarti io
    È, che dar gloria a quell' eterna pace
    Onde pende il divin che di te piace,
    E ch' ogni cor gentil fa casto e pio?
Fallace speme ha sol l' amor, che muore
    Con la beltà ch' ogni momento scema,
    Ond' è soggetta al variar d'un bel viso.
Dolce è ben quella in un pudico core
    Che per cangiar di scorza o d' ora estrema
    Non manca, e qui caparra il paradiso.

MICHELANGELO BUONARROTI

YES! HOPE MAY WITH
MY STRONG DESIRE KEEP PACE

Yes! hope may with my strong desire keep pace,
  And I be undeluded, unbetrayed;
   For if of our affections none finds grace
   In sight of Heaven, then, wherefore hath God made
The world which we inhabit? Better plea
  Love cannot have than that in loving thee
  Glory to that eternal Peace is paid,
  Who such divinity to thee imparts
As hallows and makes pure all gentle hearts.
  His hope is treacherous only whose love dies
  With beauty, which is varying every hour;
But in chaste hearts, uninfluenced by the power
  Of outward change, there blooms a deathless flower,
  That breathes on earth the air of paradise.

(WILLIAM WORDSWORTH)

MICHELANGELO BUONARROTI

BEN SARIEN DOLCE LE PREGHIERE MIE

Ben sarien dolce le preghiere mie,
se virtù mi prestassi da pregarte:
nel mio fragil terren non è già parte
da frutto buon, che da sé nato sie.
Tu sol se' seme d'opre caste e pie,
che là germuglian, dove ne fa' parte;
nessun propio valor può seguitarte,
se non gli mostri le tuo sante vie.

Sonetto mancante delle terzine.

MICHELANGELO BUONARROTI

TO THE SUPREME BEING

The prayers I make will then be sweet indeed,
If Thou the spirit give by which I pray:
My unassisted heart is barren clay,
Which of its native self can nothing feed:
Of good and pious works Thou art the seed,
Which quickens only where Thou say'st it may;
Unless Thou show to us Thine own true way,
No man can find it: Father! Thou must lead.
Do Thou, then, breathe those thoughts into my mind
By which such virtue may in me be bred
That in Thy holy footsteps I may tread;
The fetters of my tongue do Thou unbind,
That I may have the power to sing of Thee,
And sound Thy praises everlastingly.

(WILLIAM WORDSWORTH)

(Wordsworth has supplied the missing sestet—Eds.)

MICHELANGELO BUONARROTI

DANTE

Quanto dirne si de' non si può dire,
  Chè troppo agli orbi il suo splendor s'accese;
  Biasmar si può più 'l popol che l' offese,
  Ch' al suo men pregio ogni maggior salire.
Questi discese a' merti del fallire,
  Per l' util nostro, e poi a Dio ascese;
  E le porte che 'l ciel non gli contese,
  La patria chiuse al suo giusto desire.
Ingrata, dico, e della sua fortuna
  A suo danno nutrice; ond' è ben segno
  Ch' ai più perfetti abonda di più guai.
Fra mille altre ragion sol ha quest' una:
  Se par non ebbe il suo esilio indegno,
  Simil uom nè maggior non nacque mai.

MICHELANGELO BUONARROTI

DANTE

What should be said of him cannot be said;
  By too great splendor is his name attended;
  To blame is easier those who him offended,
  Than reach the faintest glory round him shed.
This man descended to the doomed and dead
  For our instruction; then to God ascended;
  Heaven opened wide to him its portals splendid,
  Who from his country's, closed against him, fled.
Ungrateful land! To its own prejudice
  Nurse of his fortunes; and this showeth well
  That the most perfect most of grief shall see.
Among the thousand proofs let one suffice,
  That as his exile hath no parallel,
  Ne'er walked the earth a greater man than he.

(HENRY WADSWORTH LONGFELLOW)

MICHELANGELO BUONARROTI

❧

QUAND'IL MINISTRO
DEL SOSPIR MIE' TANTI

Quand'il ministro de' sospir mie' tanti
Al mondo, agli occhi miei, a sé si tolse,
Natura, che fra noi degnar lo volse,
Restò in vergogna, e chi lo vide in pianti.

Ma non come degli altri oggi si vanti
Del sol del sol, ch'allor ci spense e tolse,
Morte, ch'amor ne vinse, e farlo il tolse
In terra vivo e 'n ciel fra gli altri santi.

Così credette morte iniqua e rea
Finir il suon delle virtute sparte,
E l'alma, che men bella esser potea.

Contrari effetti, alluminan le carte
Di vita, più che 'n vita non solea,
E morto ha 'l ciel, ch'allor non avea parte.

MICHELANGELO BUONARROTI

TO VITTORIA COLONNA

When the prime mover of my many sighs
  Heaven took through death from out her earthly
     place,
  Nature, that never made so fair a face,
  Remained ashamed, and tears were in all eyes.
O fate, unheeding my impassioned cries!
  O hopes fallacious! O thou spirit of grace,
  Where art thou now? Earth holds in its embrace
  Thy lovely limbs, thy holy thoughts the skies.
Vainly did cruel death attempt to stay
  The rumor of thy virtuous renown,
  That Lethe's waters could not wash away!
A thousand leaves, since he hath stricken thee down,
  Speak of thee, nor to thee could Heaven convey,
  Except through death, a refuge and a crown.

(HENRY WADSWORTH LONGFELLOW)

MICHELANGELO BUONARROTI

NON SO SE S'È LA DESIATA LUCE

Non so, se s'è la desiata luce
Del suo primo fattor, che l'alma sente,
O se dalla memoria della gente
Alcun'altra beltà nel cor traluce;

O se fama o se sogno alcun produce
Agli occhi manifesto, al cor presente,
Di sè lasciando un non so che cocente,
Ch'è forse or quel ch'a pianger mi conduce.

Quel ch'i' sento e ch'i' cerco, e chi mi guidi,
Meco non è; né so ben veder dove
Trovar mel possa, e par ch'altri mel mostri.

Questo, Signor, m'avvien, po' ch'i' vi vidi,
Ch'un dolc'e amaro, un sì e no mi muove.
Certo sarano stati gli occhi vostri.

MICHELANGELO BUONARROTI

❦

I KNOW NOT
IF FROM UNCREATED SPHERES

I know not if from uncreated spheres
Some longed-for ray it be that warms my breast,
Or lesser light, in memory expressed,
Of some once lovely face, that reappears,
Or passing rumor ringing in my ears,
Or dreamy vision, once my bosom's guest,
That left behind I know not what unrest,
Haply the reason of these wayward tears.
But what I feel and seek, what leads me on,
Comes not of me; nor can I tell aright
Where shines the hidden star that sheds this light.
Since I beheld thee, sweet and bitter fight
Within me. Resolution have I none.
Can this be, Master, what thine eyes have done?

(GEORGE SANTAYANA)

MICHELANGELO BUONARROTI

❦

IL MIO REFUGIO E 'L MIO ULTIMO SCAMPO

Il mio refugio e 'l mio ultimo scampo
qual più sicuro è, che non sia men forte
che 'l pianger e 'l pregar? e non m'aita.
Amore e crudeltà m'han posto il campo:
l'un s'arma di pietà, l'altro di morte;
questa n'ancide, e l'altra tien in vita.
Così l'alma impedita
del mio morir, che sol poria giovarne,
più volte per andarne
s'è mossa là dov'esser sempre spera,
dove'è beltà sol fuor di donna altiera;
ma l'imagine vera,
della qual vivo, allor risorge al core,
perché da morte non sia vinto amore.

MICHELANGELO BUONARROTI

THE HAVEN AND LAST REFUGE OF MY PAIN

The haven and last refuge of my pain
(A strong and safe defense)
Are tears and supplications, but in vain.
Love sets upon me banded with Disdain,
One armed with pity and one armed with death,
And as death smites me, pity lends me breath.
Else had my soul long since departed thence.
She pineth to remove
Whither her hopes of endless peace abide
And beauty dwelleth without beauty's pride,
There her last bliss to prove.
But still the living fountain of my tears
Wells in the heart when all thy truth appears,
Lest death should vanquish love.

(GEORGE SANTAYANA)

MICHELANGELO BUONARROTI

MADRIGALE 109

Gli occhi mie', vaghi delle cose belle,
E l' alma insieme della sua salute
Non ánno altra virtute
C' ascende al ciel che mirar tutte quelle.
Dalle più alte stelle
Discende uno splendore,
Che' l desir tira a quelle;
E qui si chiama amore.
Nè altro à il gentil core
Che l' innamori e arda e che' l consigli,
C' un volto che ne gli occhi lor somigli.

LA NOTTE DELLE CAPPELLE MEDICEE

Caro m'è 'l sonno e più l' esser di sasso,
Mentre che 'l danno e la vergogna dura.
Non veder, non sentir m'è gran ventura;
Però non mi destar, deh! parla basso.

MICHELANGELO BUONARROTI

MADRIGAL 109

Ravished by all that to the eyes is fair,
Yet hungry for the joys that truly bless,
My soul can find no stair
To mount to heaven, save earth's loveliness
For from the stars above
Descends a glorious light
That lifts our longing to their highest height
And bears the name of love.
Nor is there aught can move
A gentle heart, or purge or make it wise,
But beauty and the starlight of her eyes.

(GEORGE SANTAYANA)

"NIGHT" IN THE MEDICI CHAPEL

Sleep's very dear to me, but being stone's
Far more, so long as evil persevere.
It's my good fortune not to see nor hear:
Do not wake me; speak in the softest tones.

(WILLIAM JAY SMITH)

MICHELANGELO BUONARROTI

SIGNOR, SE VERO E
ALCUN PROVERBIO ANTICO

Signor, se vero è alcun proverbio antico
Questo è ben quel, che chi può mai non vuole.
Tu hai creduto a favole e parole
E premiato chi è del ver nimico.

I'sono e fui già tuo buon servo antico,
A te son dato come e' raggi al sole,
E del mio tempo non ti incresce o dole,
E men ti piaccio, se più m'affatico.

Già sperai ascender per la tua altezza,
E 'l giusto peso e la potente spada
Fusse al bisogno e non la voce d'eco.

Ma 'l cielo è quel ch'ogni virtù disprezza
Locaria al mondo se vuol ch'altri vada
A prender frutto d'un arbor ch'è se(c)co.

MICHELANGELO BUONARROTI

❦

TO POPE JULIUS II

Sir if one of the old proverbs
is true it's *He who can will not*
You have been taken in by little stories
words
and have rewarded the enemies of truth

I was faithful to you long ago and have not changed
As rays are given to the sun I gave you
myself
but my days are nothing to you
never touch you
the more I try the less I delight you

Once I hoped to be raised by your eminence
know your massive justice and the might of your sword
when I needed them
not the voice of echo

But heaven itself mocks any virtue that looks
for a place in the world
sending it to pick fruit from a dry tree

(W. S. MERWIN)

VITTORIA COLONNA
1492–1547

QUAL DIGIUNO AUGELLIN, CHE VEDE ED ODE

Qual digiuno augellin, che vede ed ode
   Batter l'ali alla madre intorno, quando
   Gli reca il nutrimento, ond'egli, amando
   Il cibo e quella, si rallegra e gode,
E dentro al nido suo si strugge e rode
   Per desio di seguirla anch'ei volando,
   E la ringrazia in tal modo cantando
   Che par ch'oltre 'l poter la lingua snode;
Tal io qualor il caldo raggio e vivo
   Del divin sole, onde nutrisco il core,
   Più dell'usato lucido lampeggia,
Muovo la penna spinta dall'amore
   Interno; e senza ch'io stessa m'avveggia
   Di quel ch'io dico, le sue lodi scrivo.

VITTORIA COLONNA

AS WHEN SOME HUNGRY FLEDGLING HEARS AND SEES

As when some hungry fledgling hears and sees
 His mother's wings beating around him, when
 She brings him nourishment, from which loving
 Both meal and her, he cheers up and rejoices,
And, deep within the nest, chafes and worries
 With desire to follow her, even flying,
 And offers thanks with such a caroling
 His tongue seems loosed beyond its usual power;
So I, at times, when warm and living rays
 Come from the heavenly sun by which my heart
 Is fed, shine forth with such a lightening,
And I find my pen moves, urged on always
 By an inner love, as if it had no part
 In what I say: it is his praise I sing.

(BARBARA HOWES)

FRANCESCO BERNI
1497–1535

ৼ

PASSERI E BECCAFICHI MAGRI ARROSTO

Passeri e beccafichi magri arrosto,
E mangiar carbonata senza bere,
Essere stracco, e non poter sedere,
Avere il fuoco presso, e il vin discosto;
    Riscuotere a bell'agio, e pagar tosto,
E dare ad altri per avere a avere;
Essere ad una festa, e non vedere,
E sudar di gennaio come d'agosto;
    Avere un sassolin 'n una scarpetta.
E una pulce drento ad una calza,
Che vadia in giù e 'n su per istaffetta;
    Una mano imbrattata ed una netta,
Una gamba calzata ed una scalza,
Esser fatto aspettare, ed aver fretta:
        Chi più n'ha, più ne metta,
E conti tutti i dispetti e le doglie,
Chè la maggior di tutte è l'aver moglie.

FRANCESCO BERNI

THE DEUCE,
A ROAST OF SCRAGGY QUAILS, A BIT

The deuce, a roast of scraggy quails, a bit
  Of salted pork to cram down a dry throat;
  To be dead tired and find nowhere to sit;
  To have the fire near by, the wine remote;
To pay cash down but to be paid at leisure;
  To be compelled to grant a profitless boon;
  Not to see aught when you've gone out on pleasure;
  To stew in January as you did in June:
To have a pebble lurking in your boot;
  To feel a flea a-running round about
  Your stirrup-leg, inside your sock; to know
One hand is clean and one is black as soot,
  One foot is with a shoe and one without;
  To be kept waiting when you're wild to go;
     Add to all this what tries you most in life,
Vexation, care, grief, every sort of strife,
  You'll find that far away the worst's a wife.

(LORNA DE' LUCCHI)

ANGELO DI COSTANZO
1507–1591

❦

SONETTO
LA MORTE DI VIRGILIO

Cigni felici, che le rive e l' acque
  Del fortunato Mincio in guardia avete,
  Deh, s' egli è ver, per Dio mi rispondete,
  Tra' vostri nidi il gran Virgilio nacque?
Dimmi, bella Sirena, ove a lui piacque
  Trapassar l'ore sue tranquille e liete
  (Così sian l' ossa tue sempre quiete),
  È ver ch' in grembo a te, morendo, giacque?
Qual maggior grazia aver dalla fortuna
  Potea? Qual fin conforme al nascer tanto?
  Qual sepolcro più simile alla cuna?
Ch' essendo nato tra 'l soave canto
  Di bianchi cigni, al fin' in veste bruna
  Esser dalle Sirene in morte pianto?

ANGELO DI COSTANZO

❦

SONNET
THE DEATH OF VIRGIL

O you fortunate swans, who sentinel
   The windings of the lucky Mincius, say
   Whether among your nests was born (reply
   If this be true) our poet, great Virgil?
May peace surround your bones, fair Siren! Tell
   Whether it pleased him those hours to pass away
   Filled with calm joy; or, when he came to die,
   Whether it was in your soft lap he fell?
What better gift or favor might he have
   From Fortune, so to end as he began?
   What was more like his cradle than his grave?
The silver-throated swans, when he was born,
   Made gentle music; destined at his death
   To be by the cloaked Sirens darkly sung.

(DAVID WRIGHT)

GASPARA STAMPA

1523-1554

❦

MESTA E PENTITA DE' MIEI GRAVI ERRORI

Mesta e pentita de' miei gravi errori
e del mio vaneggiar tanto e sì lieve,
e d'aver speso questo tempo breve
de la vita fugace in vani amori,
    a te, Signor, ch'intenerisci i cori,
e rendi calda la gelata neve,
e fai soave ogn'aspro peso e greve
a chiunque accendi di tuoi santi ardori,
    ricorro; e prego che mi porghi mano
a trarmi fuor del pelago, onde uscire,
s'io tentassi da me, sarebbe vano.
    Tu volesti per noi, Signor, morire,
tu ricomprasti tutto il seme umano;
dolce Signor, non mi lasciar perire!

GASPARA STAMPA

ℨ

WITH DEEP REPENTANCE FOR
MY WASTED DAYS

With deep repentance for my wasted days,
Trivial thoughts and sensual desires
Squandering away my days, these few rare days
Of fugitive life to kindle dying fires.
To you, to you, my God in my despair
I turn at last and let your flaming snow
Upon my heart in sacred ardor glow—
Stretch forth your hand, for I am shipwrecked, float
In a black whirlpool, drifting, sinking, gone:
A ghost that rains and tempests beat upon,
I mourn my sins, I beg your aid once more,
Hopeful I turn, O weeping I deplore;
You who for all mankind did suffer loss
Desert me not, lean down from your high cross.

(MARYA ZATURENSKA)

GASPARA STAMPA

RIMANDATEMI IL COR, EMPIO TIRANNO

Rimandatemi il cor, empio tiranno,
ch'a sì gran torto avete ed istraziate,
e di lui e di me quel proprio fate,
che le tigri e i leon di cerva fanno.

Son passati otto giorni, a me un anno,
ch'io non ho vostre lettere od imbasciate,
contro le fé che voi m'avete date,
o fonte di valor, conte, e d'inganno.

Credete ch'io sia Ercol o Sansone
a poter sostener tanto dolore,
giovane e donna e fuor d'ogni ragione,

massime essendo qui senza 'l mio core
e senza voi a mia difensione,
onde mi suol venir forza e vigore?

GASPARA STAMPA

O WICKED TYRANT, SEND ME BACK MY HEART

O wicked tyrant, send me back my heart,
which you so wrongly hold and tear to shreds,
and do to it and me that very thing
which to a hind lions and tigers do.
Eight days have passed, one entire year to me,
with neither news nor messages from you—
contrary to the oath you swore to me,
my Count, O spring of valor and deceit.

Why, do you think me Hercules or Samson
able to bear so much distress and smart—
me, young, a woman, with my wits all gone
and, worse than that, left here without my heart,
and without you, from whom I used to draw
all vigor and all strength, to shelter me?

(JOSEPH TUSIANI)

GIOVANNI BATTISTA GUARINI
1538–1612

SOGNO DELLA SUA DONNA

Occhi, stelle mortali,
Ministre di mei mali,
Ch'n sogno anco mostrate
Ch'l mio morir bramate;
Se chiusi m' uccidete
Aperti che farete?

GIOVANNI BATTISTA GUARINI

FAIR EYES, YE MORTAL STARS BELOW

Fair eyes, ye mortal stars below,
Whose aspects do portend my ill!
That sleeping cannot chuse but show
How wretched me you long to kill;
If thus you can such pleasure take,
What would you if you were awake?

(PHILIP AYRES)

GIOVANNI BATTISTA GUARINI

IL PASTOR FIDO
(Atto IV, Scena ix, Coro)

O bella età d'oro,
    Quand' era cibo il latte
    Del pargoletto mondo, e culla il bosco;
E i cari parti loro
    Godean le gregge intatte,
    Nè temea il mondo ancor ferro nè tosco!
Pensier torbido e fosco
Allor non facea velo
Al sol di luce eterna:
Or la ragion, che verna
Tra le nubi del senso, ha chiuso il cielo;
Ond' è che pellegrino
Va l'altrui terra, e'l mar turbando il pino.

Quel suon fastoso e vano,
    Quell' inutil soggetto
    Di lusinghe, di titoli e d'inganno,
Ch' Onor dal volgo insano
Indegnamente è detto,
Non era ancor degli animi tiranno,
Ma sostener affanno
Per le vere dolcezze;
Tra i boschi e tra la gregge
La fede aver per legge
Fu di quell' alme, al ben oprar avezze,
Cura d'onor felice,
Cui dettava Onestà: "Piaccia, se lice."

Allor tra prati e linfe
    Gli scherzi e le carole
    Di legittimo amor furon le faci;
Avean pastori e ninfe
Il cor nelle parole;
Dava lor Imeneo le gioie e i baci

GIOVANNI BATTISTA GUARINI

❦

THE FAITHFUL SHEPHERD
(Act IV, Scene ix, Chorus)

The Golden Age

Fair golden Age! when milk was th' onely food,
And cradle of the infant-world the wood
(Rock'd by the windes); and th' untoucht flocks did bear
Their deer young for themselves! None yet did fear
The sword or poyson: no black thoughts begun
T' eclipse the light of the eternall Sun:
Nor wandering Pines unto a forreign shore

Or War, or Riches, (a worse mischief) bore.
That pompous sound, Idoll of vanity,
Made up of Title, Pride, and Flattery,
Which they call Honour whom Ambition blindes,
Was not as yet the Tyrant of our mindes.
But to buy reall goods with honest toil
Amongst the woods and flocks, to use no guile,
Was honour to those sober souls that knew
No happinesse but what from vertue grew.

Then sports and carols amongst Brooks and Plains
Kindled a lawfull flame in Nymphs and Swains.
Their hearts and Tongues concurr'd, the kisse and joy
Which were most sweet, and yet which least did cloy
Hymen bestow'd on them. To one alone

Più dolci e più tenaci:
Un sol godeva ignude
D'amor le vive rose:
Furtivo amante ascose
Le trovò sempre, ad aspre voglie e crude
O in antro, o in selva, o in lago;
Ed era un nome sol marito e vago.

Secol rio, che velasti
Co' tuoi sozzi diletti
Il bel dell' alma, ed a nudrir la sete
Dei desiri insegnasti
Co' sembianti ristretti,
Sfrenando poi l' impurità segrete!
Così, qual tesa rete
Tra fiori e fronde sparte,
Celi pensier lascivi
Con atti santi e schivi:
Bontà stimi il parer, la vita un' arte,
Nè curi (e párti onore)
Che furto sia, purchè s' asconda, amore.

Ma tu, deh! spirti egregi
Forma ne' petti nostri,
Verace Onor, delle grand' alme donno!
O regnator de' Regi,
Deh torna in questi chiostri
Che senza te beati esser non ponno.
Déstin dal mortal sonno
Tuoi stimoli potenti
Chi per indegna e bassa
Voglia seguir te lassa,
E lassa il pregio dell' antiche genti.
Speriam, chè 'l mal fa tregua
Talor, se speme in noi non si dilegua:

Speriam, chè il sol cadente anco rinasce;
E 'l Ciel, quando men luce,
L'aspettato seren spesso n' adduce.

The lively Roses of delight were blown;
The theevish Lover found them shut on triall,
And fenc'd with prickles of a sharp denyall.
Were it in Cave or Wood, or purling Spring,
Husband and Lover signifi'd one thing.

Base present age, which dost with thy impure
Delights the beauty of the soul obscure:
Teaching to nurse a Dropsie in the veins:
Bridling the look, but giv'st desire the reins.
Thus, like a net that spread and cover'd lies
With leaves and tempting flowrs, thou dost disguise
With coy and holy arts a wanton heart;
"Mak'st life a Stage-play, vertue but a part:
"Nor thinkst it any fault Love's sweets to steal,
"So from the world thou canst the theft conceal."
But thou that art the King of Kings, create
In us true honour: Vertue's all the state
Great souls should keep. Unto these cels return
Which were thy Court, but now thy absence mourn:
From their dead sleep with thy sharp goad awake
Them who, to follow their base wils, forsake
Thee, and the glory of the ancient world.
"Let's hope: our ills have truce till we are hurled
"From that: Let's hope; the sun that's set may rise,
And within new light salute our longing eyes.

(SIR RICHARD FANSHAWE)

TORQUATO TASSO
1544-1595

☙

LE GATTE DI SANTA ANNA

Tanto le gatte son moltiplicate
    Ch' a doppio son più che l'Orse nel cielo:
    Gatte ci son c' han tutto bianco il pelo,
    Gatte nere ci son, gatte pezzate;
Gatte con coda, gatte discodate:
    Una gatta con gobba di cammelo
    Vorrei vedere e vestita di velo
    Come bertuccia: or che non la trovate?
Guardinsi i monti pur di partorire,
    Chè, s' un topo nascesse, il poverello
    Da tante gatte non potria fuggire.
Massara, io t' ammonisco, abbi 'l cervello
    E l' occhio al lavezzuol ch' è sul bollire;
    Corri, ve' ch' una se 'n porta il vitello.
        Vo farci il ritornello,
    Perchè 'l sonetto a pieno non si loda,
Se non somiglia a i gatti da la coda.

TACCIONO I BOSCHI

Tacciono i boschi e i fiumi,
E 'l mar senza onda giace,
Ne le spelonche i venti han tregua e pace,
E ne la notte bruna
Alto silenzio fa la bianca luna:
E noi teniamo ascose
Le dolcezze amorose:
Amor non parli o spiri,
Sien muti i baci e muti i miei sospiri.

234

TORQUATO TASSO

THE CATS OF SANTA ANNA

So many cats so often multiply
   They number double the stars in the Great Bear:
   Cats we observe whose coats look entirely white,
   Black cats also, and calico cats are there;
Cats with tails, and other felines tailless:
   A cat with a camel's hump I'd like to see,
   Dressed up as monkeys sometimes are, in suits
   Of velveteen: can't you find one for me?
Let mountains take care, likewise, when about
   To be delivered, that they do not bring
   Forth a mouse, who, indeed, poor fellow,
   From such a gang could never save himself.
Housewife, I warn you, keep your mind and eye
   On the stewpot boiling at the back of the stove;
   Quick, look! One's run away with the *scallopine!*
          Now I'll add the refrain:
   In the end a sonnet cannot be praised in full
   Unless it resembles cats and has a tail.

(BARBARA HOWES)

SILENT THE FORESTS

   Silent the forests, the streams,
   Waveless-sheeted the sea,
   Winds in their caves unblustering, at peace,
   Somber the night, and white
   Its moon of deepest and marmoreal quiet:
   Let us too lie like secrets
   Locked in love and its sweetness—
   Love have no breath, no voice,
   No sound a kiss, no voice or sound my sighs!

(EDWIN MORGAN)

TORQUATO TASSO

da *GERUSALEMME LIBERATA*

Vezzosi augelli infra le verdi fronde
temprano a prova lascivette note;
mormora l'aura, e fa le foglie e l'onde
garrir che variamente ella percote.
Quando taccion gli augelli alto risponde,
quando cantan gli augei più lieve scote:
sia caso od arte, or accompagna, ed ora
alterna i versi lor la musica ora.

Vola fra gli altri un che le piume ha sparte
di color vari ed ha purpureo il rostro,
e lingua snoda in guisa larga, e parte
la voce sì ch'assembra il sermon nostro.
Questi ivi allor continovò con arte
tanta il parlar che fu mirabil mostro.
Tacquero gli altri ad ascoltarlo intenti,
e fermaro i susurri in aria i venti.

"Deh mira" egli cantò "spuntar la rosa
dal verde suo modesta e verginella,
che mezzo aperta ancora e mezzo ascosa,
quanto si mostra men, tanto è più bella.
Ecco poi nudo il sen già baldanzosa
dispiega; ecco poi langue e non par quella,
quella non par che desiata inanti
fu da mille donzelle e mille amanti.

Così trapassa al trapassar d'un giorno
de la vita mortale il fiore e 'l verde;
né perché faccia indietro april ritorno,
si rinfiora ella mai, né si rinverde.
Cogliam la rosa in su 'l mattino adorno
di questo dì, che tosto il seren perde;
cogliam d'amor la rosa: amiamo or quando
esser si puote riamato amando."

TORQUATO TASSO

❧

IN ARMIDA'S GARDEN
(from *Jerusalem Delivered*)

The joyous birds, hid under greenewood shade,
Sung merrie notes on every branch and bow,
The winde (that in the leaves and waters plaid)
With murmur sweete, now song, and whistled now,
Ceased the birds, the winde loud answere made:
And while they sung, it rumbled soft and low;
   Thus, were it happe or cunning, chance or art,
   The winde in this strange musicke bore his part.

With partie coloured plumes and purple bill,
A woondrous bird among the rest there flew,
That in plaine speech sung lovelaies loud and shrill,
Her leden was like humaine language trew,
So much she talkt and with such wit and skill,
That strange it seemed how much good she knew,
   Her feathred fellowes all stood husht to heare,
   Dombe was the winde, the waters silent weare.

The gentlie budding rose (quoth she) behold,
That first scant peeping foorth with virgin beames,
Halfe ope, halfe shut, her beauties doth upfold
In their deare leaves, and lesse seene, fairer seames,
And after spreeds them foorth more broad and bold,
Then languisheth and dies in last extreames,
   Nor seemes the same, that decked bed and boure
   Of many a ladie late, and paramoure:

So, in the passing of a day, doth pas
The bud and blossome of the life of man,
Nor ere doth flourish more, but like the gras
Cut downe, becommeth withred, pale and wan:
O gather then the rose while time thou has,
Short is the day, done when it scant began,
   Gather the rose of love, while yet thou mast
   Loving, belov'd, embrasing, be embrast.

(EDWARD FAIRFAX)

TORQUATO TASSO

L'AMINTA
(Atto I, Scena ii, Coro)

O bella età de l'oro!
   Non già perchè di latte
   Se 'n corse il fiume, e stillò mèle il bosco;
   Non perchè i frutti loro
   Dièr, da l'aratro intatte,
   Le terre, e gli angui errâr senz'ira o tòsco;

   Non perchè nuvol fosco
   Non spiegò allor suo velo,
   Ma in primavera eterna,
   Ch'ora s'accende e verna,
   Rise di luce e di sereno il cielo;
   Nè portò, peregrino,
   O guerra o merce a gli altrui lidi il pino:

   Mal sol perchè quel vano
   Nome senza soggetto,
   Quell'idolo d'errori, idol d'inganno;
   Quel che da 'l volgo insano
   Onor poscia fu detto
   (Che di nostra natura il fèo tiranno),

   Non mischiava il suo affanno
   Fra le liete dolcezze
   De l'amoroso gregge;
   Nè fu sua dura legge
   Nota a quell'alme in libertate avvezze:
   Ma legge aurea e felice.
   Che Natura scolpì: *S'ei piace, ei lice.*

TORQUATO TASSO

❦

THE GOLDEN AGE
(from *Aminta*)

O lovely age of gold!
Not that the rivers rolled
With milk, or that the woods wept honeydew;
Not that the ready ground
Produced without a wound,
Or the mild serpent had no tooth that slew;
Not that a cloudless blue
For ever was in sight,
Or that the heaven, which burns
And now is cold by turns,
Looked out in glad and everlasting light;
No, nor that even the insolent ships from far
Brought war to no new lands nor riches worse than
    war:

But solely that that vain
And breath-invented pain,
That idol of mistake, that worshiped cheat,
That Honor,—since so called
By vulgar minds appalled,—
Played not the tyrant with our nature yet.
It had not come to fret
The sweet and happy fold
Of gentle human-kind;
Nor did its hard law bind
Souls nursed in freedom; but that law of gold,
That glad and golden law, all free, all fitted,
Which Nature's own hand wrote,—What pleases is
    permitted.

Allor tra fiori e linfe
   Traean dolci carole
   Gli Amoretti senz'archi e senza faci;
   Sedean pastori e ninfe,
   Meschiando a le parole
   Vezzi e sussurri, ed a i sussurri i baci
   Strettamente tenaci:
   La verginella ignude
   Scoprìa su fresche rose
   Ch'or tien ne 'l velo ascose,
   E le poma de 'l seno acerbe e crude:
   E spesso o in fiume o in lago
   Scherzar si vide con l'amata il vago.

Tu prima, Onor, velasti
   La fonte de i diletti,
   Negando l'onde a l'amorosa sete;
   Tu a' begli occhi insegnasti
   Di starne in sè ristretti,
   E tener lor bellezze altrui secrete:
   Tu raccogliesti in rete
   Le chiome a l'aura sparte:
   Tu i dolci atti lascivi
   Festi ritrosi e schivi;
   A i detti il fren ponesti, a i passi l'arte;
   Opra è tua sola, o Onore,
   Che furto sia quel che fu don d'Amore:

E son tuoi fatti egregi
   Le pene e i pianti nostri.
   Ma tu, d'Amore e di Natura donno,
   Tu, domator de' regi,
   Che fai tra questi chiostri
   Che la grandezza tua capir non ponno?
   Vàttene, e turba il sonno

Then among streams and flowers
The little winged powers
Went singing carols without torch or bow;
The nymphs and shepherds sat
Mingling with innocent chat
Sports and low whispers; and with whispers low,
Kisses that would not go.
The maiden, budding o'er,
Kept not her bloom uneyed,
Which now a veil must hide,
Nor the crisp apples which her bosom bore;
And oftentimes, in river or in a lake,
The lover and his love their merry bath would take.

'Twas thou, thou, Honor, first
That didst deny our thirst
Its drink, and on the fount thy covering set;
Thou bad'st kind eyes withdraw
Into constrained awe,
And keep the secret for their tears to wet;
Thou gather'dst in a net
The tresses from the air,
And mad'st the sports and plays
Turn all to sullen ways,
And putt'st on speech a rein, in steps a care.
Thy work it is,—thou shade, that wilt not move,—
That what was once the gift is now the theft of Love.

Our sorrows and our pains,
These are thy noble gains.
But, O, thou Love's and Nature's masterer,
Thou conqueror of the crowned,
What dost thou on this ground,
Too small a circle for thy mighty sphere?
Go, and make slumber dear

A gl'illustri e potenti:
Noi qui, negletta e bassa
Turba, senza te lassa
Viver ne l'uso de l'antiche genti.
Amiam; che non ha tregua
Con gli anni umana vita, e si dilegua:

Amiam; chè 'l Sol si muore e poi rinasce;
  A noi sua breve luce
  S'asconde, e 'l sonno eterna notte adduce.

To the renowned and high;
We here, a lowly race,
Can live without thy grace,
After the use of mild antiquity.
Go, let us love; since years
No truce allow, and life soon disappears;
Go, let us love; the daylight dies, is born;
But unto us the light
Dies once for all; and sleep brings on eternal night.

(LEIGH HUNT)

GABRIELLO CHIABRERA
1562-1637

꽃

PER IL SIGNOR ROBERTO DATI

Ancora entro i confin di fanciullezza
fui destinato a Marte; e presi in Malta
il bianco segno della nobil Croce;
nè per lo corso dell'età robusta
schifai risco o fatica: in sull'arene
fui veduto di Libia, e sulle sponde
dell'unghero Danubio assai sovente
vidi sonar le sanguinose trombe.
Così mi vissi, e non men dolgo, solo
a me rassembra di ricever torto,
che spogliato dell'armi io giungo al fine
in sulle piume del paterno albergo.
Ma pur forse per me non avrà l'Arno
di che biasmarsi: or tu non porre indugio
al tuo cammino, e nella mente serba,
come l'umana vita è fragil cosa.

GABRIELLO CHIABRERA

EPITAPH

Destined to war from very infancy
Was I, Roberto Dati, and I took
In Malta the white symbol of the Cross.
Nor in life's vigorous season did I shun
Hazard or toil; among the sands was seen
Of Libya, and not seldom, on the banks
Of wide Hungarian Danube, 't was my lot
To hear the sanguinary trumpet sounded.
So lived I, and repined not at such fate:
This only grieves me, for it seems a wrong,
That stripped of arms I to my end am brought
On the soft down of my paternal home.
Yet haply Arno shall be spared all cause
To blush for me. Thou, loiter not nor halt
In thy appointed way, and bear in mind
How fleeting and how frail is human life!

(WILLIAM WORDSWORTH)

245

TOMMASO CAMPANELLA
1568–1639

DELLA PLEBE

Il popolo è una bestia varia e grossa,
  Ch'ignora le sue forze; e però stassi
  A pesi e botte di legni e di sassi,
  Guidato da un fanciul che non ha possa,
Ch'egli potria disfar con una scossa:
  Ma lo teme, e lo serve a tutti spassi:
  Nè sa quanto è temuto, chè i bombassi
  Fanno un incanto, che i sensi gl'ingrossa.
Cosa stupenda! e' appicca e imprigiona
  Con le man proprie, e si dà morte e guerra
  Per un carlin di quanti egli al re dona.
Tutto è suo quanto sta fra cielo e terra:
  Ma no 'l conosce: e se qualche persona
  Di ciò l'avvisa, e' l'uccide ed atterra.

TOMMASO CAMPANELLA

THE PEOPLE

The people is a beast of muddy brain
  That knows not its own force, and therefore stands
  Loaded with wood and stone; the powerless hands
  Of a mere child guide it with bit and rein:
One kick would be enough to break the chain;
  But the beast fears, and what the child demands,
  It does; nor its own terror understands,
  Confused and stupefied by bugbears vain.
Most wonderful! with its own hand it ties
  And gags itself—gives itself death and war
  For pence doled out by kings from its own store.
Its own are all things between earth and heaven;
  But this it knows not; and if one arise
  To tell this truth, it kills him unforgiven.

(JOHN ADDINGTON SYMONDS)

GIOVAN BATTISTA MARINO
1569-1625

❦

LITE DEGLI OCCHI E DELLA BOCCA

Avean lite di pregio e di bellezza,
In quel volto gentil, gli occhi e la bocca.
—Da noi—gli occhi dicean—primier si scocca
L'acuto stral, ch'ogni diamante spezza.—
     La bocca poi: —Da me l'alto dolcezza
Del parlar, del baciar piove e trabocca.—
Allor gli occhi, piangendo:—E da noi fiocca
Di vive perle oriental richezza.—
     Rise la bocca, e, desserrando quelle
Porte d'un bel rubino in duo diviso,
Disse ridente a l'umidette stelle:
—Or sia giudice Amor, dove il bel viso
Discopra al paragon perle più belle:
Ne le lagrime vostre o nel mio riso?—

BELLA SCHIAVA

Nera sì, ma se' bella, o di Natura
Fra le belle d'Amor leggiadro mostro.
Fosca è l'alba appo te; perde e s'oscura
Presso l'ebeno tuo l'avorio e l'ostro.
Or quando, or dove il mondo antico o il nostro
Vide sì viva mai, sentì sì pura
O luce uscir di tenebroso inchiostro,
O di spento carbon nascere arsura?

Servo di chi m'è serva, ecco ch'avvolto
Porto di bruno laccio il core intorno,
Che per candida man non fia mai sciolto.
Là 've più ardi, o Sol, sol per tuo scorno
Un sole è nato; un Sol, che nel bel volto
Porta la notte ed ha negli occhi il giorno.

GIOVAN BATTISTA MARINO

❧

LIPS AND EYES

In Celia's face a question did arise
Which were more beautifull, her lips or eyes:
We (said the eyes,) send forth those poynted darts
Which pierce the hardest adamantine hearts.
From us (replyd the lips,) proceed those blisses
Which lovers reape by kind words and sweet kisses.
Then wept the eyes, and from their springs did powre
Of liquid orientall pearle a shower.
Whereat the lips, mov'd with delight and pleasure,
Through a sweete smile unlockt their pearlie treasure;
And bad Love judge, whether did adde more grace:
Weeping or smiling pearles to Celia's face.

(THOMAS CAREW)

THE BEAUTIFUL SLAVE

Black, yes, but beautiful. Sweet paradox
Of Nature set among Love's common beauties.
The dawn grows dark beside you. Ivory
And rose are shadows to your ebony.
For when or where in the ancient world of ours
Has any man beheld such lively, bright
Intoxicating light from sombre ink
Or felt such raging heat from blackened coal?

Servant of her who is my servant, look,
I bring my heart to you, bound in dark knots
That no white hand can now unravel.
Poor sun, where you once burned most fiercely, there
Another sun was born, whose face is night
But whose dark eyes shine brighter than your day.

(DANA GIOIA)

FRANCESCO REDI
1626–1698

ॐ

BACCO IN TOSCANA

. . . .

Non fia già che il Cioccolatte
V' adoprassi, ovvero il Tè;
Medicine così fatte
Non saran giammai per me:
Beverei prima il veleno,
Che un bicchier che fosse pieno
Dell' amaro e reo Caffè.
Cola tra gli Arabi,
E tra i Giannizzeri
Liquor sì ostico,
Sì nero e torbido
Gli schiavi ingollino.
Giù nel Tartaro,
Giù nell' Erebo
L'empie Belidi l'inventarono,
E Tesifone, e l' altre Furie
A Proserpina il ministrarono;
E se in Asia il Musulmanno
Se lo cionca a precipizio,
Mostra aver poco giudizio.

. . . .

FRANCESCO REDI

BACCHUS ON BEVERAGES
(from *Bacchus in Tuscany*)

· · · ·

Talk of Chocolate!
Talk of Tea!
Medicines, made—ye gods!—as they are,
Are no medicines made for me.
I would sooner take to poison
Than a single cup set eyes on
Of that bitter and guilty stuff ye
Talk of by the name of Coffee.
Let the Arabs and the Turks
Count it 'mongst their cruel works:
Foe of mankind, black and turbid,
Let the throats of slaves absorb it.
Down in Tartarus,
Down in Erebus,
'Twas the detestable Fifty invented it;
The Furies then took it
To grind and to cook it,
And to Proserpina all three presented it.
If the Mussulman in Asia
Doats on a beverage so unseemly,
I differ with the man extremely.

· · · ·

Chi la squallida Cervogia
Alle labbra sue congiugne,
Presto muore, o rado giugne
All' età vecchia e barbogia.
Beva il Sidro d'Inghilterra
Chi vuol gir presto sotterra;
Chi vuol gir presto alla morte
Le bevande usi del Norte.
Fanno i pazzi beveroni
Quei Norvegi e quei Lapponi:
Quei Lapponi son pur tangheri,
Son pur sozzi nel lor bere:
Solamente nel vedere,
Mi fariano uscir de' gangheri.
Ma si restin col mal die
Sì profane dicerie;
E il mio labbro profanato
Si purifichi, s'immerga,
Sì sommerga
Dentro un Pecchero indorato
Colmo in giro di quel Vino
Del Vitigno
Sì benigno,
Che fiammeggia in Sansavino.

There's a squalid thing, called Beer:
The man whose lips that thing comes near
Swiftly dies; or falling foolish,
Grows, at forty, old and owlish.
She that in the ground would hide her,
Let her take to English Cider:
He who'd have his death come quicker,
Any other Northern liquor.
Those Norwegians and those Laps
Have extraordinary taps:
Those Laps especially have strange fancies;
To see them drink,
I verily think,
Would make me lose my senses.
But a truce to such vile subjects,
With their impious, shocking objects.
Let me purify my mouth
In a holy cup o' th' South;
In a golden pitcher let me
Head and ears for comfort get me,
And drink of the wine of the vine benign
That sparkles warm in Sansovine.

(LEIGH HUNT)

VINCENZO DA FILICAIA
1642-1707

✿

ITALIA

Italia, Italia, o tu, cui feo la sorte
　Dono infelice di bellezza, ond' hai
　Funesta dote d'infiniti guai,
　Che in fronte scritti per gran doglia porte,
Deh, fossi tu men bella, o almen più forte,
　Onde assai più ti paventasse, o assai
　T'amasse men chi del tuo bello ai rai
　Par che si strugga, e pur ti sfida a morte!
Ch'or giù dall' Alpi non vedrei torrenti
　Scender d'armati, e del tuo sangue tinta
　Bever l'onda del Po gallici armenti.
Nè te vedrei del non tuo ferro cinta
　Pugnar col braccio di straniere genti,
　Per servir sempre o vincitrice o vinta.

VINCENZO DA FILICAIA

ITALY

Italia! Oh Italia! thou who hast
The fatal gift of beauty, which became
A funeral dower of present woes and past,
On thy sweet brow is sorrow plow'd by shame,
And annals graved in characters of flame.
Oh, God! that thou wert in thy nakedness
Less lovely or more powerful, and couldst claim
Thy right, and awe the robbers back, who press
To shed thy blood, and drink the tears of thy distress;

Then might'st thou more appal, or less desired,
Be homely and be peaceful, undeplored
For thy destructive charms; then, still untired,
Would not be seen the armed torrents pour'd
Down the steep Alps; nor would the hostile horde
Of many-nation'd spoilers from the Po
Quaff blood and water; nor the stranger's sword
Be thy sad weapon of defense, and so
Victor or vanquished, thou the slave of friend or foe.

(LORD BYRON)

JACOPO VITTORELLI
1749–1835

♔

SONETTO

Di due vaghe donzelle, oneste, accorte,
  Lieti e miseri padri il ciel ne feo;
  Il ciel, che degne di più nobil sorte
  L' una e l' altra veggendo, ambo chiedeo.
La mia fu tolta da veloce morte
  Alle fumanti tede d'Imeneo;
  La tua, Francesco, in suggellate porte
  Eterna prigioniera or si rendeo.
Ma tu almeno potrai della gelosa
  Irremeabil soglia, ove s' asconde,
  La sua tenera udir voce pietosa.
Io verso un fiume d'amarissim' onde,
  Corro a quel marmo in cui la figlia or posa,
  Batto e ribatto, ma nessun risponde.

JACOPO VITTORELLI

ॐ

SONNET

*Addressed by a Father Mourning His Recently
Deceased Married Daughter to the Father
Whose Daughter Had Entered a Convent*

Of two fair virgins, modest, though admired,
   Heaven made us happy; and now, wretched sires,
   Heaven for a nobler doom their worth desires,
And gazing upon either, both required.
Mine, while the torch of Hymen newly fired,
   Becomes extinguished, soon, too soon, expires;
   But thine, within the closing grate retired,
Eternal captive, to her God aspires.
But thou at least from out the jealous door
   Which shuts between your never-meeting eyes,
Mayst hear her sweet and pious voice once more;
   I, to the marble where my daughter lies,
Rush—the swoln flood of bitterness I pour,
   And knock, and knock, and knock—but none replies.

(LORD BYRON)

VITTORIO ALFIERI
1749-1803

❦

SULLA VITA SUA

Sperar, temere, rimembrar, dolersi;
sempre bramar, non appagarsi mai;
dietro al ben falso sospirare assai,
nè il ver (che ognun ha in sè) giammai godersi;
spesso da più, talor da men tenersi;
nè appien conoscer sè che in braccio a' guai;
e, giunto all' orlo del sepolcro omai,
della mal spesa vita ravvedersi;

   tal, credo, è l' uomo, o tale almen son io;
benchè il core in ricchezze o in vili onori
non ponga, e gloria e amore a me sien Dio.
L' un mi fa di me stesso viver fuori:
dell' altra in me ritrammi il bel desio:
nulla ho d' ambi finor che i lor furori.

AL SUO CAVALLO

Fido destiero, mansueto e ardente,
che dell' alato piè giovato hai spesso
al tuo signor sì ch' ei seguía dappresso
il cervo rapidissimo fuggente;
tu riedi a me, da non gran tempo assente;
ma pur più non ritrovi in me lo stesso,
ch' io son da mille e mille cure oppresso
egro di core, d' animo e di mente.

   M'è il rivederti doglia e, in un, diletto;
di là tu vieni, ov' è il mio sol pensiero ....
sovvienti ancor, quand' ella il collo e il petto
t' iva palpando, indi con dolce impero
tuo fren reggeva? E tu, pien d'intelletto,
del caro peso te ne andavi altero.

VITTORIO ALFIERI

ॐ

ON HIS LIFE

To hope, to fear, remember, suffer pain;
Always desiring, never satisfied;
Longing for some base falsehood constantly,
Never to know that truth all have within;
Often to grasp for more, then clutch at less;
Only to know oneself in trouble's arms;
And having reached the very edge of the grave
To call to mind the error of one's ways.
  Such is man's lot, I find, and such is mine;
Because I value neither wealth nor vain
Honors, then Love and Glory are from God.
One causes me to live beyond myself:
The other draws me back from pure desire:
Nothing I know of either but its rage.

(BARBARA HOWES)

TO FIDO, HIS HORSE

My trusty warhorse, spirited yet mild,
Whose winged feet so often served me well
That I, your master, might pursue the wild
Stag who flees so rapidly away;
After a short-lived absence you return
But somehow find me not at all the same,
For now I am oppressed by countless woes,
And sick at heart, in spirit and in mind.
  Now I am flooded by both pain and joy
Seeing you back from her who holds my thought . . .
Do you remember when she stroked your neck
And chest, and afterward, with sweet dominion
Curbed you well? And you, with sound good sense,
Bore that dear burden proudly on her way.

(BARBARA HOWES)

259

UGO FOSCOLO
1778–1827

IL PROPRIO RITRATTO

Solcata ho fronte, occhi incavati intenti;
crin fulvo, emunte guance, ardito aspetto;
labbri tumidi, arguti, al riso lenti,
capo chino, bel collo, irsuto petto;
membra esatte; vestir semplice eletto;
ratti i passi, il pensier, gli atti, gli accenti:
prodigo, sobrio; umano, ispido, schietto;
avverso al mondo, avversi a me gli eventi.

Mesto i più giorni e solo; ognor pensoso,
alle speranze incredulo e al timore;
il pudor mi fa vile; e prode l'ira;
cauta in me parla la ragion; ma il core,
ricco di vizi e di virtù, delira—
Morte, tu mi darai fama e riposo.

UGO FOSCOLO

SELF-PORTRAIT

My forehead's lined, my eyes intense, deep-set;
My hair full-blown, cheeks gaunt, a proud aspect;
Full curving lips, slow to give way to wit;
Fine neck with head inclined to hairy chest;
Compact in build, elegant but simply dressed;
Quick in step, in thought, in act and word;
Prodigal but sober, bristling but sincere—
When it's hostile to me, I'm hostile to the world.

Sad most days and alone; always contemplative,
Believing not in hope, not fearing fear,
Modesty makes me craven; anger, brave;
Reason counsels, but the heart will never hear,
Both vile and virtuous must wildly rave—
Death, you alone can give me fame and rest.

(WILLIAM JAY SMITH)

UGO FOSCOLO

❧

IN MORTE DEL PADRE

Era la notte; e sul funereo letto
agonizzante il genitor vid' io
tergersi gli occhi, e con pietoso aspetto
mirarmi e dirmi in suon languido: "Addio."
Quindi scordato ogni terreno obbietto,
erger la fronte ed affissarsi in Dio;
mentre, discolta il crin, batteasi il petto
la madre rispondendo al pianto mio.
   Ei, volte a noi le luci lacrimose,
"Deh, basti!" disse, e alla mal ferma palma
appoggiò il capo, tacque e si nascose.
E tacque ognun: ma alfin, spirata l' alma,
cessò il silenzio, e alle strida amorose
la notturna gemea terribil calma.

UGO FOSCOLO

MY FATHER'S DEATH

It was at night; I saw my father lie
Wearily on his bed of agony;
His eyes grew dim, faintly he breathed: "Good-bye,"
The while he gazed upon me piteously.
Then worldly things were put away to rest,
And his whole thought uplifted to God's grace;
My mother wept with me and beat her breast,
Her hair unbraided fell about her face.
   Then once again he turned his tear-veiled eyes
Towards us all and sighed, "Enough," before
His head sank quietly on his tremulous palm.
We too were hushed, but when unto the skies
His spirit fled, then silence reigned no more;
Our love's despair shattered night's awful calm.

(LORNA DE' LUCCHI)

GIUSEPPE GIOACCHINO BELLI

1791-1863

❦

ER CAFFETTIERE FISOLOFO

L'ommini de sto monno sò ll'istesso
Che vvaghi de caffè nner mascinino:
C'uno prima, uno doppo, e un antro appresso,
Tutti cuanti però vvanno a un distino.

Spesso muteno sito, e ccaccia spesso
Er vago grosso er vago piccinino,
E ss'incarzeno tutti in zu l'ingresso
Der ferro che li sfraggne in porverino.

E ll'ommini accusí vviveno ar monno
Misticati pe mmano de la sorte
Che sse li ggira tutti in tonno in tonno;

E mmovennose oggnuno, o ppiano, o fforte,
Senza capillo mai caleno a ffonno
Pe ccascà nne la gola de la morte.

GIUSEPPE GIOACCHINO BELLI

THE COFFEE-HOUSE PHILOSOPHER

Human beings in this world are the same
As coffee-beans before the *espresso* machine:
First one, and then another, a steady stream,
All of 'em going alike to one sure fate.

  Often they change places, and often the big bean
Presses against and crushes the little bean,
And they all crowd each other at the entrance gate
Of iron that grinds them down into a powder.

  And so in this way men live, soft or hard,
Mixed together by the hand of God
That stirs them round and round and round in circles;

  And, gently or roughly, everyone moves, draws breath
Without ever understanding why and falls
Down to the bottom through the throat of death.

(HAROLD NORSE)

GIUSEPPE GIOACCHINO BELLI

❧

ER BON PADRE SPIRITUALE

Accúsati, figliuola.—Me vergoggno.—
Niente: ti aiuto io con tutto il cuore.
Hai dette parolacce?—A un ber ziggnore.—
E cosa, figlia mia?—Bbrutto caroggno.—

Hai mai rubato?—Padre sì, un cotoggno.—
A chi?— Ar zor Titta.—Figlia, fai l'amore?—
Padre sí.—E come fai?—Da un cacatore
Ciarlamo.—E dite?—Cuer che cc'è bbisoggno.—

La notte dormi sola?—Padre sí.—
Ciài pensieri cattivi?—Padre, oibbò.—
Dove tieni le mani?—O cqui o llí ... —

Non ti stuzzichi?—E cc'ho da stuzzicà?—
Lí fra le cosce ... —Sin' adesso no,
(Ma sta notte sce vojjo un po' pprovà).

GIUSEPPE GIOACCHINO BELLI

THE GOOD SPIRITUAL FATHER

"Confess, my daughter." "I'm ashamed to start."
"Don't be afraid; I'll help you all I can.
Have you said bad words?" "Once, to a nice old man."
"What was it, child?" "I called him an old fart."

"Have you ever stolen?" "Yes, Father." "What did you steal?"
"A scarf, from old Dotty." "Do you make love?"
"Behind the outhouse, Father, I guess I have.
We just talk." "And you say?" "Whatever we feel."

"Daughter, do you sleep alone at night?"
"Yes." "Do you have bad thoughts?" "Father, please."
"What do you do with your hands?" "What, you mean these?"

"Do you play with yourself?" "Father, I wouldn't know how."
"There, between your thighs." "Well, not till now,"
(but when I get in bed, I think I might).

(MILLER WILLIAMS)

GIUSEPPE GIOACCHINO BELLI

❦

LA NUNZIATA

Ner mentre che la Verginemmaria
Se maggnava un piattino di minestra,
L'Angiolo Grabbïello vïa vïa
Vieniva com'un zasso di bbalestra.

Per un vetro sfassciato de finestra
J'entrò in casa er curiero der Messia;
E cco un gijjo a mman dritta de man destra
Prima je rescitò 'na vemmaria.

Poi disse a la Madonna: "Sora sposa,
Sete gravida lei senza sapello
Pe ppremission de Ddio da Pascua-rosa."

Lei allora arispose ar Grabbïello:
"Come pò èsse mai sta simir cosa
S'io nun zo mmanco cosa sia l'uscello?"

GIUSEPPE GIOACCHINO BELLI

ANNUNCIATION

You know the day, the month, even the year.
While Mary ate her noonday plate of soup,
The Angel Gabriel, like a heaven-hurled hoop,
Was bowling towards her through the atmosphere.
She watched him crash the window without fear
And enter through the hole in one swift swoop.
A lily in his fist, his wings adroop,
"Ave," he said, and after that, "Maria.

Rejoice, because the Lord's eternal love
Has made you pregnant—not by orthodox
Methods, of course. The Pentecostal Dove
Came when you slept and nested in your box."
"A hen?" she blushed, "for I know nothing of—"
The Angel nodded, knowing she meant cocks.

(ANTHONY BURGESS)

GIUSEPPE GIOACCHINO BELLI

❧

ER GIORNO DER GIUDIZZIO

Cuattro angioloni co le tromme in bocca
Se metteranno uno pe ccantone
A ssonà: poi co ttanto de voscione
Cominceranno a ddì: "Ffora a cchi ttocca."

Allora vierà ssú una filastrocca
De schertri da la terra a ppecorone,
Pe rripijjà ffigura de perzone,
Come purcini attorno de la bbiocca.

E sta bbiocca sarà Ddio bbenedetto,
Che ne farà du' parte, bbianca, e nnera:
Una pe annà in cantina, una sur tetto.

All'urtimo usscirà 'na sonajjera
D'angioli, e, ccome si ss'annassi a lletto,
Smorzeranno li lumi, e bbona sera.

GIUSEPPE GIOACCHINO BELLI

℣

THE LAST JUDGMENT

At the round earth's imagined corners let
Angels regale us with a brass quartet,
Capping that concord with a fourfold shout:
"Out, everybody, everybody out!"
Then skeletons will rattle all about
Forming in file, on all fours, tail to snout,
Putting on flesh and face until they get,
Upright, to where the Judgment Seat is set.

There the All High, maternal, systematic,
Will separate the black souls from the white:
That lot there for the cellar, this the attic.
The wing'd musicians now will chime or blare a
Brief final tune, then they'll put out the light:
Er-phwhoo.
   And so to bed.
      Owwwwwww.
        Bona sera.

(ANTHONY BURGESS)

GIACOMO LEOPARDI
1798-1837

L'INFINITO

Sempre caro mi fu quest' ermo colle,
E questa siepe, che da tanta parte
Dell' ultimo orizzonte il guardo esclude.
Ma sedendo e mirando, interminati
Spazi di là da quella, e sovrumani
Silenzi, e profondissima quiete
Io nel pensier mi fingo; ove per poco
Il cor non si spaura. E come il vento
Odo stormir tra queste piante, io quello
Infinito silenzio a questa voce
Vo comparando: e mi sovvien l' eterno,
E le morte stagioni, e la presente
E viva, e il suon di lei. Così tra questa
Immensità s' annega il pensier mio:
E il naufragar m' è dolce in questo mare.

GIACOMO LEOPARDI

THE INFINITE

I've always liked this lonely hill
crowned with a thicket cutting from view
so great a part of the far horizon.
Sitting and gazing out, I can imagine
interminable spaces beyond, supernatural
silences, and that profound calm
in which the heart comes near
to terror. And as I hear
the wind flutter the branches around me,
I weigh its voice against that infinite
silence; and summon up Eternity,
the dead seasons, and the present one
alive with sound. And so in this Immensity
my thoughts drown; and I find how sweet
it is to shipwreck in that sea.

(WILLIAM JAY SMITH)

GIACOMO LEOPARDI

A SE STESSO

Or poserai per sempre,
Stanco mio cor. Perì l'inganno estremo
Ch'eterno io mi credei. Perì. Ben sento,
In noi di cari inganni,
Non che la speme, il desiderio è spento.
Posa per sempre. Assai
Palpitasti. Non val cosa nessuna
I moti tuoi, nè di sospiri è degna
La terra. Amaro e noia
La vita, altro mai nulla; e fango è il mondo.
T'acqueta omai. Dispera
L'ultima volta. Al gener nostro il fato
Non donò che il morire. Omai disprezza
Te, la natura, il brutto
Poter che, ascoso, a comun danno impera,
E l'infinita vanità del tutto.

GIACOMO LEOPARDI

TO HIMSELF

Now be for ever still,
Weary my heart. For the last cheat is dead,
I thought eternal. Dead. For us, I know
Not only the dear hope
Of being deluded gone, but the desire.
Rest still for ever. You
Have beaten long enough. And to no purpose
Were all your stirrings; earth not worth your sighs.
For spleen and bitterness
Is life; and the rest, nothing; the world is dirt.
Lie quiet now. Despair
For the last time. Fate granted to our kind
Only the dying. Now you may despise
Yourself, nature, the brute
Power which, hidden, ordains the common doom,
And all the immeasurable emptiness of things.

(JOHN HEATH-STUBBS)

GIACOMO LEOPARDI

IL SABATO DEL VILLAGIO

La donzelletta vien dalla campagna,
In sul calar del sole,
Col suo fascio dell'erba; e reca in mano
Un mazzolin di rose e di viole,
Onde, siccome suole,
Ornare ella si appresta
Dimani, al dì di festa, il petto e il crine.
Siede con le vicine
Su la scala a filar la vecchierella,
Incontro là dove si perde il giorno;
E novellando vien del suo buon tempo,
Quando ai dì della festa ella si ornava,
Ed ancor sana e snella
Solea danzar la sera intra di quei
Ch'ebbe compagni dell'età più bella.
Già tutta l'aria imbruna,
Torna azzurro il sereno, e tornan l'ombre
Giù da' colli e da' tetti,
Al biancheggiar della recente luna.
Or la squilla dà segno
Della festa che viene;
Ed a quel suon diresti
Che il cor si riconforta.
I fanciulli gridando
Su la piazzuola in frotta,
E qua e là saltando,

GIACOMO LEOPARDI

SATURDAY EVENING IN THE VILLAGE

The young girl now comes back from the open fields,
About the set of sun,
Bearing her swathe of grasses, and in hand
A bunch of roses and of violets,
As is her custom, for
Tomorrow's holiday,
To make more beautiful her breast and hair.
And the old woman sits
Upon the steps among her neighbours, spinning.
Turning herself to where the day goes down,
And telling tales how she, in better times,
Decked herself out against the holiday,
And graceful still, and fresh,
Would dance the evening through among the rest,
Who were companions of her lovely prime.
Darkens the air, the sky
Takes on a deeper blue, and shadows fall
Cast by the roofs and hills
Beneath the whiteness of the rising moon.
And now the bell proclaims
The holy day's approach,
And at that sound, it seems,
Each heart is cheered once more.
The small boys shouting in troops
About the village square
Go leaping hither and thither

Fanno un lieto romore:
E intanto riede alla sua parca mensa,
Fischiando, il zappatore,
E seco pensa al dì del suo riposo.

Poi quando intorno è spenta ogni altra face,
E tutto l'altro tace,
Odi il martel picchiare, odi la sega
Del legnaiuol, che veglia
Nella chiusa bottega alla lucerna,
E s'affretta, e s'adopra
Di fornir l'opra anzi il chiarir dell'alba.

Questo di sette è il più gradito giorno,
Pien di speme e di gioia:
Diman tristezza e noia
Recheran l'ore, ed al travaglio usato
Ciascuno in suo pensier farà ritorno.

Garzoncello scherzoso
Cotesta età fiorita
È come un giorno d'allegrezza pieno,
Giorno chiaro, sereno,
Che precorre alla festa di tua vita.
Godi, fanciullo mio, stato soave,
Stagion lieta è cotesta.
Altro dirti non vo'; ma la tua festa
Ch'anco tardi a venir non ti sia grave.

And make a cheerful noise;
Meanwhile the labourer goes whistling home,
Back to his frugal meal,
And thinks about the coming day of rest.

When every other light around is out,
All other sound is mute,
Hark to the hammer knocking, and the saw—
The carpenter is up,
Working by lamplight in his shuttered shop,
And labours on, in haste
To get all finished before morning comes.

This is the best-loved day of all the week,
Most full of hope and joy;
The morrow will bring back
Sadness and tedium, and each within his thought
Returns once more to find his usual labour.

You little playful boy,
Even this your flowering time
Is like a day filled up with grace and joy—
A clear, calm day that comes
As a precursor to life's festival.
Be happy, little boy;
A joyful time is this.
More I'd tell you; but if your holiday
Seems somewhat tardy yet, let not that grieve you.

(JOHN HEATH-STUBBS)

GIACOMO LEOPARDI

ALLA LUNA

O graziosa luna, io mi rammento
Che, or volge l'anno, sovra questo colle
Io venia pien d'angoscia a rimirarti:
E tu pendevi allor su quella selva
Siccome or fai, che tutta la rischiari.
Ma nebuloso e tremulo dal pianto
Che mi sorgea sul ciglio, alle mie luci
Il tuo volto apparia, che travagliosa
Era mia vita: ed è, né canglia stile,
O mia diletta luna. E pur mi giova
La ricordanza, e il noverar l'etate
Del mio dolore. Oh come grato occorre
Nel tempo giovanil, quando ancor lungo
La speme e breve ha la memoria il corso,
Il rimembrar delle passate cose,
Ancor che triste, e che l'affanno duri!

GIACOMO LEOPARDI

TO THE MOON

O gracious Moon, I call to mind again
It was a year ago I climbed this hill
To gaze upon you in my agony;
And you were hanging then above that wood,
Filling it all with light, as you do now.
But dim and tremulous your face appeared,
Seen through the tears that rose beneath my eyelids,
My life being full of travail; as it is still—
It does not change, O my sweet Moon. And yet
Remembrance helps, and reckoning up
The cycles of my sorrow. How sweet the thought
That brings to mind things past, when we are young—
When long's the road for Hope, for Memory brief—
Though they were sad, and though our pain endures.

(JOHN HEATH-STUBBS)

GIACOMO LEOPARDI

č

ULTIMO CANTO DI SAFFO

Placida notte, e verecondo raggio
Della cadente luna; e tu che spunti
Fra la tacita selva in su la rupe,
Nunzio del giorno; oh dilettose e care
Mentre ignote mi fur l'erinni e il fato,
Sembianze agli occhi miei; già non arride
Spettacol molle ai disperati affetti.
Noi l'insueto allor gaudio ravviva
Quando per l'etra liquido si volve
E per li campi trepidanti il flutto
Polveroso de' Noti, e quando il carro,
Grave carro di Giove a noi sul capo,
Tonando, il tenebroso aere divide.
Noi per le balze e le profonde valli
Natar giova tra' nembi, e noi la vasta
Fuga de' greggi sbigottiti, o d'alto
Fiume alla dubbia sponda
Il suono e la vittrice ira dell'onda.

Bello il tuo manto, o divo cielo, e bella
Sei tu, rorida terra. Ahi di cotesta
Infinita beltà parte nessuna
Alla misera Saffo i numi e l'empia
Sorte non fenno. A' tuoi superbi regni
Vile, o natura, e grave ospite addetta,
E dispregiata amante, alle vezzose
Tue forme il core e le pupille invano
Supplichevole intendo. A me non ride
L'aprico margo, e dall'eterea porta
Il mattutino albor; me non il canto
De' colorati augelli, e non de' faggi
Il murmure saluta: e dove all'ombra
Degl' inchinati salice dispiega
Candido rivo il puro seno, al mio
Lubrico piè le flessuose linfe
Disdegnando sottragge,
E preme in fuga l'odorate spiagge.

GIACOMO LEOPARDI

꙳

THE LAST SONG OF SAPPHO

Peaceful night and the unassuming gleam
Of the declining moon, and you who rise
Out of the silent woods, above the hilltop,
Herald of daybreak: presences dear to me
And pleasing, when I was ignorant of my fate
And knew not passion's furies; now no tender
Vision soothes our inconsolable loves.
In us that rarest exultation kindles
Only when the dusty race of the winds
Goes swirling through the fluid aether, rolls
Over the shuddering fields, and the chariot,
Jove's heavy chariot hard above our heads
Thundering, severs the tenebrous air.
Now in the valleys and steep gorges we
Must wrap ourselves in rainclouds, match the vast
Stampede of the bewildered herds, beside
The treacherous banks, the deep river's
Sounding triumphant roar and rage of the tide.

Beautiful is your mantle, sacred sky,
Beautiful are you, O dewy earth. Alas
Of all that infinite beauty nothing, nothing
Did the gods and pitiless fate bestow
On this luckless Sappho. In your proud realms
Mean, O nature, and an unwanted guest,
And a discarded lover, upon your gracious
Forms I turn my heart and eyes in vain
Suppliance. And the apricated places
Smile not upon me, nor the morning light
From the ethereal gates; nor do the voices
Of colored birds sing to me, or the murmurs
Of beeches greet me; also in the shade of
Leaning willows, where the shining stream
Lays her pure bosom bare, at the approach
Of my uncertain foot, she scornfully
Recoils her pliant waters,
Pressing in flight on the sweet-scenting shore.

283

Qual fallo mai, qual sì nefando eccesso
Macchiommi anzi il natale, onde sì torvo
Il ciel mi fosse e di fortuna il volto?
In che peccai bambina, allor che ignara
Di misfatto è la vita, onde poi scemo
Di giovanezza, e disfiorato, al fuso
Dell'indomita Parca si volvesse
Il ferrigno mio stame? Incaute voci
Spande il tuo labbro: i destinati eventi
Move arcano consiglio. Arcano è tutto,
Fuor che il nostro dolor. Negletta prole
Nascemmo al pianto, e la ragione in grembo
De' celesti si posa. Oh cure, oh speme
De' più verd'anni! Alle sembianze il Padre,
Alle amene sembianze eterno regno
Diè nelle genti; e per virili imprese,
Per dotta lira o canto,
Virtù non luce in disadorno ammanto.

Morremo. Il velo indegno a terra sparto,
Rifuggirà l'ignudo animo a Dite,
E il crudo fallo emenderà del cieco
Dispensator de' casi. E tu cui lungo
Amore indarno, e lunga fede, e vano
D'implacato desio furor mi strinse,
Vivi felice, se felice in terra
Visse nato mortal. Me non asperse
Del soave licor del doglio avaro
Giove, poi che perìr gl'inganni e il sogno
Della mia fanciullezza. Ogni più lieto
Giorno di nostra età primo s'invola.
Sottentra il morbo, e la vecchiezza, e l'ombra
Della gelida morte. Ecco di tante
Sperate palme e dilettosi errori,
Il Tartaro m'avanza; e il prode ingegno
Han la tenaria Diva,
E l'atra notte, e la silente riva.

What possible crime, what foul atrocity
Stained me before my birth, that the heavens
Themselves, and the face of chance, scowled so upon me?
How did I sin, a little girl, when our
Life knows nothing of wickedness, to be
Bereft of youth, and the flourish of it, while
Pitiless Lachesis on her spindle
Wound my iron-grey thread?—Your lips are spilling
Dangerous words; unsearchable dispose
Ordains predestined things. Unsearchable
Is all, except our grief: rejected children
Born unto sorrow, and the reason lies
In the lap of the gods. Alas, the hopes, the fervors
Of our green years! To appearances, to fair
Appearances the Father gave eternal
Rule over men; whatever the deeds of worth,
However skilled the lyre or song,
In vile apparel virtue shines not forth.

We shall die. Her mean veil shed to earth
My naked spirit shall flee back to Dis,
And there amend this crude blunder the blind
Dispenser of chances made. And you for whom
Long unrequited love, long faith, and vain
Rage of implacable desire compelled me,
Live and be happy, if happily on earth
Ever lived mortal man. I was never
Aspersed with that soave liquor from the miserly
Phial of Jove, since the deceits, the dream
I loved in girlhood, perished. First of all
Each of our cherished moments steals away,
Then sickness enters in, old age, the spectre
Of gelid death. And so, of the many, many
Coveted laurels and joyful errors only
Death is left to me; and brave genius falls
Prey to the queen of hell,
And goes to sombre night, and the silent shore.

(PATRICK CREAGH)

GIACOMO LEOPARDI

❧

IL TRAMONTO DELLA LUNA

Quale in notte solinga,
Sovra campagne inargentate ed acque,
Là 've zefiro aleggia,
E mille vaghi aspetti
E ingannevoli obbietti
Fingon l'ombre lontane
Infra l'onde tranquille
E rami e siepi e collinette e ville;
Giunta al confin del cielo,
Dietro Apennino od Alpe, o del Tirreno
Nell'infinito seno
Scende la luna; e si scolora il mondo;
Spariscon l'ombre, ed una
Oscurità la valle e il monte imbruna;
Orba la notte resta,
E cantando, con mesta melodia,
L'estremo albor della fuggente luce,
Che dianzi gli fu duce,
Saluta il carrettier dalla sua via;

Tal si dilegua, e tale
Lascia l'età mortale
La giovinezza. In fuga
Van l'ombre e le sembianze
Dei dilettosi inganni; e vengon meno
Le lontane speranze,
Ove s'appoggia la mortal natura.
Abbandonata, oscura
Resta la vita. In lei porgendo il guardo,
Cerca il confuso viatore invano
Del cammin lungo che avanzar si sente
Meta o ragione; e vede
Che a se l'umana sede,
Esso a lei veramente è fatto estrano.

GIACOMO LEOPARDI

THE SETTING OF THE MOON

As in the lonely night,
Above the waters and the silvered plains,
Where fluttering breezes move,
And distant shadows feign
A thousand images,
Illusory and fair,
Among the quiet waves,
Hedgerows, and trees, and hills, and villages—
Having reached the sky's confine,
Past Apennine, or Alp, or in the Tyrrhene
Sea's unsounded bosom,
The moon descends, and all the world grows dim,
The shadows disappear,
And one same darkness blots out vale and mountain.
While night remains, bereaved,
And singing, with a mournful melody,
The wagoner hails the last gleam of that light
Which now is vanishing
And on his journey still had been his guide;

Thus disappears, even so
From human life must go,
The season of youth. Away
Depart the shadowy forms
And beautiful illusions; less now seem
Those far-off hopes on which
Our suffering mortal nature learned to lean.
Desolate, full of darkness,
Our life remains. And gazing round on it,
Bewildered, vainly would the traveler trace
On the long road which lies before him yet
Reason or bourn; he finds
That he has now become
A stranger here where dwells the human race.

Troppo felice e lieta
Nostra misera sorte
Parve lassù, se il giovanile stato,
Dove ogni ben di mille pene è frutto,
Durasse tutto della vita il corso.
Troppo mite decreto
Quel che sentenzia ogni animale a morte,
S'anco mezza la via
Lor non si desse in pria
Della terribil morte assai più dura.
D'intelletti immmortali
Degno trovato, estremo
Di tutti i mali ritrovàr gli eterni
La vecchiezza, ove fosse
Incolume il desio, la speme estinta,
Secche le fonti del piacer, le pene
Maggiori sempre, e non più dato il bene.

Voi, collinette e piagge,
Caduto lo splendor che all'occidente
Inargentava della notte il velo,
Orfane ancor gran tempo
Non resterete; che dall'altra parte
Tosto vedrete il cielo
Imbiancar novamente, e sorger l'alba:
Alla qual poscia seguitando il sole,
E folgorando intorno
Con sue fiamme possenti,
Di lucidi torrenti
Inonderà con voi gli eterei campi.
Ma la vita mortal, poi che la bella
Giovinezza sparì, non si colora
D'altra luce giammai, nè d'altra aurora.
Vedova è insino al fine; ed alla notte
Che l'altre etadi oscura,
Segno poser gli Dei la sepoltura.

Too sweet, too full of joy,
Had seemed our mortal state
To those above, if our first youthful time,
Whose every good is bred from thousand pains,
Had lasted out the whole course of our life.
Too mild were that decree
Which sentences to death each living thing,
Did not the path to it,
Though half completed yet,
first show itself more harsh than terrible death.
The Eternal Ones devised
The last of all our ills,
Worthy invention of immortal minds—
Old age, where still desire
Survives, with hope extinct,
When pleasure's founts run dry, and every pain
Grows more and more, while good comes not again.

You, banks and little hills,
Though hidden be the light which from the west
Had silvered all the mantle of the night,
Orphaned you shall not long
Remain, for very soon you may discern
Once more the eastern skies
Grow pale with morning, till the dawn arise,
Whom the sun follows after, and comes forth,
Blazing and bright again,
And with his ardent beams,
His shining streams of light,
Floods all your summits and the ethereal plain.
But mortal life, when the fair time of youth
Has vanished, never then grows bright again
With any radiance more, or second dawn.
Widowed until the end; and in the night,
Where through the dark we come,
The gods have set a sign for us, the tomb.

(JOHN HEATH-STUBBS)

GIUSEPPE GIUSTI
1809–1850

·

LA GUIGLIOTTINA A VAPORE

Hanno fatto nella China
una macchina a vapore
per mandar la guigliottina:
questa macchina in tre ore
fa la testa a cento mila
           messi in fila.

L'istrumento ha fatto chiasso,
e quei preti han presagito
che il paese passo passo
sarà presto incivilito;
rimarrà come un babbeo
           l'Europeo.

L'imperante è un uomo onesto;
un po' duro, un po' tirato,
un po' ciuco, ma del resto
ama i sudditi e lo Stato,
e protegge i bell' ingegni
           de' suoi regni.

V'era un popolo ribelle
che pagava a malincuore
i catasti e le gabelle:
il benigno imperatore
ha provato in quel paese
           quest' arnese.

GIUSEPPE GIUSTI

THE LATEST IN GUILLOTINES

China's got a machine
That goes by steam
And works a guillotine.
If a thousand form line,
In three hours it lops
          Their tops.

The puffer is such a wow
That the bonzes of the nation
Say China heads civilization.
Westerners must now
Stop putting on dog
          And stand agog.

The Emperor's full of probity,
Gruff, a bit stingy, on the dry side;
But he loves the commonalty
And he has sworn to provide
Scope for the inventor
          Under his sceptre.

E.g., in a certain region
Folk were looking out of sorts
About taxes and duty on imports.
His Majesty sent them the invention,
And now you won't trace
          A long face.

La virtù dell' istrumento
ha fruttato una pensione
a quel boia di talento,
col brevetto d'invenzione,
e l'ha fatto Mandarino
        di Pekino.

Grida un frate: oh! bella cosa!
gli va dato anco il battesimo.
ah perchè, (dice al Canosa
un Tiberio in diciottesimo),
questo genio non m'è nato
        nel Ducato!

LA CHIOCCIOLA

Viva la chiocciola,
viva una bestia
che unisce il merito
alla modestia.
Essa all'astronomo
e all'architetto
forse nell'animo
destò il concetto
del cannocchiale,
e delle scale:
        viva la chiocciola,
        caro animale.

His work's so highly regarded
That the genius has been awarded
Sole patent rights in his engine.
In addition, he has been given
A pension: he's now a mandarin
    In Pekin.

I heard a priest cry: "What a wingding!
Let's get it—only needs christening."
And I heard a howl from Tiberius
To his Premier: "This is serious!
Why don't brains under *my* sway
    Make headway?"

      (NIGEL DENNIS)

THE SNAIL

Here's a toast to the snail!
A health to a beast
That is brimming with merit
But extremely modest.
In matters architectural,
The spiral stair
Was inspired, certainly, by its shell;
While in matters astronomical,
To its horns we owe the telescope as well.
So, long live the snail!
A beneficial animal.

Contenta ai comodi
che Dio la fece,
può dirsi il Diogene
della sua spece.
Per prender aria
non passa l'uscio;
nelle abitudini
del proprio guscio
sta persuasa
e non intasa:
 viva la chiocciola
 bestia da casa.

Di cibi estranei
acre prurito
svegli uno stomaco
senza appetito:
essa, sentendosi
bene in arnese,
ha gusto a rodere
del suo paese
tranquillamente
l'erba nascente:
 viva la chiocciola,
 bestia astinente.

Nessun procedere
sa colle buone,
e più d'un asino
fa da leone.
Essa al contrario,
bestia com'è,
tira a proposito
le corna a sè;
non fa l'audace,
ma frigge e tace:
 viva la chiocciola,
 bestia di pace.

Content with the station
That God has put it in,
One could call it the Diogenes
Of the species.
It can take the air without
Crossing its threshold
And is so much at home in a shell
That it neither catches cold
Nor feels ever unwell.
So, long live the snail!
A proper Abigail.

When appetite languishes,
The bored belly craves
The savoury juices
Of outlandish dishes.
But the bonny snail
Sticks without fail
To the young growth
Of its home country,
Gnawing shoots, ruminatively.
So, long live the snail!
An abstemious animal.

Simple kindliness isn't
The way to success,
So we're forced to ape the lion,
Not the meek jackass.
But the snail has, inborn,
The urge to retract its horns;
Nettles, it never seizes;
It blows bubbles, and wheezes:
So, here's to the snail!
A pacifistical animal.

Natura, varia
ne' suoi portenti,
la privilegia
sopra i viventi
perchè (carnefici,
sentite questa)
le fa rinascere
perfin la testa;
cosa mirabile,
ma indubitabile;
    viva la chiocciola,
    bestia invidiabile.

Gufi dottissimi,
che predicate
e al vostro simile
nulla insegnate;
e, voi, girovaghi,
ghiotti, scapati,
padroni idrofobi,
servi arrembati,
prego a cantare
l'intercalare:
    viva la chiocciola,
    bestia esemplare.

Nature, we know, is capable
Of every kind of miracle,
But (listen to this,
Executioners all!)
The snail is so favoured
That, on losing its head,
It grows a new one instead—
Yes, this sounds exaggerated,
But mustn't be deprecated;
So, long live the snail!
An example to us all.

Listen now, you homely owls,
Who pour stuffy maxims
Out of fatuous skulls;
Listen, Bohemian playboys and gourmands,
Drivelling masters, lickspittle servants:
Listen, I tell you, and with
One voice raise that chorus:
Long live the snail!
An example to all of us.

(NIGEL DENNIS)

GIOSUÈ CARDUCCI
1835–1907

NEVICATA

Lenta fiocca la neve pe 'l cielo cinerëo: gridi,
suoni di vita più non salgon da la città,

non d'erbaiola il grido o corrente rumor di carro,
non d'amor la canzon ilare e di gioventù.

De la torre di piazza roche per l' aere le ore
gemon, come sospir d' un mondo lungi dal dì.

Picchiano uccelli raminghi a' vetri appannati: gli amici
spiriti reduci son, guardano e chiamano a me.

In breve, o cari, in breve—tu càlmati, indomito cuore—
giù al silenzio verrò, ne l' ombra riposerò.

CONGEDIO

Fior tricolore,
tramontano le stelle in mezzo al mare
e si spengono i canti entro il mio core.

GIOSUÈ CARDUCCI

A SNOW-STORM

Large, slow snowflakes fall from an ashen heaven: the noisy
Hum and hubbub of life no more go up from the town.
Hushed is the cry of the vendor of herbs, the rumble of
  wagons,
Hushed are the voices that sang blithely of youth and of love.
Harsh thro' the throbbing air the chimes from the tower o'er
  the market
Moan, like the sigh of a world far from the daylight with-
  drawn.
Tap on the frosted panes, birdlike, forlorn, the beloved
Ghosts of old friends who return, calling on me to depart.
Soon, dear ones, very soon—O strong heart, calm thyself—
  I too
Shall to the silence descend, lay me to rest in the gloom.

(G. L. BICKERSTETH)

LEAVE-TAKING

Tri-colored flower:
stars go down far out at sea
and in my heart songs die.

(WILLIAM JAY SMITH)

GIOVANNI PASCOLI
1855–1912

🎶

NOVEMBRE

Gemmea l'aria, il sole così chiaro
che tu ricerchi gli albicocchi in fiore,
e del prunalbo l'odorino amaro
      senti nel cuore ...

Ma secco è il pruno, e le stecchite piante
di nere trame segnano il sereno,
e vuoto il cielo, e cavo al piè sonante
      sembra il terreno.

Silenzio, intorno: solo, alle ventate,
odi lontano, da giardini ed orti,
di foglie un cader fragile. È l'estate,
      fredda, dei morti.

GIOVANNI PASCOLI

NOVEMBER

The air gemlike, the sun so clear
that you seek apricots in flower
and find in your heart only the white
            thorn's bitter scent.

The thornbush is dry; stick-like the plants
stand now revealed in somber silhouette
against a vacant sky; and earth resounds
            with hollow step.

Silence: but hear in the distant wind
descending faintly on orchard and flowerbed
the crackling leaves—in this, the cold
            summer of the dead.

(WILLIAM JAY SMITH)

GIOVANNI PASCOLI

LA TESSITRICE

Mi son seduto su la panchetta
come una volta ... quanti anni fa?
Ella, come una volta, s'è stretta
su la panchetta.
   E non il suono d'una parola;
solo un sorriso tutto pietà.
La bianca mano lascia la spola.

   Piango, e le dico: Come ho potuto,
dolce mio bene, partir da te?
Piange, e mi dice d'un cenno muto:
Come hai potuto?
   Con un sospiro quindi la cassa
tira del muto pettine a sé.
Muta la spola passa e ripassa.

   Piango, e le chiedo: Perché non suona
dunque l'arguto pettine piú?
Ella mi fissa timida e buona:
Perché non suona?
   E piange, piange—Mio dolce amore,
non t'hanno detto? non lo sai tu?
Io non son viva che nel tuo cuore.

   Morta! Sí, morta! Se tesso, tesso
per te soltanto; come, non so:
in questa tela, sotto il cipresso,
accanto alfine ti dormirò.

GIOVANNI PASCOLI

THE WEAVER

I come to the bench in front of the loom,
Just as I used to in years out of mind.
She, as she used to, moves to make room
In front of the loom.
And never a sound, no word at all.
Only her smile comes, gentle and kind.
Her white hand lets the shuttle fall.

With tears I ask: How could I have gone?
How could I have left you, my long-desired?
Silent she answers with tears alone:
How could you have gone?
And draws towards her, sadly and slow,
The silent comb; and never a word.
Silent the shuttle flies to and fro.

With tears I ask: Why does it not sing,
The treble comb, as it did long ago?
Gentle she echoes me, wondering:
Why does it not sing?
And: O my love—says, weeping, weeping—
Have they not told you? Do you not know?
I have no life now but in your keeping.

Dead, I am dead, yes; weaving, I weave
In your heart only. So it must be
Till wrapped in this sheet at last, my love,
I sleep by you, near the cypress tree.

(E. J. SCOVELL)

GABRIELE D'ANNUNZIO
1863–1938

FALCE DI LUNA

O falce di luna calante
Che brilli su l'acque deserte,
O falce d'argento, qual messe di sogni
Ondeggia al tuo mite chiarore qua giù!

Aneliti brevi di foglie,
Sospiri di fiori dal bosco
Esalano al mare: non canto non grido
Non suono pe 'l vasto silenzio va.

Oppresso d'amor, di piacere,
Il popol de' vivi s'addorme . . .
O falce calante, qual messe di sogni
Ondeggia al tuo mite chiarore qua giù!

GABRIELE D'ANNUNZIO

CRESCENT MOON

O crescent of the waning moon
Glittering on these deserted waters,
O silver sickle, what harvest of dreams
Now sways beneath your glowing blade.

The nervous breathing of leaves,
The sighing of forest flowers
Are borne out to sea; no song, no cry,
No sound breaks the vast silence.

Overcome with love and pleasure
The world of the living sleeps . . .
O waning sickle, what harvest of dreams
Now sways beneath your glowing blade.

(GEORGE CAMPSTER)

GABRIELE D'ANNUNZIO

LA PIOGGIA NEL PINETO

Taci. Su le soglie
del bosco non odo
parole che dici
umane; ma odo
parole più nuove
che parlano gocciole e foglie
lontane.
Ascolta. Piove
dalle nuvole sparse.
Piove su le tamerici
salmastre ed arse,
piove su i pini
scagliosi ed irti,
piove su i mirti
divini,
su le ginestre fulgenti
di fiori accolti,
su i ginepri folti
di coccole aulenti,
piove su i nostri volti
silvani,
piove su le nostre mani
ignude,
su i nostri vestimenti
leggieri,
su i freschi pensieri
che l'anima schiude
novella,
su la favola bella
che ieri
t'illuse, che oggi m'illude,
o Ermione.

Odi? La pioggia cade
su la solitaria
verdura
con un crepitio che dura
e varia nell'aria
secondo le fronde
più rade, men rade.
Ascolta. Risponde
al pianto il canto
delle cicale
che il pianto australe
non impaura,
nè il ciel cinerino.
E il pino
ha un suono, e il mirto
altro suono, e il ginepro
altro ancora, stromenti
diversi
sotto innumerevoli dita.
E immersi
noi siam nello spirto
silvestre,
d'arborea vita viventi:
e il tuo volto ebro
e molle di pioggia
come una foglia,
e le tue chiome
auliscono come
le chiare ginestre,
o creatura terretre
che hai nome
Ermione.

GABRIELE D'ANNUNZIO

THE RAIN IN THE PINE GROVE

You keep silent. On the threshold
of the forest I don't hear
the words you say,
human words, but I do hear
new words
which raindrops and leaves utter
far away.
Listen. Rain falls
from the scattered clouds.
It falls on the tamerisks
salt-laden and parched,
it falls on the pines
scaly and straight,
it falls on the myrtle
sacred to Venus,
on the broom plant, refulgent
with clusters of flowers,
on the juniper thick
with fragrant berries,
it falls on our faces
sylvan faces,
it falls on our hands
naked hands,
on our clothing
light clothing,
on the fresh thoughts
our souls unfold
new souls,
on the beautiful tale
that yesterday
beguiled you, that today beguiles me,
Oh Hermione.

You hear? The rain falls
on the lonely
verdure
with a patter that endures
and varies in the air
according to the leaves,
some thick, some thin.
Listen. An answer
to the weeping is the singing
of the cicada
whom the southern lament
does not terrify,
nor the ashen sky.
And the pine
has one sound, and the myrtle
another sound, and the juniper
yet another, instruments
diverse
under innumerable fingers.
And immersed
are we in the spirit
of the wood-land,
pulsating with arboreal life:
and your inebriated face
is moist with rain
like a leaf,
and your tresses
are fragrant like
the bright broom plant,
oh terrestial creature
by name
Hermione.

(WILLIAM GIULIANO)

307

FILIPPO TOMMASO MARINETTI
1876-1944

※

L'AVIATORE FUTURISTA
PARLA CON SUO PADRE, IL VULCANO

Io vengo a te, Vulcano, e mi burlo
delle tue furibonde sghignazzate da ventriloquio.
Credimi: io non sono in tua balía!
Vorresti, lo so, imprigionarmi
nelle tue reti di lava,
come fai con i giovani sognatori ambiziosi
quando affrontano sui tuoi fianchi
l'orribile tristezza dell'enorme tramonto
che si sganascia a ridere a crepapelle, talvolta,
in un gran terremoto!
Io non temo né i simboli, né le minacce dello spazio
che può a piacer suo seppellire le città
sotto mucchi di rame o di oro o di grumi di sangue!
Io sono il futurista possente e invincibile
tratto in alto da un cuore instancabile e folle.
È per ciò che mi siedo alla tavola dell'Aurora,
per saziarmi alla sua mostra di frutti multicolori.
Schiaccio i meriggi, fumanti piramidi di bombe,
scavalco i tramonti, eserciti sanguinanti in fuga,
e mi trascino dietro
i singhiozzanti crepuscoli nostalgici.

Etna! chi mai potrà danzare meglio di me
e dondolarsi sulla tua bocca fiera
che mugghia a mille metri sotto i miei piedi? . . .
Ecco io scendo e m'immergo nel tuo fiato solfidrico
tra i globi colossali dei tuoi fumi rossigni,
e odo il pesante rimbombo echeggiante
del tuo stomaco vasto che frana
sordamente come una capitale sotterranea.
Invano, la rabbia carbonosa della terra
vorrebbe respingermi in cielo!
Tengo ben strette fra le dita le leve . . .

FILIPPO TOMMASO MARINETTI

THE FUTURIST AVIATOR SPEAKS
TO HIS FATHER, VULCAN

I come to you, Vulcan, to give back the laugh
to you, sputtering, old ventriloquist.
Believe me, I'm out of your reach!
You'd snare me if you could,
in your coils of lava,
that luck you have with foolish dreamers
who climb your slopes
when the hypnotizing sadness of your monolithic sunsets
convulses into horrid, titanic guffaws,
and sometimes an earthquake.
I fear neither omens, nor menace of the abyss
that at your whim can bury a city
beneath a tumulus of ore and ash and blood.
I am the Futurist, strong and indomitable,
hauling aloft my wild and enduring heart:
and so it is I sit me down at Aurora's board,
and feast upon her color-shows of fruits;
or trample meridians, launch my bombs,
pursue the fleeing armies of the sunset,
dragging the wistful, sighing twilight
in tow behind me.

Etna, Etna, who dances better than I
pirouetting above your fearsome maw
bellowing a thousand meters below?
Watch me descend and dip toward your sulphurous breath
and dart between your columns of reddening clouds
to listen to the rumblings of that vast belly,
your heaving, gulping, deafening landslide,
your war at the center of the earth.
In vain your carbon rage
that would buffet me back to the sky!
I grip the flight-stick firmly in my hands ...

Io sono in mezzo, nello squarcio sinistro
delle tue labbra piú alte e piú grosse
che le montagne ...
E scendo ancora, guardando intorno a me
le tue mostruose gengive rigonfie ...
Che è mai questa flora di molli fumacchi
che tu vorresti masticare
come grossi baffi azzurri? ...

O Vulcano!
smaschera la tua faccia dalle verruche di fosforo!
Metti in moto i tuoi muscoli boccali,
apri le tue labbra rocciose incrostate di graniti,
e gridami, gridami qual è il destino
quali sono i doveri che s'impongono alla mia razza!

I enter now, through the wide gap of your mouth,
a sprawl of peaks,
and drop still further down
to inspect your monstrous gums ...
Vulcan! what weeds are these
limp plumes of smoke
you nibble at,
like an ogre's blue moustache? ...

O Vulcan! ...
strip from your face that mask of gleaming warts!
Set working the sinews of your jaw,
open those lips of stone grown over with rubble,
and cry, cry out to me what is the destiny
what are the duties to be borne by my race!

(FELIX STEFANILE)

GUIDO GOZZANO
1883–1916

☙

LA DIFFERENZA

Penso e ripenso:—Che mai pensa l'oca
gracidante alla riva del canale?
Pare felice! Al vespero invernale
protende il collo, giubilando roca.

Salta starnazza si rituffa gioca:
nè certo sogna d'essere mortale
nè certo sogna il prossimo Natale
nè l'armi corruscanti della cuoca.

—O pàpera, mia candida sorella,
tu insegni che la Morte non esiste:
solo si muore de che s'è pensato.

Ma tu non pensi. La tua sorte è bella!
Chè l'esser cucinato non è triste,
triste è il pensare d'esser cucinato.

GUIDO GOZZANO

~č

THE DIFFERENCE

I think and think again:—What thinks the goose
on the canal bank croaking with all her might?
She seems happy! In the winter twilight
stretching her neck out jubilant and raucous.

She jumps, dives, flutters her gay wings loose,
and surely doesn't dream how short her flight
and surely doesn't dream of Christmas night
or of the cook's bright weapons and their use.

O gosling, my sister, most candid mate,
Death does not exist, you teach us all:
only as he thought did man begin to die.

But you don't think. Yours is a happy fate!
Since to be fried is not sad at all,
What's sad is the thought that we must fry.

(CARLO L. GOLINO)

GUIDO GOZZANO

č

INVERNALE

« . . . cri . . . i . . . i . . . i . . . icch» . . .
l'incrinatura
il ghiaccio rabescò, stridula e viva.
«A riva!» Ognuno guadagnò, la riva.
disertando la crosta malsicura.
«A riva! A riva! . . .» un soffio di paura
disperse la brigata fuggitiva.

«Resta!» Ella chiuse il mio braccio conserto,
le sue dita intrecciò, vivi legami,
alle mie dita. «Resta, se tu m'ami!»
E sullo specchio subdolo e deserto
soli restammo, in largo volo aperto,
ebbri d'immensità, sordi ai richiami.

Fatto lieve cosí come uno spetro,
senza passato piú, senza ricordo,
m'abbandonai con lei, nel folle accordo,
di larghe rote disegnando il vetro.
Dall'orlo il ghiaccio fece cricch, più tetro . . .
dall'orlo il ghiaccio fece cricch, piú sordo . . .

Rabbrividii cosí, come chi ascolti
lo stridulo sogghigno della Morte,
e mi chinai, con le pupille assorte,
e trasparire vidi i nostri volti
già risupini lividi sepolti . . .
Dall'orlo il ghiaccio fece cricch, piú forte . . .

GUIDO GOZZANO

WINTER PIECE

'. . . cree . . . ee . . . ee . . . ee . . . eak . . .':
                              the spreading fracture
arabesqued the ice: strident, it seems it lives.
'Back to the edge!' Each one of them arrives
safe by the brink, beyond the insecure
abandoned crust. 'The edge!' One breath of fear
disperses the brigade of fugitives.

'Stay here!' I felt her fingers interlace
my own in living links, my arm in custody
as she entwined it: 'Stay, if you love me!'
And on that cunning and deserted glass
we sped alone in wide and winging grace,
deaf to their shouts, drunk with the immensity.

Ghostlike and gliding there with all weight gone,
robbed of my past, robbed of my memory,
two minds abandoned in a single folly,
we cut enormous circles on the pane.
Creak, said the split ice in a duller tone . . .
Creak with a groan of darker melancholy . . .

At which I shuddered, and like one who hears
the shrill and laughing mockery of Death,
stared down with eyes intent and saw beneath
two faces through transparency appear,
livid as though we stretched out on a bier . . .
Creak, from the ice, as with a deeper breath . . .

315

Oh! Come, come, a quelle dita avvinto,
rimpiansi il mondo e la mia dolce vita!
O voce imperïosa dell'istinto!
O voluttà di vivere infinita!
Le dita liberai da quelle dita,
e guadagnai la ripa, ansante, vinto . . .

Ella sola restò, sorda al suo nome,
rotando a lungo nel suo regno solo.
Le piacque, alfine, ritoccare il suolo;
e ridendo approdò, sfatta le chiome,
e bella ardita palpitante come
la procellaria che raccoglie il volo.

Non curante l'affanno e le riprese
dello stuolo gaietto femminile,
mi cercò, mi raggiunse tra le file
degli amici con ridere cortese:
«Signor mio caro, grazie!» E mi protese
la mano breve, sibilando:—Vile!—

Guido Gozzano

Oh how, bound by those fingers, could I doubt,
or how could world and comfort signify?
O voice of instinct, your imperious shout,
O fleshly wish to live eternally!
My fingers from her fingers tearing free,
panting and overcome, I scrambled out ...

Alone, she stayed on, circling wide across
her solitary realm, ignored her name;
decided to return, in her own time,
laughing approached with wind-dishevelled tress,
and fluttering, beautifully fearless,
swept in like a stormy petrel where she came.

She passed the flock of females, as uncaring
for their admonishment as their alarm;
sought for and found me standing in a swarm
of friends, and joined me courteously laughing:
'Belovèd sir, I thank you!' offering
her small hand to me as she hissed—'You worm!'

(CHARLES TOMLINSON)

317

GUIDO GOZZANO

L'ULTIMA INFEDELTÀ

Dolce tristezza, pur t'aveva seco,
non è molt'anni, il pallido bambino
sbocconcellante la merenda, chino
sul tedioso compito di greco . . .

Più tardi seco t'ebbe in suo cammino
sentimentale, adolescente cieco
di desiderio, se giungeva l'eco
d'una voce, d'un passo femminino.

Oggi pur la tristezza si dilegua
per sempre da quest'anima corrosa
dove un riso amarissimo persiste,

un riso che mi torce senza tregua
la bocca . . . Ah! veramente non so cosa
più triste che non più essere triste!

GUIDO GOZZANO

❦

THE LAST BETRAYAL

Sweet sadness, you were never far to seek,
not many years ago the milk-faced lad
nibbling a cracker, bent with a writing pad
over some boring exercise in Greek . . .

Later you were the only friend he had
on his sentimental pathway, green and weak,
hearing a girl walk, hearing a woman speak,
blind with desire, driven nearly mad.

Yet now from this corroded soul of mine
I feel the sadness fade away forever
before an endless bitter laugh, before

a laugh that makes my mouth a twisted line
of mockery . . . Ah, truly I can discover
nothing more sad than to be sad no more!

(MICHAEL PALMA)

GUIDO GOZZANO

ॐ

TOTÒ MERÚMENI

I

Col suo giardino incolto, le sale vaste, i bei
balconi secentisti guarniti di verzura,
la villa sembra tolta da certi versi miei,
sembra la villa-tipo, del Libro di Lettura ...

Pensa migliori giorni la villa triste, pensa
gaie brigate sotto gli alberi centenari,
banchetti illustri nella sala da pranzo immensa
e danze nel salone spoglio da gli antiquari.

Ma dove in altri tempi giungeva Casa Ansaldo,
Casa Rattazzi, Casa d'Azeglio, Casa Oddone,
s'arresta un'automobile fremendo e sobbalzando,
villosi forestieri picchiano la gorgòne.

S'ode un latrato e un passo, si schiude cautamente
la porta ... In quel silenzio di chiostro e di caserma
vive Totò Merúmeni con una madre inferma,
una prozia canuta ed uno zio demente.

II

Totò ha venticinque anni, tempra sdegnosa,
molta cultura e gusto in opere d'inchiostro,
scarso cervello, scarsa morale, spaventosa
chiaroveggenza: è il vero figlio del tempo nostro.

Non ricco, giunta l'ora di «vender parolette»
(il suo Petrarca! ...) e farsi baratto o gazzettiere,
Totò scelse l'esilio. E in libertà riflette
ai suoi trascorsi che sarà bello tacere.

GUIDO GOZZANO

❦

TOTÒ MERÙMENI

I

With its untended garden, its spacious rooms, and its fine
seventeenth-century balconies alive with verdure,
the villa appears to be taken from certain verses of mine,
a model villa almost, out of a children's reader ...

Sadly the villa dreams of better days, it dreams
of happy parties under hundred-year-old trees,
of lustrous banquets in enormous dining-rooms,
of dances in the hall despoiled by antiquaries.

But where in another age the Ansaldos used to come,
The Rattazzis, d'Azeglios, Oddones, now a motor-car
arrives and grinds to a kind of shuddering halt and some
shaggy stranger rattles the Gorgon on the door.

Somewhere a dog barks, and somewhere a step is heard,
the door half-opens ... That silence, cloistral, barrack-like,
is where Totò lives with a mother who is sick,
a whitehaired great-aunt, and an uncle who is mad.

II

Totò is twenty-five, his temper is disdainful,
he is cultured, and he has a taste for inkhorn terms,
slight brain, and slighter scruple, and a rather painful
clearsightedness: in fact, the true child of our times.

Not rich, when the dreadful hour arrived for 'selling ink'
(as Petrarch almost put it), a drunken journalist,
Totò chose exile. Now he's at liberty to think
of his errors, on which silence were no doubt best.

Non è cattivo. Manda soccorso di danaro
al povero, all'amico un cesto di primizie;
non è cattivo. A lui ricorre lo scolaro
pel tema, l'emigrante per le commendatizie.

Gelido, consapevole di sé e dei suoi torti,
non è cattivo. È il *buono* che derideva il Nietzsche
« ... in verità derido l'inetto che si dice
buono, perché non ha l'ugne abbastanza forti ...»

Dopo lo studio grave, scende in giardino, gioca
coi suoi dolci compagni sull'erba che l'invita;
i suoi compagni sono: una ghiandaia rôca,
un micio, una bertuccia che ha nome Makakita ...

III

La Vita si ritolse tutte le sue promesse.
Egli sognò per anni l'Amore che non venne,
sognò pel suo martirio attrici e principesse
ed oggi ha per amante la cuoca diciottenne.

Quando la casa dorme, la giovinetta scalza,
fresca come una prugna al gelo mattutino,
giunge nella sua stanza, lo bacia in bocca, balza
su lui che la possiede, beato e resupino ...

IV

Totò non può sentire. Un lento male indomo
inaridì le fonti prime del sentimento;
l'analisi e il sofisma fecero di quest'uomo
ciò che le fiamme fanno d'un edificio al vento.

Ma come le ruine che già seppero il fuoco
esprimono i giaggioli dai bei vividi fiori,
quell'anima riarsa esprime a poco a poco
una fiorita d'esili versi consolatori ...

He is not bad. He sends cash to the needy man;
his friend gets choice fruit out of season in a basket;
the schoolboy runs to him, who wants his homework done;
the emigrant who needs a word is right to ask it.

So cold, so conscious of himself and every wrong,
he is not bad. He is the *good man* mocked by Nietzsche:
'... in truth I have to mock that ninny of a creature
who is called good because his talons are not strong.'

Hard on his serious studies he goes down to play
with his best friends on the inviting garden plot.
And these best friends of his are: a loud-mouthed raucous
jay,
an ape called Makakita, and a pussy-cat.

III

Life took back every promise she ever made to him.
He dreamed of actresses, princesses (it was torture),
he dreamed for years of a love that never ever came,
and now today the eighteen-year-old cook's his lover.

While all the house is asleep, that girl, her feet quite bare,
fresh as a ripened plum in the coldness of daybreak,
comes to his room, kisses his mouth, and then and there
leaps onto him in bed, flat on his blessèd back.

IV

Totò knows no emotion. A slow uncured distress
has dried up at their source the very founts of feeling;
of this man has been made, by dry analysis,
what flames make of a house through which the wind is
howling.

But as a ruin fire has gutted may express
a swarm of irises, those marvellously bright things,
just so this withered soul puts forth, but less and less,
some few consolatory verses, rather slight things.

V

Così Totò Merúmeni, dopo tristi vicende,
quasi è felice. Alterna l'indagine e la rima.
Chiuso in se stesso, medita, s'accresce, esplora, intende
la vita dello Spirito che non intese prima.

Perché la voce è poca, e l'arte prediletta
immensa, perché il Tempo — mentre ch'io parlo! — va,
Totò opra in disparte, sorride, e meglio aspetta.
E vive. Un giorno è nato. Un giorno morirà.

V

And so Totò Merùmeni, after sad days,
is almost happy. He alternates research and rhyme.
Shut in himself, he thinks, he grows, explores, and knows
the Life of the Spirit which he never knew one-time.

Because the voice is tiny, and so wide the scope
of the chosen art, and Time — while I am speaking — flies,
he works in isolation, smiles, and lives in hope.
He's living still. One day he's born. One day he dies.

(J. G. NICHOLS)

UMBERTO SABA
1883–1957

ẽ

LA CAPRA

Ho parlato a una capra.
Era sola sul prato, era legata.
Sazia d'erbe, bagnata
dalla pioggia, belava.

Quell'uguale belato era fraterno
al mio dolore. Ed io risposi, prima
per celia, poi perchè il dolore è eterno
ha una voce e non varia.
Questa voce sentivo
gemere in una capra solitaria.

In una capra dal viso semita
sentivo querelarsi ogni altro male,
ogni altra vita.

UNA NOTTE

Verrebbe il sonno come l'altre notti,
s'insinua già tra i miei pensieri.
                              Allora,
come una lavandaia un panno, torce
la nuova angoscia il mio cuore. Vorrei
gridare, ma non posso. La tortura,
che si soffre una volta, soffro muto.

Ahi, quello che ho perduto so io solo.

UMBERTO SABA

THE GOAT

I have spoken with a goat.
She was alone in the meadow, tied to a post.
Satiated with grass and her coat
rain-sodden, she was bleating.

The incessant bleat I felt blending
with my own grief and I answered,
in mockery first and then after
(for sorrow timeless unending
has but the one unvarying note)
because of the message that came
borne over the field from the goat.

From a goat with semitic muzzle
I heard the lamenting
of all living things and their trouble.

(T. G. BERGIN)

ONE NIGHT

If only sleep would come, as it has come
on other nights, already slipping through
my thoughts.
        Instead now
like an old washerwoman wringing clothes,
anguish wrings another pain from my heart.
I would cry out, but cannot. As for torment—
suffered once—I suffer on in silence.

Ah, that which I have lost, only I know.

(FELIX STEFANILE)

UMBERTO SABA

ૐ

FRUTTA ERBAGGI

Erbe, frutta colori della bella
stagione. Poche ceste ove alla sete
si rivelano dolci polpe crude.

Entra un fanciullo colle gambe nude,
imperioso, fugge via.
    S'oscura
l'umile botteguccia, invecchia come
una madre.
   Di fuori egli nel sole
si allontana, con l'ombra sua, leggero.

IL FANCIULLO E L'AVERLA

S'innamorò un fanciullo d'un'averla.
Vago del nuovo—interessate udiva
di lei, dal cacciatore, meraviglie—
quante promesse fece per averla!

L'ebbe; e all'istante, l'obliò. La trista,
nella sua gabbia alla finestra appesa,
piangeva sola e in silenzio, del cielo
lontano irraggiungibile alla vista.

Si ricordò di lei solo quel giorno
che, per noia o malvagio animo, volle
stringerla in pugno. La quasi rapace
gli fece male e s'involò. Quel giorno,

per quel male l'amò senza ritorno.

UMBERTO SABA

FRUITS AND VEGETABLES

Greens and fruit the color of the loveliest
time of year. Some baskets which display
the pulps, sweet, fresh, and raw, tempting to desire.

A bare-legged youth comes in
imperious, then quickly leaves.
      Darkness descends
upon the humble shop, which ages
like a mother.
    Outside in the sun,
he departs on light feet, with his shadow.

(HENRY TAYLOR)

THE BOY AND THE SHRIKE

A boy became enamored of a shrike.
It was the novelty of what he heard
a hunter say about that marvellous bird:
How many vows he made to own a shrike!

He got one, and forgot her, just like that.
Poor bird, strung up inside her window-cage,
she mourned alone in silence for the sky
far off, and irretrievable to her sight.

He only thought of her a certain day
when, out of boredom, or some kind of spite,
he clenched her in his fist, and felt a pain.
She bit him, and flew off. And since that day,

and for that hurt, he loves her all in vain.

(FELIX STEFANILE)

UMBERTO SABA

ULISSE

Nella mia giovanezza ho navigato
lungo le coste dalmate. Isolotti
a fior d'onda emergevano, ove raro
un uccello sostava intento a prede,
coperti d'alghe, scivolosi, al sole
belli come smeraldi. Quando l'alta
marea e la notte li annulava, vele
sottovento sbandavano più al largo,
per fuggirne l'insidia. Oggi il mio regno
è quella terra di nessuno. Il porto
accende ad altri i suoi lumi; me al largo
sospinge ancora il non domato spirito,
e della vita il doloroso amore.

UMBERTO SABA

ULYSSES

I sailed, in the days of my youth,
the length of the Dalmatian coast. Small islands
would rise from the waves; there, intent on his prey,
an occasional sea-bird would alight;
slippery, covered with sea-moss, those islands
gleamed in the sunlight like emeralds.
But when they lay beneath high tides or darkness,
boats sailing to leeward swung wide of them,
steering clear of their treachery.
                              Now I am king
of Noman's land. The harbor-lights
kindle for others; once more I turn out to sea,
driven by an unconquered spirit
and a sorrowful love for all life.

(HENRY TAYLOR)

UMBERTO SABA

ϫ

CUCINA ECONOMICA

Immensa gratitudine alla vita
che ha conservate queste care cose;
oceano di delizie, anima mia.

Oh come tutto al suo posto si trova!
Oh come tutto al suo posto è restato!
In grande povertà anche è salvezza.
Della gialla polenta la bellezza
mi commuove per gli occhi; il cuore sale,
per fascini piú occulti, ad un estremo
dell'umano possibile sentire.
Io, se potessi, io qui vorrei morire,
qui mi trasse un istinto. Indifferenti
cenano accanto a me due muratori;
e un vecchietto che il pasto senza vino
ha consumato, in sé si è chiuso e al caldo
dolce accogliente, come nascituro
dentro il grembo materno. Egli assomiglia
forse al mio povero padre ramingo,
cui malediva mia madre; un bambino
esterreffatto ascoltava. Vicino
mi sento alle mie origini; mi sento,
se non erro, ad un mio luogo tornato;

al popolo in cui muoio, onde son nato.

UMBERTO SABA

❧

KITCHEN RANGE

What immense gratitude one feels toward life
for having saved these dear things,
what an ocean of delights, my soul!

Everything is so in place!
Everything still so in place!
In great poverty there is also salvation.
The beauty of the yellow polenta
moves my eye; my heart, through
the most occult charms, attains the possible
extremity of human feeling.
If I could, I would die here
where instinct drew me. Beside me
two masons dine in stony silence
and an old man who has consumed
a meal without wine
has shut himself in on himself
in the welcome heat like an unborn child
in its mother's womb. He looks a bit
like my poor wandering father
as he cursed my mother while a terrified
child listened. I feel close
to my origins: I feel,
if not mistaken, that I've returned to my own place;

to the people in whom I die, to where I was born.

(WILLIAM JAY SMITH)

CORRADO GOVONI
1884-1965

č

LA TROMBETTINA

Ecco che cosa resta
di tutta la magia della fiera:
quella trombettina,
di latta azzurra e verde,
che suona una bambina
camminando, scalza, per i campi.
Ma, in quella nota sforzata,
ci sono dentro i pagliacci bianchi e rossi,
c'è la banda d'oro rumoroso,
la giostra coi cavalli, l'organo, i lumini.
Come, nel sgocciolare della gronda,
c'è tutto lo spavento della bufera,
la bellezza dei lampi e dell'arcobaleno;
nell'umido cerino d'una lucciola
che si sfa su una foglia di brughiera,
tutta la meraviglia della primavera.

CORRADO GOVONI

THE LITTLE TRUMPET

All that is left
of the magic of the fair
is this little trumpet
of blue and green tin,
blown by a girl
as she walks, barefoot, through the fields.
But within its forced note
are all the clowns, white ones and red ones,
the band all dressed in gaudy gold,
the merry-go-round, the calliope, the lights.
Just as in the dripping of the gutter
is all the fearfulness of the storm
the beauty of lightning and the rainbow;
and in the damp flickers of a firefly
whose light dissolves on a heather branch
is all the wondrousness of spring.

(CARLO L. GOLINO)

335

CORRADO GOVONI

ℰ

PAESI

Esplodon le simpatiche campane
d'un bianco campanile, sopra tetti
grigi: donne, con rossi fazzoletti,
cavano da un rotondo forno il pane.

Ammazzano un maiale nella neve,
tra un gruppo di bambini affascinati
dal sangue, che, con gli occhi spalancati,
aspettan la crudele agonia breve.

Gettano i galli vittoriosi squilli.
I buoi escono dai fienili neri;
si sporgono su l'argine tranquilli,

scendono a bere, gravi, acqua d'argento.
Nei campi, rosei, bianchi, i cimiteri
sperano in mezzo al verde del frumento.

CORRADO GOVONI

VILLAGES

From the white campanile a cannonade
of friendly bells that breaks on the gray roofs:
below, their hair bound in red handkerchiefs,
the women at the oven drawing bread.

A pig is being killed out in the snow
among a band of children. Stupefied
and thrilled by the blood, they witness, goggle-eyed,
the cruel agony of the brief show.

The roosters raise a victorious hue and cry.
The oxen leave the haystacks for the trail
down to the riverside, where ponderously

they drape themselves, and drink the silver up.
In the green fields the graveyards, rosy pale,
amid the ranks of burgeoning wheat, take hope.

(FELIX STEFANILE)

ALDO PALAZZESCHI

1885-1974

❦

E LASCIATEMI DIVERTIRE!
Canzonetta

Tri tri tri,
fru fru fru,
ihu ihu ihu,
uhi uhi uhi!

Il poeta si diverte,
pazzamente,
smisuratamente!
Non lo state a insolentire,
lasciatelo divertire
poveretto,
queste piccole corbellerie
sono il suo diletto.

Cucú rurú,
rurú cucú,
cuccuccurucú!

Cosa sono queste indecenze?
Queste strofe bisbetiche?
Licenze, licenze,
licenze poetiche!
Sono la mia passione.

Farafarafarafa,
taratarataratа,
paraparaparapa,
laralaralarala!

Sapete cosa sono?
Sono robe avanzate,
non sono grullerie,
sono la spazzatura
delle altre poesie.

Bubububu,
fufufufu.
Friu!
Friu!

Ma se d'un qualunque nesso
son prive,
perché le scrive
quel fesso?

Bilobilobilobilobilo
blum!
Filofilofilofilofilo
flum!
Bilolú. Filolú.
U.

Non è vero che non voglion dire
voglion dire qualcosa.
Voglion dire . . .

ALDO PALAZZESCHI

SO LET ME HAVE MY FUN

Tri tri tri,
fru fru fru,
ihu ihu ihu,
uhi uhi uhi!

The poet's having fun;
he's mad
and out of control!
But don't say anything bad,
let him have his fun,
poor soul:
these harmless little tricks
that give him his kicks.

Cucu ruru,
ruru cucu,
cucucucurucu!

What are these obscenities?
These stanzas, who can read them?
Freedom, freedom,
poetic freedom!
They're my passion.

Farafarafarafa,
tarataratarata,
paraparaparapa,
laralaralarala!

Do you know what they are?
Avant-garde stuff:
not mere grotesqueries
but the finishing off
of other poetries.

Bubububu,
fufufufu,
Friu!
Friu!

It hasn't a shred
of wit—
so why does he write it,
the block-head?

Bilobilobilobilobilo
blum!
Filofilofilofilofilo
flum!
Bilolu. Filolu.
U.

It isn't true they have no meaning,
they mean something;
what they mean's

339

come quando uno
si mette a cantare
senza saper le parole.
Una cosa molto volgare.
Ebbene, cosí mi piace di fare.

Aaaaa!
Eeeee!
Iiiii!
Ooooo!
Uuuuu!
A! E! I! O! U!

Ma giovinotto,
ditemi un poco una cosa,
non è la vostra una posa,
di voler con cosí poco
tenere alimentato
un sí gran foco?

Huisc .... Huiusc ...
Sciu sciu sciu,
koku koku koku.

Ma come si deve fare a capire?
  Avete
delle belle pretese, sembra ormai
che scriviate in giapponese.

Abí, alí, alarí.
Riririri!
Ri.

Lasciate pure che si sbizzarisca,
anzi è bene che non la finisca.
Il divertimento gli costerà caro,
gli daranno del somaro.

Labala
falala
falala
eppoi lala.
Lalala lalala.

Certo è un azzardo un po' forte,
scrivere delle cose cosí,
che ci son professori oggidí
a tutte le porte.

Ahahahahahahah!
Ahahahahahahah!
ahahahahahahah!

Infine io ò pienamente ragione,
i tempi sono molto cambiati,
gli uomini non dimandano
piú nulla dai poeti,
e lasciatemi divertire!

Aldo Palazzeschi

as when
one starts to sing
and doesn't know the words . . .
a very vulgar thing,
and yet it's to my liking!

Aaaaa!
Eeeee!
Iiiii!
Ooooo!
Uuuuu!
A!E!I!O!U!

But young man
will you tell me this:
isn't your act a pose,

to claim with such little justification
you're going to cause
a conflagration?

Whish . . . . . whish . . . .
Shoo shoo shoo
Koku koku koku.

But how is one to understand?
You make pretences
   that are meant to please,
but all the same
   they sound like Japanese.

Abi, ali, alari,
Ririririri!
Ri.

Don't go off on a spree;
it's better not to be so free.
Your fun will cost you quite a bit,
and you'll be called an ass for it.

Labala
falala
falala
and even lala.
Lalala lalala!

The risk is certainly great
to write the way you do.
Like guards at every gate
the professors are watching you.

Ahahahahahaha!
Ahahahahahaha!
Ahahahahahaha!

When all is said and done
I'm right, the times have changed,
and men don't ask a thing
of poets anymore,
so let me have my fun!

(FELIX STEFANILE)

DINO CAMPANA

1885-1932

꙰

LA CHIMERA

Non so se tra roccie il tuo pallido
Viso m'apparve, o sorriso
Di lontananze ignote
Fosti, la china eburnea
Fronte fulgente o giovine
Suora de la Gioconda:
O delle primavere
Spente, per i tuoi mitici pallori
O Regina o Regina adolescente:
Ma per il tuo ignoto poema
Di voluttà e di dolore
Musica fanciulla esangue,
Segnato di linea di sangue
Nel cerchio delle labbra sinuose,
Regina de la melodia:
Ma per il vergine capo
Reclino, io poeta notturno
Vegliai le stelle vivide nei pelaghi del cielo,
Io per il tuo dolce mistero
Io per il tuo divenir taciturno.
No so se la fiamma pallida
Fu dei capelli il vivente
Segno del suo pallore,
Non so se fu un dolce vapore,
Dolce sul mio dolore,
Sorriso di un volto notturno:
Guardo le bianche rocce le mute fonti dei venti
E l'immobilità dei firmamenti
E i gonfii rivi che vanno piangenti
E l'ombre del lavoro umano curve là sui poggi algenti
E ancora per teneri cieli lontane chiare ombre correnti
E ancora ti chiamo ti chiamo Chimera.

DINO CAMPANA

THE CHIMERA

I know not if among rocks
Your pale face appeared to me,
Or if you were a smile
From unknown distances,
The bent, ivoried, gleaming
Forehead, O young sister
Of the Gioconda:
Or of the springtimes extinguished
In your mythical pallors,
O Queen, O adolescent Queen:
But it was for your unknown poem
Of voluptuousness and grief
Musical, bloodless girl,
Poem marked by a line of blood
In the circle of the sinuous lips,
Queen of melody:
But for your maidenly head
Reclined, that I, nocturnal poet,
Kept vigil over the vivid stars in the seas of the sky,
I, for your soft mystery,
I, for your taciturn growth.
I know not if the pallid flame of your hair
Was the living mark of your pallor
Or perhaps a sweet vapor,
Sweet to my sadness,
Smile of a nocturnal visage:
I watch the white rocks, the mute sources of the winds,
And the immobility of the firmaments
And the swollen rivers that flow weeping
And the shadows of human labor bent there over the gelid hills
And still through tender heavens distant clear shadows running
And still I call you I call you Chimera.

(WILLIAM WEAVER)

DINO CAMPANA

GIARDINO AUTUNNALE

Al giardino spettrale al lauro muto
De le verdi ghirlande
A la terra autunnale
Un ultimo saluto!
A l'aride pendici
Aspre arrossate nell'estremo sole
Confusa di rumori
Rauchi grida la lontana vita:
Grida al morente sole
Che insanguina le aiole.
S'intende una fanfara
Che straziante sale: il fiume spare
Ne le arene dorate: nel silenzio
Stanno le bianche statue a capo i ponti
Volte: e le cose già non sono più.
E del fondo silenzio come un coro
Tenero e grandioso
Sorge ed anela in alto al mio balcone:
E in aroma d'alloro,
In aroma d'alloro acre languente,
Tra le statue immortali nel tramonto
Ella m'appar, presente.

DINO CAMPANA

❦

AUTUMN GARDEN
(Florence)

To the spectral garden to the silent laurel
Of green garlands
To the autumnal earth
A last goodbye!
To the hard dry hillsides
Reddened in the hand-heavy sun
A confusion of raw noises
From life far away:
it cries to the setting sun
That bloodies the flower beds in its going down.

You hear the fanfare
That rises like a rip in the old fabric: the river
    disappears
In the gold sands: in the silence
The white statues on top of the bridgeheads
Have turned: and things that once were are no
    longer so.
And from down below like a chorus
Soft and majestic
Silence rises and gasps to the height of my
    balcony:
And in the smell of laurel,
In the sharp and persistent laurel smell,
Among the immortal statues against the sunset
She appears to me, here and present.

(CHARLES WRIGHT)

DINO CAMPANA

dalle *QUATTRO LIRICHE PER SIBILLA ALERAMO*

In un momento
Sono sfiorite le rose
I petali caduti
Perchè io non potevo dimenticare le rose
Le cercavamo insieme
Abbiamo trovato delle rose
Erano le sue rose erano le mie rose
Questo viaggio chiamavamo amore
Col nostro sangue e colle nostre lagrime facevamo le rose
Che brillavano un momento al sole del mattino
Le abbiamo sfiorite sotto il sole tra i rovi
Le rose che non erano le nostre rose
Le mie rose le sue rose

P.S.E così dimenticammo le rose.

DINO CAMPANA

from *FOUR LYRICS FOR SIBILLA ALERAMO*

In a moment
The roses have faded
Their petals fallen
Because I could not forget the roses
We looked for them together
We found some roses
They were her roses they were my roses
This journey we called love
With our blood and our tears we made the roses
That shone for a moment in the morning sun
We have withered them under the sun among the brambles
The roses which were not our roses
My roses her roses.

P.S. And so we forgot the roses.

(L. R. LIND)

DINO CAMPANA

DONNA GENOVESE

Tu mi portasti un po' d'alga marina
Nei tuoi capelli, ed un odor di vento,
Che è corso di lontano e giunge grave
D'ardore, era nel tuo corpo bronzino:
— Oh la divina
Semplicità delle tue forme snelle —
Non amore non spasimo, un fantasma,
Un'ombra della necessità che vaga
Serena e ineluttabile per l'anima
E la discioglie in gioia, in incanto serena
Perchè per l'infinito lo scirocco
Se la possa portare.
Come è piccolo il mondo e leggero nelle tue mani!

DINO CAMPANA

GENOA WOMAN

You brought me a little seaweed
In your hair, and a wind odor
That came in from hundreds of miles away and
    arrives
Heavy with meaning, smuggled in your tanned
    skin:
— O the divine
Simplicity of your acrobat's body —
Not love not spasm, but something untouchable,
Necessity's ghost that walks aimlessly
Serene and ineluctable through the soul
And unties it with joy, as though under a sweet
    spell,
So that the desert wind
Can carry it out through infinity.
How small the world is
        and how light it is in your hands.

(CHARLES WRIGHT)

DIEGO VALERI
1887-1976

VIOLETTE A SAN MARCO

Quel viso cosí pallido, irrorato
di rosa, i tiepidi occhi di nocciola
e il bruno mazzolino di violette
fiorito in cima della bianca mano
fecero a un tratto primavera, nella
piazza di pura pietra e pura idea,
sotto il cielo di zinco e fumo e quarzo
del novissimo marzo.

I GIORNI, I MESI, GLI ANNI

I giorni, i mesi, gli anni,
dove mai sono andati?
Questo piccolo vento
che trema alla mia porta,
uno a uno, in silenzio,
se li è portati via.
Questo piccolo vento
foglia a foglia mi spoglia
dell'ultimo mio verde
già spento. E così sia.

DIEGO VALERI

VIOLETS IN SAINT MARK'S SQUARE

That face so faintly colored, rose-
sprinkled, the warm eyes hazel
and the dark small bunch of violets
blossoming on top of the white hand
suddenly made spring in the square
of pure stone and pure idea
under a zinc sky and smoke and quartz
in new-come March.

(I. L. SALOMON)

THE DAYS, THE MONTHS, THE YEARS

The days, the months, the years,
where have they disappeared?
This little bit of wind
that trembles at my door,
in silence, one by one,
has taken them from me.
This little bit of wind
has stripped me leaf by leaf
of my last bit of green.
It's gone. And let it be.

(MICHAEL PALMA)

GIUSEPPE UNGARETTI
1888–1970

č

MATTINA

M'illumino
d'immenso

QUIETE

L'uva è matura, il campo arato,

Si stacca il monte dalle nuvole.

Sui polverosi specchi dell'estate
Caduta è l'ombra,

Tra le dita incerte
Il loro lume è chiaro
E lontano.

Colle rondini fugge
L'ultimo strazio

GIUSEPPE UNGARETTI

MORNING

On the edge of night
I fill with the light
Of immensity.

(WILLIAM JAY SMITH)

QUIET

The grapes are ripe, the field is plowed,

The mountain comes loose from the clouds.

On the dusty mirrors of summer
The shadow has fallen,

Between unsure fingers
The light is clear
And far off.

With the swallows flies
The final agony.

(HENRY TAYLOR)

GIUSEPPE UNGARETTI

ĕ

IN MEMORIA

Si chiamava
Moammed Sceab

Discendente
di emiri di nomadi
suicida
perchè non aveva più
Patria

Amò la Francia
e mutò nome

Fu Marcel
ma non era Francese
e non sapeva più
vivere
nella tenda dei suoi
dove si ascolta la cantilena
del Corano
gustando un caffè

E non sapeva
sciogliere
il canto
del suo abbandono

L'ho accompagnato
insieme alla padrona dell'albergo
dove abitavamo
a Parigi
dal numero 5 della rue des Carmes
appassito vicolo in discesa

GIUSEPPE UNGARETTI

IN MEMORIAM

His name was
Mohammed Sceab

A descendant
of the emirs of the nomads
he killed himself
because he no longer had
a homeland

He loved France
and changed his name

He became Marcel
but he was not French
and he forgot
how to live
in the tents of his people
where they listen to choruses
of the Koran
and sip coffee

And he forgot
how to set loose
the song
of his abandonment

I went with him
and the woman who owned the hotel
where we lived
in Paris
from number 5, rue des Carmes
a faded descending alley

Riposa
nel camposanto d'Ivry
sobborgo che pare
sempre
in una giornata
di una
decomposta fiera

E forse io solo
so ancora
che visse

SENTIMENTO DEL TEMPO

E per la luce giusta,
Cadendo solo un'ombra viola
Sopra il giogo meno alto,
La lontananza aperta alla misura,
Ogni mio palpito, come usa il cuore,
Ma ora l'ascolto,
T'affretta, tempo, a pormi sulle labbra
Le tue labbra ultime.

He rests
in the graveyard at Ivry
a suburb which
always
seems like the last day
of a broken-down carnival

And perhaps I alone
still know
that he lived

(HENRY TAYLOR)

FEELING OF TIME

And when the light is exact
And only the shade of memory falls
Across the little peak that is no Alp,
In the distance bared by perspective I face the past,
My pulse as usual beats, in accord with heart's habit,
But now I listen to it,
And Time, I hurry you, harry you and would marry you,
Time, to our final embrace.

(ISABELLA GARDNER)

GIUSEPPE UNGARETTI

❦

SENZA PIÙ PESO

Per un Iddio che rida come un bimbo,
Tanti gridi di passeri,
Tante danze nei rami,

Un'anima si fa senza più peso,
I prati hanno una tale tenerezza,
Tale pudore negli occhi rivive,

Le mani come foglie
S'incantano nell'aria . . .

Chi teme più, chi giudica?

VANITÀ

D'improvviso
è alto
sulle macerie
il limpido
stupore
dell'immensità

E l'uomo
curvato
sull'acqua
sorpresa
dal sole
si rinviene
un'ombra

Cullata e
piano
franta

GIUSEPPE UNGARETTI

🦎

WEIGHTLESS NOW

For a God who is laughing like a child
So many cries of sparrows,
So many hoppings high in the branches,

A soul grows weightless now,
Such tenderness is on the fields,
Such chastity refills the eyes,

The hands like leaves
Float breathless in the air . . .

Who fears, who judges now?

(RICHARD WILBUR)

VANITY

Suddenly
there towers
above the rubble
the limpid
wonder
of immensity

And the man
bent
over the sun-
startled water
comes to
as a shadow

Rocked and
softly
shattered

(CHARLES TOMLINSON)

GIUSEPPE UNGARETTI

AGONIA

Morire come le allodole assetate
sul miraggio

O come la quaglia
passato il mare
nei primi cespugli
perché di volare
non ha più voglia

Ma non vivere di lamento
come un cardellino accecato

NOIA

Anche questa notte passerà

Questa solitudine in giro
titubante ombra dei fili tranviari
sull'umido asfalto

Guardo le teste dei brumisti
nel mezzo sonno
tentennare

GIUSEPPE UNGARETTI

AGONY

To die like thirsty larks
upon the mirage

Or as the quail
the sea once past
having no more
will to fly
dies in the first thickets

But not to live on lamentation
like a blinded goldfinch

(PATRICK CREAGH)

TEDIUM

Even tonight will pass

This going round and round in solitude
irresolute shadow of the tram-wires
on the wet asphalt

I watch the heads of the cabmen
in half-sleep
wavering

(CHARLES TOMLINSON)

GIUSEPPE UNGARETTI

❧

VEGLIA
Cima Quattro il 23 dicembre 1915

Un'intera nottata
buttato vicino
a un compagno
massacrato
con la sua bocca
digrignata
volta al plenilunio
con la congestione
delle sue mani
penetrata
nel mio silenzio
ho scritto
lettere piene d'amore

Non sono mai stato
tanto
attaccato alla vita

GIUSEPPE UNGARETTI

VIGIL

A whole night through
flung down beside
a comrade
slaughtered
his mouth
grimacing
turned to the full moon
his stiffened
hands
penetrating
into my silence
I wrote
letters full of love

Never have I
clung so
close to life

(CHARLES TOMLINSON)

EUGENIO MONTALE
1896-1981

❦

da *ACCORDI*
(Sensi e fantasmi di una adolescente)

I
VIOLINI

Gioventù troppe strade
distendi innanzi alle pupille
mie smarrite:
quali si snodano, erbite,
indecise curve in piane tranquille,
quali s'avventano alla roccia dura
dei monti,
o ad orizzonti vanno ove barbaglia
la calura!
Sono qui nell'attesa di un prodigio
e le mani mi chiudo nelle mani.
Forse è in questa incertezza,
mattino che trabocchi
dal cielo,
la più vera ricchezza e tu ne innimbi
tutto che tocchi!
Occhi corolle s'aprono
in me — chissà — o nel suolo:
tutto vaneggia e nella luce nuova
volere non so più né disvolere.
Solo
m'è dato nel miracolo del giorno,
o cuore fatto muto,
scordare gioie o crucci,
ed offrirti alla vita
tra un mattinare arguto
di balestrucci!

EUGENIO MONTALE

❧

from *CHORDS*
(Feelings and fantasies of an adolescent girl)

I
VIOLINS

Youth, you lay out
too many streets
before my bewildered eyes;
some unravel, grassy,
indecisive curves in quiet plains;
some run up the hard rock
of the mountains,
or go to the horizons where the heat
dazzles!
I'm here waiting for a miracle
clasping my hands.
Maybe in this uncertainty,
morning brimming over from the sky,
lies the truest wealth
and with it you enhalo
everything you touch!
Eyes, blossoms, open
in me—who knows—or the earth:
everything drifts and in the new light
I no longer know desire or non-desire.
Still
it is given to me in the miracle of the day,
O heart struck dumb,
to forget joys and sorrows
and offer you to life
in a morning bright
with martins!

5
OBOE

Ci son ore rare
che ogni apparenza dintorno vacilla s'umilia scompare,
come le stinte
quinte
d'un boccascena, ad atto finito, tra il parapiglia

I sensi sono intorpiditi,
il minuto si piace di sé;
e nasce nei nostri occhi un po' stupiti
un sorriso senza perché.

5
OBOE

There are rare moments
when all appearances around us waver, decline, disappear
like the faded
screens
of a stage set, in the turmoil, when the play's over.

The senses are numb,
the moment is pleased with itself;
and in our eyes, a bit amazed
a smile begins for no reason.

(JONATHAN GALASSI)

EUGENIO MONTALE

ℨ

MERIGGIARE PALLIDO E ASSORTO

Meriggiare pallido e assorto
presso un rovente muro d'orto,
ascoltare tra i pruni e gli sterpi
schiocchi di merli, frusci di serpi.

Nelle crepe del suolo o su la veccia
spiar le file di rosse formiche
ch'ora si rompono ed ora s'intrecciano
a sommo di minuscole biche.

Osservare tra frondi il palpitare
lontano di scaglie di mare
mentre si levano tremuli scricchi
di cicale dai calvi picchi.

E andando nel sole che abbaglia
sentire con triste meraviglia
com'è tutta la vita e il suo travaglio
in questo sequitare una muraglia
che ha in cima cocci aguzzi di bottiglia.

EUGENIO MONTALE

THE WALL

To lie in shadow on the lawn
By a crumbling wall, pale and withdrawn,
And spy in the weeds the gliding snake
And hear the rustle blackbirds make—

To watch in the cracked earth and the grass
Battalions of red ants at drill,
That break and form ranks, pass and repass
In busy marches on some tiny hill—

To catch, each time the leaves blow free,
The faint and pulsing motion of the sea,
While ceaseless, tremulous and shrill,
The cicadas chatter on the bald hill—

Rising, to wander in bewilderment
With the sun's dazzle, and the sorry thought
How all our life, and all its labors spent,
Are like a man upon a journey sent
Along a wall that's sheer and steep and endless, dressed
With bits of broken bottles on its crest.

(MAURICE ENGLISH)

EUGENIO MONTALE

PORTAMI IL GIRASOLE
CH'IO LO TRAPIANTI

Portami il girasole ch'io lo trapianti
nel mio terreno bruciato dal salino,
e mostri tutto il giorno agli azzurri specchianti
del cielo l'ansietà del suo volto giallino.

Tendono all chiarità le cose oscure,
si esauriscono i corpi in un fluire
di tinte: queste in musiche. Svanire
e dunque la ventura delle venture.

Portami tu la pianta che conduce
dove sorgono bionde trasparenze
e vapora la vita quale essenza;
portami il girasole impazzito di luce.

EUGENIO MONTALE

THE SUNFLOWER

Bring me the sunflower to plant in my garden here
Where the salt of the flung spray has parched a space,
And all day long to the blue and mirroring air
Let it turn the ardor of its yellow face.

These dark things to the source of brightness turn,
In a flow of colors into music flowing, spend
Themselves forever. Thus to burn
Is consummation, of all ends the end.

Bring me within your hands that flower which yearns
Up to the ultimate transparent white
Where all of life into its essence burns:
Bring me that flower impassioned of the light.

(MAURICE ENGLISH)

EUGENIO MONTALE

ℭ

NEL PARCO

Nell' ombra della magnolia
che sempre più si restringe,
a un soffio di cerbottana
la freccia mi sfiora e si perde.

Pareva una foglia caduta
dal pioppo che a un colpo di vento
si stinge—e fors' era una mano
scorrente da lungi tra il verde.

Un riso che non m'appartiene
trapassa da fronde canute
fino al mio petto, lo scuote
un trillo che punge le vene,

e rido con te sulla ruota
deforme dell' ombra, mi allungo
disfatto di me sulle ossute
radici che sporgono e pungo

con fili di paglia il tuo viso.

EUGENIO MONTALE

IN THE PARK

In the magnolia's ever
stricter shade, at one
puff from a blowgun
the dart grazes me and is gone.

It was like a leaf let fall
by the poplar a gust of wind
uncolors—perhaps a hand
roving through green from afar.

A laughter not my own
pierces through hoary branches
into my breast, a thrill
shakes me, stabs my veins,

and I laugh with you on the warped
wheel of shade, I stretch out
discharged of myself on the sharp
protruding roots, and needle

your face with bits of straw. . . .

(JAMES MERRILL)

EUGENIO MONTALE

L'ANGUILLA

L'anguilla, la sirena
dei mari freddi che lascia il Baltico
per giungere ai nostri mari,
ai nostri estuari, ai fiumi
che risale in profondo, sotto la piena avversa,
di ramo in ramo e poi
di capello in capello, assottigliati,
sempre più addentro, sempre più nel cuore
del macigno, filtrando
tra gorielli di melma finchè un giorno
una luce scoccata dai castagni
ne accende il guizzo in pozze d'acquamorta,
nei fossi che declinano
dai balzi d'Appennino alla Romagna;
l'anguilla, torcia, frusta,
freccia d'Amore in terra
che solo i nostri botri o i disseccati
ruscelli pirenaici riconducono
a paradisi di fecondazione;
l'anima verde che cerca
vita dove là solo
morde l'arsura e la desolazione,
la scintilla che dice
tutto comincia quando tutto pare
incarbonirsi, bronco seppellito;
l'iride breve, gemella
di quella che incastoni in mezzo ai cigli
e fai brillare intatta in mezzo ai figli
dell'uomo, immersi nel tuo fango, puoi tu
non crederla sorella?

EUGENIO MONTALE

THE EEL

The eel, that North Sea
siren who leaves the cold Baltic
for our warm seas,
our estuaries, our rivers,
swimming upstream against their currents,
climbing from branch to branch,
from stem to thinner stem,
penetrating ever deeper the core
of stone, threading
narrowing channels of ooze until one day
a flare from flowering chestnuts
kindles its flickering thread in those stagnant pools,
those hollows sweeping down
from the terraced Appenines to the Romagna,
the eel, that torch, that whip,
that arrow of Earthly Love,
which only our gullies and fiery, dried
creek beds can lead back
to paradises of fertility;
green soul that looks for life
where only drought and desolation gnaw,
spark proclaiming
that everything begins only
when it is burned out, rotted away like a stump;
brief rainbow, iris, twin
of that one you set between your lashes
and let shine in the midst of the sons
of man, sunk as they are in your primeval mud—
can you believe she is not your sister?

(WILLIAM JAY SMITH)

EUGENIO MONTALE

č

DORA MARKUS

I

Fu dove il ponte di legno
mette a Porto Corsini sul mare alto
e rari uomini, quasi immoti, affondano
o salpano le reti. Con un segno
della mano additavi all'altra sponda
invisibile la tua patria vera.
Poi seguimmo il canale fino alla darsena
della città, lucida di fuliggine,
nella bassura dove s'affondava
una primavera inerte, senza memoria.

E qui dove un'antica vita
si screzia in una dolce
ansietà d'Oriente,
le tue parole iridavano come le scaglie
della triglia moribonda.

La tua irrequietudine mi fa pensare
agli uccelli di passo che urtano ai fari
nelle sere tempestose:
è una tempesta anche la tua dolcezza,
turbina e non appare,
e i suoi riposi sono anche piú rari.
Non so come stremata tu resisti
in questo lago
d'indifferenza ch'è il tuo cuore; forse
ti salva un amuleto che tu tieni
vicino alla matita delle labbra,
al piumino, alla lima: un topo bianco,
d'avorio; e cosí esisti!

376

EUGENIO MONTALE

❦

DORA MARKUS

1.

It was where the wooden bridge
crosses to Porto Corsini on the open sea
and a few men, in slow motion, lower
or haul in their nets. With a wave
of your hand you gestured toward the other
invisible shore, your true homeland.
Then we followed the canal as far as the wharves
of the town, glistening with soot,
in that lowland where a cold spring
slowly settled down, outside memory.

And here, where a classical age
begins to break up under delicate
Asiatic tensions,
your words shimmered like rainbows on the scales
of a trout drowning in air.

Your restlessness calls to mind
birds of passage that crash against lighthouses
on stormy nights—
but your tenderness, too, is a storm,
always lowering, never breaking;
and its lulls are rarer still.
Pushed so far, how do you stay
afloat in that lake
of indifference, your heart? Perhaps
an amulet protects you, one you keep
next to your lipstick, your nail-file,
your compact: a white mouse,
in ivory. *Somehow you survive!*

2

Ormai nella tua Carinzia
di mirti fioriti e di stagni,
china sul bordo sorvegli
la carpa che timida abbocca
o segui sui tigli, tra gl'irti
pinnacoli le accensioni
del vespro e nell'acque un avvampo
di tende da scali e pensioni.

La sera che si protende
sull'umida conca non porta
col palpito dei motori
che gemiti d'oche e un interno
di nivee maioliche dice
allo specchio annerito che ti vide
diversa una storia di errori
imperturbati e la incide
dove la spugna non giunge.

La tua leggenda, Dora!
Ma è scritta già in quegli sguardi
di uomini che hanno fedine
altere e deboli in grandi
ritratti d'oro e ritorna
ad ogni accordo che esprime
l'armonica guasta nell'ora
che abbuia, sempre piú tardi.

E scritta là. Il sempreverde
alloro per la cucina
resiste, la voce non muta,
Ravenna è lontana, distilla
veleno una fede feroce.
Che vuole da te? Non si cede
voce, leggenda o destino . . .
Ma è tardi, sempre piú tardi.

2.

Now, in your Carinthia,
with its flowering myrtles and little ponds,
leaning over the edge you look down
at the timid carp that gapes and swallows;
or stroll under the lindens, their crowns
thrusting up into sunset
bonfires, the waters ablaze
with awnings of landings and hotels.

The evening that stretches out
over a misty inlet brings,
above the stutter of motors,
only the cries of geese; and an interior
of snowy tiles tells
the blackened mirror that hardly
recognized you a story of errors
calmly acknowledged, engraving it within
where the dustcloth doesn't reach.

Your golden legend, Dora—
but it is already written in the fixed stares
of those men with fluffy sidewhiskers,
dignified and weak, portraits
in big, gilt frames; a refrain
that comes back with every chord wrung
from the cracked barrel-organ at the hour
when dusk falls, always later and later.

It is written there. The evergreen
bayleaf all through the kitchen
survives, the voice does not fail,
Ravenna is far away; and a barbarous
creed keeps secreting its poison.
What can it want from you? None surrenders,
voice, legend, nor destiny. . . .
But it is late, always later and later.

(ALFRED CORN)

EUGENIO MONTALE

&

da *I MOTTETTI*

I.

Lo sai: debbo riperderti e non posso.
Come un tiro aggiustato mi sommuove
ogni opera, ogni grido e anche lo spiro
salino che straripa
dai moli e fa l'oscura primavera
di Sottoripa.

Paese di ferrame e alberature
a selva nella polvere del vespro.
Un ronzío lungo viene dall'aperto,
strazia com'unghia ai vetri. Cerco il segno
smarrito, il pegno solo ch'ebbi in grazia
da te.
      E l'inferno è certo.

X.

Perché tardi? Nel pino lo scoiattolo
batte la coda a torcia sulla scorza.
La mezzaluna scende col suo picco
nel sole che la smorza. È giorno fatto.

A un soffio il pigro fumo trasalisce,
si difende nel punto che ti chiude.
Nulla finisce, o tutto, se tu fólgore
lasci la nube.

EUGENIO MONTALE

from *THE MOTETS*

I.

You know this: I must lose you again and cannot.
Every action, every cry strikes me
like a well-aimed shot, even the salt spray
that spills over the harbor walls
and makes spring
dark against the gates of Genoa.

Country of ironwork and ship masts
like a forest in the dust of evening.
A long drone comes from the open spaces
scraping like a nail on a windowpane. I look
for the sign I have lost, the only pledge
I had from you.
                    Now hell is certain.

X.

Why are you waiting? The squirrel in the pine tree
beats its torch-like tail on the bark.
Half of the moon is sinking with one horn
touching the sun and fading. The day is finished.

The lazy smoke is startled by a breeze
but gathers itself to cover you.
Nothing will end, or everything, if you,
the flash of lightning, leave the cloud.

XII.

Ti libero la fronte dai ghiaccioli
che raccogliesti traversando l'alte
nebulose; hai le penne lacerate
dai cicloni, ti desti a soprassalti.

Mezzodí: allunga nel riquadro il nespolo
l'ombra nera, s'ostina in cielo un sole
freddoloso; e l'altre ombre che scantonano
nel vicolo non sanno che sei qui.

XIII.

La gondola che scivola in un forte
bagliore di catrame e di papaveri,
la subdola canzone che s'alzava
da masse di cordame, l'alte porte
rinchiuse su di te e risa di maschere
che fuggivano a frotte—

una sera tra mille e la mia notte
è piú profonda! S'agita laggiú
uno smorto groviglio che m'avviva
a stratti e mi fa eguale a quell'assorto
pescatore d'anguille dalla riva.

XII.

I run my hand across your forehead
to wipe away the ice
that formed there as you crossed
the highest clouds. Your wings
have been torn by cyclones.
You wake in sudden starts.

Noon: and the black shadows of the medlars
stretch themselves across the square,
a cold sun
persists in heaven, and the other
shadows turning in the alley
don't know that you are here.

XIII.

The gondola that glides
forward in the dark
splendor of its polished
tar and poppies, the insinuating
song that rises from beyond
the heaps of rigging, the tall
doors that close behind you,
and the smiles of the masqueraders
who run away in packs—

only one evening out of many,
but my night goes deeper still.
Down there a pale mass
writhing in the water startles
me awake and makes me
like the self-absorbed old man
fishing for eels on the bank.

XIX.

La canna che dispiuma
mollemente il suo rosso
flabello a primavera;
la rédola nel fosso, su la nera
correntía sorvolata di libellule;
e il cane trafelato che rincasa
col suo fardello in bocca,

oggi qui non mi tocca riconoscere;
ma là dove il riverbero piú cuoce
e il nuvolo s'abbassa, oltre le sue
pupille ormai remote, solo due
fasci di luce in croce.
                              E il tempo passa.

XIX.

The reed that sheds its
soft, red crescent
in the spring; the gravel path
above the gulley where dragonflies
are hovering on the slow
dark current; the dog,
breathless, coming home
with a bundle in its mouth.

Today there is nothing here
which I can recognize:
only there
where the reflection burns
more fiercely, and the clouds
are sinking, there beyond the eyes
which are so far away
by now, only these
two beams of light
that cross.

And time passes.

(DANA GIOIA)

EUGENIO MONTALE

✺

PICCOLO TESTAMENTO

Questo che a notte balugina
nella calotta del mio pensiero,
traccia madreperlacea di lumaca
o smeriglio di vetro calpestato,
non è lume di chiesa o d'officina
che alimenti
chierico rosso, o nero.
Solo quest'iride posso
lasciarti a testimonianza
d'una fede che fu combattuta,
d'una speranza che bruciò piú lenta
di un duro ceppo nel focolare.
Conservane la cipria nello specchietto
quando spenta ogni lampada
la sardana si farà infernale
e un ombroso Lucifero scenderà su una prora
del Tamigi, del Hudson, della Senna
scuotendo l'ali di bitume semi-
mozze dalla fatica, a dirti: è l'ora.
Non è un'eredità, un portafortuna
che può reggere all'urto dei monsoni
sul fil di ragno della memoria,
ma una storia non dura che nella cenere
e persistenza è solo l'estinzione.
Giusto era il segno: chi l'ha ravvisato
non può fallire nel ritrovarti.
Ognuno riconosce i suoi: l'orgoglio
non era fuga, l'umiltà non era
vile, il tenue bagliore strofinato
laggiú non era quello di un fiammifero.

EUGENIO MONTALE

❧

LITTLE TESTAMENT

This thing the night flashes
like marshlight through the skull of my mind,
this pearl necklace snail's trail,
this ground glass, diamond-dust sparkle—
it is not the lamp in any church or office,
tended by some adolescent altar boy,
Communist or papist,
in black or red.
I have only this rainbow
to leave you, this testimonial
of a faith, often invaded,
of a hope that burned more slowly
than a green log on the fire.
Keep its spectrum in your pocket-mirror,
when every lamp goes out,
when hell's orchestra trembles,
and the torch-bearing Lucifer
lands on some bowsprit
in the Thames, Hudson or Seine—
rotating his hard coal wings,
half lopped by fatigue, to tell you, "Now."
It's hardly an heirloom or charm
that can tranquillize monsoons
with the transparent spider web of contemplation—
but an autobiography can only survive in ashes,
persistence is extinction.
It is certainly a sign: whoever has seen it,
will always return to you.
Each knows his own: his pride
was not an escape, his humility
was not a meanness, his obscure
earth-bound flash
was not the fizzle of a wet match.

(ROBERT LOWELL)

EUGENIO MONTALE

č

LA BELLE DAME SANS MERCI

Certo i gabbiani cantonali hanno atteso invano
le briciole di pane che io gettavo
sul tuo balcone perché tu sentissi
anche chiusa nel sonno le loro strida.

Oggi manchiamo all'appuntamento tutti e due
e il nostro breakfast gela tra cataste
per me di libri inutili e per te di reliquie
che non so: calendari, astucci, fiale e creme.

Stupefacente il tuo volto s'ostina ancora, stagliato
sui fondali di calce del mattino;
ma una vita senz'ali non lo raggiunge e il suo fuoco
soffocato è il bagliore dell'accendìno.

EUGENIO MONTALE

ઝ

LA BELLE DAME SANS MERCI

To be sure the cantonal seagulls
waited in vain for the crumbs
I used to throw on your balcony,
that you might hear their cries even when asleep.

Today neither of us turns up for the appointment,
our breakfast grows cold among piles
of my useless books and your various relics:
calendars, jewel cases, medicine
bottles and creams.

Your astounding face lingers still,
carved against the morning's chalky
background; but a life without wings
can't reach it and its suffocated fire
is no more than the flash of a lighter.

(G. SINGH)

CARLO BETOCCHI
1899–

❧

DIARIETTO INVECCHIANDO

Guardo, nel mezzodí, splendere il sole
sugli intonaci vecchi, sotto il tetto,
nel rettangolo intenso del cortile.
Han rifatto le docce, odora il tenero
grigio della vernice al caldo autunno,
presso l'orlo dei coppi che boccheggiano,
vecchi, di fresco incalcinati, immersi
nell'azzurro. Ronza una vespa intorno
alle crepe del muro, ai turpi intonaci
cadenti, che sprofondano nel buio.
E il difendersi mite delle cose
dal morire, e il loro offrirsi, insieme,
alla morte, è di tale innocenza,
e c'è, latente, un'amicizia
cosí tenera, tra quel corrotto esistere
ed il cielo, che rifatta bambina
la mia anima, dentro, è come
un nòcciolo di pesca, la mia vita
niente di più, senza polpa, rugosa.

CARLO BETOCCHI

LITTLE DIARY ON GROWING OLD

At noon I watch the sun shine
on the old plaster under the roof,
in the sharply defined rectangle of the courtyard.
They have repaired the eaves: the soft gray
paint is a subdued scent in the heat of autumn,
close to the edge of the rounded tiles,
gasping for breath, old, freshly limed, immersed
in the blue of the sky. A wasp hums about
the cracks in the wall and about the ugly
falling plaster, subsiding to darkness.
And the gentle self-defense of things
from dying (and at the same time their self-surrender
to death) is of such innocence,
and there is hidden beneath a friendship
so tender between that miserable existence
and heaven that my soul
made child again within is like
a peach stone, my life
nothing more, without pulp, wrinkled.

(I. L. SALOMON)

CARLO BETOCCHI

ૐ

DAI TETTI

È un mare fermo, rosso,
un mare cotto, in un'increspatura
di tegole. È un mare di pensieri.
Arido mare. E mi basta vederlo
tra le persiane appena schiuse: e sento
che mi parla. Da una tegola all'altra,
come da bocca a bocca, l'acre
discorso fulmina il mio cuore.
Il suo muto discorso: quel suo esistere
anonimo. Quel provocarmi verso
la molteplice essenza del dolore:
dell'unico dolore:
immerso nel sopore,
unico anch'esso, del cielo. E vi posa
ora una luce come di colomba,
quieta, che vi si piuma: ed ora l'ira
sterminata, la vampa che rimbalza
d'embrice in embrice. E sempre la stessa
risposta, da mille bocche d'ombra.
—Siamo—dicono al cielo i tetti—
la tua infima progenie. Copriamo
la custodita messe ai tuoi granai.
O come divino spazia su di noi
il tuo occhio, dal senso inafferrabile.

CARLO BETOCCHI

FROM THE ROOFTOPS

It is a red motionless sea,
a rippling sea of baked tiles.
It is a sea of thoughts.
An arid sea. And it is enough for me to view it
through the slightly open shutters: and I feel
it speaks to me. From one tile to another,
as from mouth to mouth, the harsh speech
strikes my heart.
Its mute speech: its anonymous
existence. This provokes me toward
the manysided essence of suffering:
the only suffering:
immersed in the torpor,
also unique, of the sky. And now
a tranquil light as of a dove
that sheds its down comes to rest there; and now
endless anger, the blaze that rebounds
from rooftile to rooftile. And always the same
answer from a thousand mouths of shadow.
—We are—roofs tell the sky—
your lowliest progeny. We cover
the granaries to protect the harvest.
O how divinely your eye wanders over us
in a sense incomprehensible!

(I. L. SALOMON)

SALVATORE QUASIMODO
1901–1968

ED È SUBITO SERA

Ognuno sta solo sul cuor della terra
trafitto da un raggio di sole:
ed è subito sera.

STRADA DI AGRIGENTUM

Là dura un vento che ricordo acceso
nelle criniere dei cavalli obliqui
in corsa lungo le pianure, vento
che macchia e rode l'arenaria e il cuore
dei telamoni lugubri, riversi
sopra l'erba. Anima antica, grigia
di rancori, torni a quel vento, annusi
il delicato muschio che riveste
i giganti sospinti giù dal cielo.
Come sola allo spazio che ti resta!
E più t'accori s'odi ancora il suono
che s'allontana largo verso il mare
dove Èspero già striscia mattutino:
il marranzano tristemente vibra
nella gola di carraio che risale
il colle nitido di luna, lento
tra il murmure d'ulivi saraceni.

SALVATORE QUASIMODO

AND THEN SUDDENLY IT'S DARK

Alone at the earth's core stands each man,
Pierced by a ray of light; and then
Suddenly it's dark.

(WILLIAM JAY SMITH)

THE AGRIGENTUM ROAD

That wind's still there that I remember afire
In the manes of the racing horses
Veering across the plains; a wind
That stains the sandstone and erodes the hearts
Of downed columnar statues in the grass.
Oh antique soul, bled white
By rancor, back you lean to that wind again,
Catching the delicate fetor of the moss
That clothes those giants tumbled down by heaven.
How lonely it will be, the time that is left you!
    Worse, worse, if you should hear
That sound again, borne toward the far-off sea
Which Hesperus already pinks with morning:
The jew's-harp quavering sadly in the mouth
Of the wagon-maker climbing
Slowly his moon-washed hill, amidst
The murmur of the Saracen olive trees.

(RICHARD WILBUR)

SALVATORE QUASIMODO

I MORTI

Mi parve s'aprissero voci,
che labbra cercassero acque,
che mani s'alzassero a cieli.

Che cieli! Piú bianchi dei morti
che sempre mi destano piano;
i piedi hanno scalzi; non vanno lontano.

Gazzelle alle fonti bevevano,
vento a frugare ginepri
e rami ad alzare le stelle?

IMITAZIONE DELLA GIOIA

Dove gli alberi ancora
abbandonata piú fanno la sera,
come indolente
è svanito l'ultimo tuo passo,
che appare appena il fiore
sui tigli e insiste alla sua sorte.

Una ragione cerchi agli affetti,
provi il silenzio nella tua vita.
Altra ventura a me rivela
il tempo specchiato. Addolora
come la morte, bellezza ormai
in altri volti fulminea.
Perduto ho ogni cosa innocente,
anche in questa voce, superstite
a imitare la gioia.

SALVATORE QUASIMODO

THE DEAD

It seemed as if voices were raised,
lips sought waters,
hands were raised to skies.

What skies! Whiter than the dead
that always waken me gently;
barefoot, they do not go far away.

Gazelles were drinking at the springs;
wind stirring junipers,
and branches lifting the stars?

(JACK BEVAN)

IMITATION OF JOY

Where trees deepen
the evening's abandon
your last step has vanished
indolent, like the flower
that on the linden
barely appears, urging its destiny.

You seek a motive for feeling,
find in your life, silence.
Another fate is revealed for me
by mirrored time. It is pain
like death to see beauty
aflame now in other faces;
lost to me each innocent thing,
even this voice, enduring
in imitation of joy.

(JACK BEVAN)

SALVATORE QUASIMODO

❦

LETTERA ALLA MADRE

«*Mater dulcissima*, ora scendono le nebbie,
il Naviglio urta confusamente sulle dighe,
gli alberi si gonfiano d'acqua, bruciano di neve;
non sono triste nel Nord: non sono
in pace con me, ma non aspetto
perdono da nessuno, molti mi devono lacrime
da uomo a uomo. So che non stai bene, che vivi
come tutte le madri dei poeti, povera
e giusta nella misura d'amore
per i figli lontani. Oggi sono io
che ti scrivo.»—Finalmente, dirai, due parole
di quel ragazzo che fuggí di notte con un mantello corto
e alcuni versi in tasca. Povero, cosí pronto di cuore,
lo uccideranno un giorno in qualche luogo.—
«Certo, ricordo, fu da quel grigio scalo
di treni lenti che portavano mandorle e arance,
alla foce dell'Imera, il fiume pieno di gazze,
di sale, d'eucalyptus. Ma ora ti ringrazio,
questo voglio, dell'ironia che hai messo
sul mio labbro, mite come la tua.
Quel sorriso m'ha salvato da pianti e da dolori.
E non importa se ora ho qualche lacrima per te,
per tutti quelli che come te aspettano,
e non sanno che cosa. Ah, gentile morte,
non toccare l'orologio in cucina che batte sopra il muro
tutta la mia infanzia è passata sullo smalto
del suo quadrante, su quei fiori dipinti:
non toccare le mani il cuore dei vecchi.
Ma forse qualcuno risponde? O morte di pietà,
morte di pudore. Addio, cara, addio, mia *dulcissima mater*.»

SALVATORE QUASIMODO

LETTER TO MY MOTHER

"Mater dulcissima, now the mists are descending,
the Naviglio thrusts disorderly on the locks,
the trees swell with water, burn with snow;
I am not unhappy in the north: I am not
at peace with myself, but seek
pardon from no one, and many owe me tears.
I know you are ailing, live
like all mothers of poets, poor
and just in the measure of their love
for distant sons. Today it is I
who write to you" . . . At last, you will say, a line
from the boy who ran away at night
in a skimpy coat with a few lines
of poetry in his pocket. Poor thing, so ready-hearted.
One day, somewhere, they will kill him—
"Yes, I remember that grey stopping place
for slow trains loaded with almonds, oranges,
at the mouth of the Imera, the river full of magpies,
salt and eucalyptus. But now I want to thank you
truly for the wry smile you set
on my lips, a smile as mild as your own:
it has saved me pain and grief.
And if now I shed a tear for you
and all who wait like you and do not know
what they wait for, it does not matter.
O gentle death,
do not touch the clock in the kitchen that ticks on the wall;
all my childhood was passed away on the enamel
of its dial, on those painted flowers:
do not touch the hands, the heart of the old.
Does anyone answer? O death of pity,
death of shame. Goodbye, dear one, farewell my
dulcissima mater."

(JACK BEVAN)

SALVATORE QUASIMODO

MILANO, AGOSTO 1943

Invano cerchi tra la polvere,
povera mano, la città è morta.
È morta: s'è udito l'ultimo rombo
sul cuore del Naviglio. E l'usignolo
è caduto dall'antenna, alta sul convento,
dove cantava prima del tramonto.
Non scavate pozzi nei cortili:
i vivi non hanno piú sete.
Non toccate i morti, cosí rossi. cosí gonfi:
lasciateli nella terra delle loro case:
la città è morta, è morta.

IN QUESTA CITTÀ

In questa città c'è pure la macchina
che stritola i sogni: con un gettone
vivo, un piccolo disco di dolore
sei subito di là, su questa terra,
ignoto in mezzo ad ombre deliranti
su alghe di fosforo funghi di fumo:
una giostra di mostri
che gira su conchiglie
che si spezzano putride sonando.
È in un bar d'angolo laggiú alla svolta
dei platani, qui nella mia metropoli
o altrove. Su, già scatta la manopola.

SALVATORE QUASIMODO

MILAN AUGUST 1943

In vain you search in the dust,
poor hand, the city is dead.
Dead: on the heart of the Naviglio
the last hum has been heard.
The nightingale has fallen from the flagpole
high on the convent where once he sang before sunset.
Dig no wells in the courtyards,
the living have lost their thirst.
The dead, so red, so swollen, do not touch them:
leave them in the earth of their houses:
the city is dead. Dead.

(JACK BEVAN)

IN THIS CITY

This city has even got the machine
that grinds out dreams: with a quick
token, a little disk of pain,
in no time you're off, upon this earth,
unknown in a pack of raving shadows
on phosphorus seaweed, mushrooms of smoke:
a merry-go-round of monsters
revolving on conch shells
that fall to putrid pieces when they play.
It's in a bar down there at the turn
of the plane trees, here in my metropolis
or elsewhere. Come, the switch is on!

(ALLEN MANDELBAUM)

SALVATORE QUASIMODO

NEVE

Scende la sera: ancora ci lasciate,
o immagini care della terra, alberi,
animali, povera gente chiusa
dentro i mantelli dei soldati, madri
dal ventre inaridito dalle lacrime.
E la neve ci illumina dai prati
come luna. Oh, questi morti. Battete
sulla fronte, battete fino al cuore.
Che urli almeno qualcuno nel silenzio,
in questo cerchio bianco di sepolti.

SALVATORE QUASIMODO

SNOW

Evening descends: again you leave us,
O dear images of the earth, trees,
animals, poor people wrapped
in the cloaks of soldiers, mothers
with womb made barren by tears.
And the snow lights us from the meadows
like a moon. Oh, these dead. Beat
on the forehead, strike deep to the heart.
Let someone at least cry out in the silence,
in this white circle of the entombed.

(WILLIAM WEAVER)

LUCIO PICCOLO

1903-1969

❦

da *ANNA PERENNA*

Sul tetto
subito s'alza, sovrasta il monte—
ingombro a manca di dumoso
verde su verde, di coltri di sfatto
fogliame, di cortecce vetuste, di sterpi—
e il cappero, l'euforbia, pendono alle venture
dei venti; dove volge la costa
e chiama l'ombra e la stende sugli increspamenti,
al dorso della salita s'aprono pieghe,
conche di verde piú denso, s'indovina
vescia, ranuncolo, porro, su foglia
spessa, su bronchi carponi, schiuma,
saliva di bosco, oscura rugiada di gambo
tumido, di spino, di gozzo di fusto
che trasuda, quel ch'è viscido d'iridi, che mai
vede sole (e assidue le invisibili spole
tessono, mutano, ma il giro è sempre lo stesso)
nutrito d'umido antico, di vegetale ruggine ...
e forse sfugge la lucertola senz' occhi ...

LUCIO PICCOLO

ℰ

LANDSCAPE
(from *Anna Perenna*)

Above the roof
ascends, impends all at once
the mountain—to the left, encumbered
with a thorny green on green, with blankets
of a shed leafage, agèd tree-rinds, brush:
and caper, euphorbia hang at the winds'
mercy; where the coastline bends
and summons the shadow in, spreading it across
the scape of wrinklings, at the slope's
summit, folds fall open: valleys
of thicker green, there you can seek
and find puffball, buttercup and wild leek:
on dense leaf, on creeping bronchia
scum, wood spit, dark dew
of the swollen stalk, the thorn, the goitred
and oozing stem, that which remains
clammy with rainbow-coloured stains, which never sees
sunlight (and assiduously the invisible shuttles
weave, mutate, but the cycle will stay
the same forever) fed with an ancient moisture,
a mildew of vegetation . . .
and perhaps an eyeless lizard slides away . . .

(CHARLES TOMLINSON)

LUCIO PICCOLO

MOBILE UNIVERSO DI FOLATE

Mobile universo di folate
di raggi, d'ore senza colore, di perenni
transiti, di sfarzo
di nubi: un attimo ed ecco mutate
splendon le forme, ondeggian millenni.
   E l'arco della porta bassa e il gradino liso
di troppi inverni, favola sono nell'improvviso
raggiare del sole di marzo.

LUCIO PICCOLO

UNSTILL UNIVERSE

Unstill universe of gusts
of rays, of hours without colour, of perennial
transits, vain displays
of cloud: an instant and—
look, the changed forms
blaze out, millennia grow unstable.
And the arch of the low door and the step
worn by too many winters, are a fable
in the unforseen burst from the March sun.

(CHARLES TOMLINSON)

SANDRO PENNA
1906-1977

❦

PASSANDO SOPRA UN PONTE

Passando sopra un ponte
alto sull 'imbrunire
guardando l'orizzonte
ti pare di svanire.

Ma la campagna resta
piena di cose vere
e tante azzure sfere
non valgono una festa.

IL TRENNO TARDERÀ DI ALMENO UN'ORA

Il treno tarderà di almeno un'ora.
L'acqua del mare si fa più turchina.
Sul muro calcinato il campanello
casalingo non suona. La panchina
di ferro scotta al sole. Le cicale
sono le sole padrone dell'ora.

AMAVO OGNI COSA NEL MONDO

Amavo ogni cosa nel mondo. E non avevo
che il mio bianco taccuino sotto il sole.

SANDRO PENNA

AS YOU PASS HIGH UPON

As you pass high upon
a bridge as night falls there
you gaze at the horizon
and seem to disappear.

But still the fields are full
of things that still are true
and all the spheres of blue
aren't worth one festival.

(HENRY TAYLOR)

THE TRAIN WILL BE
AT LEAST AN HOUR LATE

The train will be at least an hour late.
The blue-green of the water darkens.
The doorbell on the whitewashed wall
doesn't ring. The iron
bench burns in the sun. The cicadas
are sole masters of the hour.

(W.S. DI PIERO)

I LOVED EVERYTHING IN THE WORLD

I loved everything in the world. And all I had
was my small blank notebook in the sunlight.

(W.S. DI PIERO)

CESARE PAVESE

1908-1950

❧

VERRÀ LA MORTE E AVRÀ
I TUOI OCCHI

Verrà la morte e avrà i tuoi occhi —
questa morte che ci accompagna
dal mattino alla sera, insonne,
sorda, come un vecchio rimorso
o un vizio assurdo. I tuoi occhi
saranno una vana parola,
un grido taciuto, un silenzio.
Così li vedi ogni mattina
quando su te sola ti pieghi
nello specchio. O cara speranza,
quel giorno sapremo anche noi
che sei la vita e sei il nulla.

Per tutti la morte ha uno sguardo.
Verrà la morte e avrà i tuoi occhi.
Sarà come smettere un vizio,
come vedere nello specchio
riemergere un viso morto,
come ascoltare un labbro chiuso.
Scenderemo nel gorgo muti.

CESARE PAVESE

DEATH WILL COME
AND WILL HAVE YOUR EYES

Death will come and will have your eyes—
this death which attends us
from morning to night, sleepless,
deaf, like an old remorse
or absurd vice. Your eyes
will be a vain word,
a stilled cry, a silence.
So you see them each morning
when upon yourself alone you bend
into the mirror. O dear hope,
on that day we too will know
you are life and nothingness.

For all death has one glance.
Death will come and will have your eyes.
It will be like quitting a vice,
like seeing in the mirror
a dead visage unfold,
like heeding closed lips.
We will descend into the abyss muted.

(NORMAN THOMAS DI GIOVANNI)

CESARE PAVESE

❦

LO STEDDAZZU

L'uomo solo si leva che il mare è ancora buio
e le stelle vacillano. Un tepore di fiato
sale su dalla riva, dov'è il letto del mare
e addolcisce il respiro. Quest'è l'ora in cui nulla
può accadere. Perfino la pipa tra i denti
pende spenta. Notturno è il sommesso sciacquio.
L'uomo solo ha già acceso un gran fuoco di rami
e lo guarda arrossare il terreno. Anche il mare
tra non molto sarà come il fuoco, avvampante.

Non c'è cosa più amara che l'alba di un giorno
in cui nulla accadrà. Non c'è cosa più amara
che l'inutilità. Pende stanca nel cielo
una stella verdognola, sorpresa dall'alba.
Vede il mare ancor buio e la macchia di fuoco
a cui l'uomo, per fare qualcosa, si scalda;
vede, e cade dal sonno tra le fosche montagne
dov'è un letto di neve. La lentezza dell'ora
è spietata, per chi non aspetta più nulla.

Val la pena che il sole si levi dal mare
e la lunga giornata cominci? Domani
tornerà l'alba tiepida con la diafana luce
e sarà come ieri e mai nulla accadrà.
L'uomo solo vorrebbe soltanto dormire.
Quando l'ultima stella si spegne nel cielo,
l'uomo adagio prepara la pipa e l'accende.

CESARE PAVESE

MORNING STAR

The man alone gets up while the sea's still dark
and the stars still flicker. A warmth like breathing
drifts from the shore where the sea has its bed,
sweetening the air he breathes. This is the hour when nothing
can happen. Even the pipe dangling from his teeth
is out. The sea at night makes a muffled plash.
By now the man alone has kindled a big fire of brush,
he watches it redden the ground. Before long
the sea will be like the fire, a blaze of heat.

Nothing's more bitter than the dawning of a day
when nothing will happen. Nothing's more bitter
than being useless. A greenish star, surprised
by the dawn, still droops feebly in the sky.
It looks down on the sea, still dark, and the brushwood fire
where the man, simply to do something, is warming himself.
It looks, then drops sleepily down among the dusky mountains.
to its bed of snow. The hour drags by, cruelly
slow for a man who's waiting for nothing at all.

Why should the sun bother to rise from the sea
or the long day bother to begin? Tomorrow
the warm dawn with its transparent light will be back,
and everything will be like yesterday, and nothing will happen.
The man alone would like nothing more than to sleep.
When the last star in the sky is quenched and gone,
the man quietly tamps his tobacco and lights his pipe.

(WILLIAM ARROWSMITH)

VITTORIO SERENI
1913-1983

❧

TERRAZZA

Improvvisa ci coglie la sera.
               Più non sai
dove il lago finisca:
un murmure soltanto
sfiora la nostra vita
sotto una pensile terrazza.

Siamo tutti sospesi
a un tacito evento questa sera
entro quel raggio di torpediniera
che ci scruta poi gira se ne va.

I VERSI

Se ne scrivono ancora.
Si pensa ad essi mentendo
ai trepidi occhi che ti fanno gli auguri
l'ultima sera dell'anno.
Se ne scrivono solo in negativo
dentro un nero di anni
come pagando un fastidioso debito
che era vecchio di anni.
No, non è più felice l'esercizio.
Ridono alcuni: tu scrivevi per l'Arte.
Nemmeno io volevo questo che volevo ben altro.
Si fanno versi per scrollare un peso
e passare al seguente. Ma c'è sempre
qualche peso di troppo, non c'è mai
alcun verso che basti
se domani tu stesso te ne scordi.

VITTORIO SERENI

č

THE TERRACE

Sudden nightfall around us.
               You no longer know
where the edge of the lake is;
only a whisper
moves over our life
under a hanging terrace.

We are completely suspended
from the silent event of this evening
caught in the light from a torpedo boat
which peers at us, then turns and vanishes.

(HENRY TAYLOR)

POEMS

We still write them.
We think of them lying
to anxious eyes that wish us
a Happy New Year.
We write them only in negatives
in a darkness of years,
as if we were paying an annoying debt
many years old.
No there is no more happiness in my job.
Some laugh: you wrote for Art's sake.
Not even I wanted this, I wanted something more.
One writes poems to shake off a weight
and pass it on to him who follows us. But there is always
too much weight, no line
that is ever enough
if you yourself forget it tomorrow.

(PAUL VANGELISTI)

415

MARIO LUZI

1914–

༄

AVORIO

Parla il cipresso equinoziale, oscuro
e montuoso esulta il capriolo,
dentro le fonti rosse le criniere
dai baci adagio lavan le cavalle.
Giù da foreste vaporose immensi
alle eccelse città battono i fiumi
lungamente, si muovano in un sogno
affettuose vele verso Olimpia.
Correranno le intense vie d'Oriente
ventilate fanciulle e dai mercati
salmastri guarderanno ilari il mondo.
Ma dove attingerò io la mia vita
ora che il tremebondo amore è morto?
Violavano le rose l'orizzonte,
esitanti città stavano in cielo
asperse di giardini tormentosi,
la sua voce nell'aria era una roccia
deserta e incolmabile di fiori.

LA NOTTE LAVA LA MENTE

La notte lava la mente.

Poco dopo si è qui come sai bene,
fila d'anime lungo la cornice,
chi pronto al balzo, chi quasi in catene.

Qualcuno sulla pagina del mare
traccia un segno di vita, figge un punto.
Raramente qualche gabbiano appare.

MARIO LUZI

༒

IVORY

The ever-dark cypress is alive,
the somber mountain buck is elated;
in reddened springs the mares
slowly wash caresses out of their manes.
Down from misty forests immense
rivers lash against the towering cities
constantly; quivering sails move
in a dream towards Olympia.
Airy girls will travel the crowded roads
of the Orient and from brackish markets
will look cheerfully at the world.
But where will I draw my life from
now that flickering love is dead?
Roses corrupted the horizon;
faltering cities sprinkled with troubled
gardens remained in the sky;
her voice on the air was a desert rock
never to be heaped with flowers.

(I. L. SALOMON)

NIGHT WASHES OVER THE MIND

Night washes over the mind.

After a while we are here, as you well know,
a line of ghosts along the mountain ledge,
ready to leap, almost in chains.

On the page of the sea someone
traces a sign of life, fixes a point.
Rarely does a gull appear.

(DANA GIOIA)

417

MARIO LUZI

LAS ANIMAS

Fuoco dovunque, fuoco mite di sterpi, fuoco
sui muri dove fiotta un'ombra fievole
che non ha forza di stamparsi, fuoco
più oltre che a gugliate sale e scende
il colle per la sua tesa di cenere,
fuoco a fiocchi dai rami, dalle pergole.

Qui né prima né poi nel tempo giusto
ora che tutt'intorno la vallata
festosa e triste perde vita, perde
fuoco, mi volgo, enumero i miei morti
e la teoria pare più lunga, freme
di foglia in foglia fino al primo ceppo.

Da' loro pace, pace eterna, portali
in salvo, via da questo mulinare
di cenere e di fiamme che s'accalca
strozzato nelle gole, si disperde
nelle viottole, vola incerto, spare;
fa' che la morte sia morte, non altro
da morte, senza lotta, senza vita.
Da' loro pace, pace eterna, placali.

Laggiù dov'è più fitta la falcidia
arano, spingono tini alle fonti,
parlottano nei quieti mutamenti
da ora a ora. Il cucciolo s'allunga
nell'orto pressso l'angolo, s'appisola.

Un fuoco così mite basta appena,
se basta, a rischiarare finché duri
questa vita di sottobosco. Un altro,
solo un altro potrebbe fare il resto
e il più: consumare quelle spoglie,
mutarle in luce chiara, incorruttibile.

MARIO LUZI

❦

LAS ANIMAS

Fire everywhere, the gentle fire of brushwood,
fire on the walls where a feeble shadow floating
hasn't the strength to imprint itself; fire
further off rises and sinks in loops of thread
downhill across a length of ashes,
fire in flakes from the branches and trellises.

Here not before not later but at the proper time,
now that everything about the festive
and sad valley loses life and fire,
I turn round; I count my dead,
the procession seems longer, trembles
from leaf to leaf as far as the first stump.

Give them peace, eternal peace, carry them
to safety away from the ashes and flames
of this whirlwind that presses
strangulated in the ravines, is lost
on trails, flies uncertainly, vanishes.
Make death what it is, nothing but
death, struggle done with and lifeless.
Give them peace, eternal peace, quiet them.

Down there where the cutting is thicker
they plow, push vats to the springs,
whisper during the hushed mutations
from hour to hour. In a corner
of the garden a puppy stretches himself and dozes.

A fire so gentle is hardly enough,
if enough to illuminate as long as
this undergrowth under life may last. Another,
only another could do the rest
and more; to consume these spoils,
to change them to light, clear and incorruptible.

Requie dai morti per i vivi, requie
di vivi e morti in una fiamma. Attizzala:
la notte è qui, la notte si propaga,
tende tra i monti il suo vibrìo di ragna,
presto l'occhio non serve più, rimane
la conoscenza per ardore o il buio.

Requiems from the dead for the living, requiems
for the living and dead in one flame. Poke it:
night is here and overspreading,
stretches its quivering cobweb between the mountains;
soon the eye will no longer serve; what remains
is awareness for ardor or the dark.

(I.L. SALOMON)

NELO RISI

1920-

❧

IL TEATRO PRIVATO

Che bellezza scaricare tutto sull'inconscio!
purché l'inconscio lo si lavi in famiglia
si può uccidere il padre fottere la madre

La psicoanalisi è una indagine borghese
un processo simbolico tanto rispettabile
(conta il denaro la cura è interminabile)

Fughe e censure sono piaceri da narciso
un murarsi dentro la scena familiare
che l'uomo di fabbrica l'uomo della terra

neanche sospettano—per i subalterni
vale ancora la vecchia coscienza

NELO RISI

❦

THE PRIVATE THEATER

What a beautiful thing to dump everything on the unconscious!
if the unconscious would cleanse the whole family
you could kill your father fuck your mother

Psychoanalysis is a bourgeois inquiry
such a respectable symbolic process
(only money matters the cure never ends)

Escapes and censures are narcissistic pleasures
a self-enclosure in the familial scene
which the factory worker the man of the earth

don't even suspect—for the lower ranks
it's still the old conscience that counts

(LAWRENCE R. SMITH)

NELO RISI

da *PENSIERI ELEMENTARI*

20

Negare quello che sappiamo
come se non ci riguardasse,
non inquietare il prossimo
e tanto meno se stessi,
creare un diversivo
senza allarmi né scosse,
non venire mai al punto—
purché in qualche modo si viva!
Ecco il comandamento nuovo.

21

Ci vogliono voci forti
ugole di ferro, oggi, per dire
una sola sommessa parola d'amore.

NELO RISI

❧

from *ELEMENTARY THOUGHTS*

POEM 20

To deny what we know
as if it did not concern us,
not to upset our neighbour
and ourselves even less,
to create a diversion
without alarm or shock,
never to come to the point—
so that somehow one can live!
This is the new Commandment.

POEM 21

Loud voices are needed,
uvulas of iron, today, to speak
a single gentle word of love.

(GAVIN EWART)

PIER PAOLO PASOLINI
1922-1975

❦

IL PIANTO DELLA SCAVATRICE

I

Solo l'amare, solo il conoscere
conta, non l'aver amato,
non l'aver conosciuto. Dà angoscia

il vivere di un consumato
amore. L'anima non cresce più.
Ecco nel calore incantato

della notte che piena quaggiù
tra le curve del fiume e le sopite
visioni della città sparsa di luci,

echeggia ancora di mille vite,
disamore, mistero, e miseria
dei sensi, mi rendono nemiche

le forme del mondo, che fino a ieri
erano la mia ragione d'esistere.
Annoiato, stanco, rincaso, per neri

piazzali di mercati, tristi
strade intorno al porto fluviale,
tra le baracche e i magazzini misti

agli ultimi prati. Lì mortale
è il silenzio: ma giù, a viale Marconi,
alla stazione di Trastevere, appare

ancora dolce la sera. Ai loro rioni,
alle loro borgate, tornano su motori
leggeri—in tuta o coi calzoni

PIER PAOLO PASOLINI

THE TEARS OF THE EXCAVATOR

I

Only loving, only knowing
matter, not past love
nor past knowledge. Living

a consummated love
is agonizing. The soul no longer grows.
And in the dark enchanted heat,

down here along the curving
river with its drowsy sights
of the city touched with lights,

the night still echoes with a thousand lives;
while the estrangement, mystery, misery
of the senses cut me off from

the world's shapes, which were till
yesterday my reason for living.
Bored, tired, I return home, across

dark marketplaces, down sad streets
near the river docks between shacks
and warehouses mingling with the countryside's

last fields, where there's a deathly
silence, though farther along, at Viale Marconi,
at Trastevere Station, the evening's

still sweet. To their neighborhoods,
their slums, the young return on light
motorbikes, in overalls and workpants;

di lavoro, ma spinti da un festivo ardore—
i giovani, coi compagni sui sellini,
ridenti, sporchi. Gli ultimi avventori

chiacchierano in piedi con voci
alte nella notte, qua e là, ai tavolini
dei locali ancora lucenti e semivuoti.

Stupenda e misera città,
che m'hai insegnato ciò che allegri e feroci
gli uomini imparano bambini,

le piccole cose in cui la grandezza
della vita in pace si scopre, come
andare duri e pronti nella ressa

delle strade, rivolgersi a un altro uomo
senza tremare, non vergognarsi
di guardare il denaro contato

con pigre dita dal fattorino
che suda contro le facciate in corsa
in un colore eterno d'estate;

a difendermi, a offendere, ad avere
il mondo davanti algi occhi e non
soltanto in cuore, a capire

che pochi conoscono le passioni
in cui io sono vissuto:
che non mi sono fraterni, eppure sono

fratelli proprio nell'avere
passioni di uomini
che allegri, inconsci, interi

vivono di esperienze
ignote a me. Stupenda e misera
città che mi hai fatto fare

but propelled by festive fire,
with a friend behind on the saddle
laughing and dirty. In the night

the last customers stand talking
loudly, amid the little tables of nearly
empty but still brightly lit cafés.

Stupendous, miserable city,
you taught me what men learn
joyously and ferociously as children,

those little things in which we
discover life's grandeur in peace:
going tough and ready into crowded

streets, addressing another man
without trembling, not ashamed
to check the change counted

by the lazy fingers of the conductor
sweating along passing façades
in the eternal red of summer;

to defend myself, to attack, to have
the world before my eyes and not
just in my heart, to understand

that few know the passions
in which I've lived; that they're
not brotherly to me, and yet they are

my brothers because they have
passions of men
who, joyous, unknowing, whole,

live experiences
unknown to me. Stupendous, miserable
city, you made me

esperienza di quella vita
ignota: fino a farmi scoprire
ciò che, in ognuno, era il mondo.

Una luna morente nel silenzio,
che di lei vive, sbianca tra violenti
ardori, che miseramente sulla terra

muta di vita, coi bei viali, le vecchie
viuzze, senza dar luce abbagliano
e, in tutto il mondo, le riflette

lassù, un po' di calda nuvolaglia.
È la notte più bella dell'estate.
Trastevere, in un odore di paglia

di vecchie stalle, di svuotate
osterie, non dorme ancora.
Gli angoli bui, le pareti placide

risuonano d'incantati rumori.
Uomini e ragazzi se ne tornano a casa
—sotto festoni di luci ormai sole—

verso i loro vicoli, che intasano
buio e immondizia, con quel passo blando
da cui più l'anima era invasa

quando veramente amavo, quando
veramente volevo capire.
E, come allora, scompaiono cantando.

experience that unknown
life, you made me discover
what the world was for everyone.

A moon dying in the silence that she
feeds goes white amid violent glowing,
which, miserably, on the silent earth,

with its beautiful avenues and old
lanes, dazzles them without shedding
light, while a few hot cloud masses

reflect them to her, above, all over the world.
It's the most beautiful night of summer.
Trastevere, which smells of emptied

taverns and straw from old
stables, isn't asleep yet.
Its dark corners and peaceful walls

resound with enchanted sounds.
Men and boys are strolling home
—beneath abandoned garlands of lights—

toward their alleyways clogged by
darkness and garbage, with that slow pace
which invaded the depths of my soul

when I truly loved, when
I truly wanted to understand.
And, as then, they disappear, singing.

(NORMAN MACAFEE with LUCIANO MARTINENGO)

PIER PAOLO PASOLINI

SUPPLICA A MIA MADRE

È difficile dire con parole di figlio
ciò a cui nel cuore ben poco assomiglio.

Tu sei la sola al mondo che sa, del mio cuore,
ciò che è stato sempre, prima d'ogni altro amore.

Per questo devo dirti ciò ch'è orrendo conoscere:
è dentro la tua grazia che nasce la mia angoscia.

Sei insostituibile. Per questo è dannata
alla solitudine la vita che mi hai data.

E non voglio esser solo. Ho un'infinita fame
d'amore, dell'amore di corpi senza anima.

Perchè l'anima è in te, sei tu, ma tu
sei mia madre e il tuo amore è la mia schiavitù:

ho passato l'infanzia schiavo di questo senso
alto, irrimediabile, di un impegno immenso.

Era l'unico modo per sentire la vita,
l'unica tinta, l'unica forma: ora è finita.

Sopravviviamo: ed è la confusione
di una vita rinata fuori dalla ragione.

Ti supplico, ah, ti supplico: non voler morire.
Sono qui, solo, con te, in un futuro aprile . . .

PIER PAOLO PASOLINI

❧

PRAYER TO MY MOTHER

It's so hard to say in a son's words
what I'm so little like in my heart.

Only you in all the world know what my
heart always held, before any other love.

So, I must tell you something terrible to know:
From within your kindness my anguish grew.

You're irreplaceable. And because you are,
the life you gave me is condemned to loneliness.

And I don't want to be alone. I have an infinite
hunger for love, love of bodies without souls.

For the soul is inside you, it is you, but
you're my mother and your love's my slavery:

My childhood I lived a slave to this lofty
incurable sense of an immense obligation.

It was the only way to feel life,
the unique form, sole color; now, it's over.

We survive, in the confusion
of a life reborn outside reason.

I pray you, oh, I pray: Don't die.
I'm here, alone, with you, in a future April . . .

(NORMAN MACAFEE with LUCIANO MARTINENGO)

ROCCO SCOTELLARO

1923-1953

❦

ALLA FIGLIA DEL TRAINANTE

Io non so piú viverti accanto
qualcuno mi lega la voce nel petto
sei la figlia del trainante
che mi toglie il respiro sulla bocca.
Perché qui sotto di noi nella stalla
i muli si muovono nel sonno
perché tuo padre sbuffa a noi vicino
e non ancora va alto sul carro
a scacciare le stelle con la frusta.

LA TREBBIATURA

Cessa il motore della trebbia,
le foglie del granturco tremano,
il paese è nella trama bruna.

Case, madonne incagnate,
stasera non ci aspettate,
dormiremo alla mèta della paglia,
già il cielo si frastaglia,
nel contrasto dei venti
nasce per noi la punta della luna.

ROCCO SCOTELLARO

TO THE CARTER'S DAUGHTER

I don't know how I can live near you any longer
someone ties the voice in my chest
you are the carter's daughter
who takes the breath from my mouth.
Because below in the stall
mules kick in their sleep
because your father snores close to us
and does not yet mount high on his wagon
to chase away the stars with his whip.

(PAUL VANGELISTI)

THE THRESHING

The thresher motor stops,
the leaves of the corn shiver,
the town is in the brown weft.

Houses, raging madonnas,
tonight don't wait up for us,
we will sleep in the hay,
already the sky is growing ragged,
for us in the wind's dissonance
the tip of the moon is flowering.

(PAUL VANGELISTI)

ROCCO SCOTELLARO

LEZIONI DI ECONOMIA

Ti ho chiesto un giorno chi mise
le sentinelle di abeti
visti alle Dolomiti.
Ti ho chiesto tante altre cose
del cisto, del mirto,
dell'inula viscosa,
nomi senza economia.
Mi hai risposto tra l'altro,
che un padre che ama i figli
può solo vederli andar via.

ROCCO SCOTELLARO

č

ECONOMICS LESSON

I asked you one day who posted
the sentinels of spruce
up there in the Dolomites.
I asked you many other things
of the rock rose, of myrtle,
of the gummy inula,
names of nothing to do with economy.
You answered me
that a father who loves his children
can only watch them go away.

(PAUL VANGELISTI)

BIOGRAPHIES OF THE
POETS

BIOGRAPHIES OF THE POETS

Albizzi, Niccolò degli (fl. 1300). Although no biographical information on this poet is available, the poem printed here, in the brilliant translation by Rossetti, is certainly one of the most powerful war poems ever written.

Alfieri, Vittorio (1749-1803). Born in Asti of a wealthy, French-speaking aristocratic family; travelled extensively in his dissipated early life; learned Italian well only after deciding to devote himself to literature. To his contemporaries, Alfieri was best known for his verse tragedies which helped galvanize Italian national identity.

Angiolieri, Cecco (1258?-1320). Born at Siena, from which he was exiled because of his dissipated life. Three of his sonnets are addressed to Dante. Boccaccio (*Decameron*, IX, 4) tells of how one of Cecco's friends robbed him of his clothes.

Annunzio, Gabriele d' (see D'*Annunzio, Gabriele, 1863–1938.*)

Aquino, Rinaldo d' (fl. 1240–1250). Probably a Sicilian nobleman of the house of Aquino. In the canzone printed here, a woman laments the departure of her lover on a Crusade, possibly the one in 1228 led by Frederick II of Sicily.

Ariosto, Lodovico (1474—1533). Born in Reggio, Emilia; son of a nobleman. Ariosto studied law at Ferrara and led a career as a diplomat. His major reputation rests almost solely on his masterpiece, *Orlando Furioso*, which is generally considered the finest romance epic of the Renaissance.

Barberini, Francesco da (1264–1348). Another of the early poets translated by Rossetti.

Belli, Giuseppe Gioacchino (1791–1863). Wrote more than two thousand sonnets in the Roman dialect, a veritable monument to the life and language of the people of Rome. Many of these are bitterly satirical and anticlerical. Ironically, he ended his life as a censor and official writer for the papal authorities he had criticized, and at one point even thought of destroying his work.

Berni, Francesco (1497–1535). Born in Tuscany; went to Rome at the age of nineteen, and spent many years in the service of cardinals and papal dignitaries. Is supposed to have been poisoned in revenge for his refusal to poison Cardinal Salviati. Wrote a number of sonnets and *Capitoli* (poems in *terza rima*) in a comic, burlesque manner that came to be known as "bernesque." The sonnet quoted here is a fine example.

Betocchi, Carlo (1899–   ). Born at Turin; graduated as a land surveyor from the Technical Institute in Florence. For almost twenty-five years worked on various construction enterprises. "Work was my bath of innocence," he says. A fervent Catholic, he was awarded the Premio Viareggio for his *Poesia* (1955) and on the appearance of *L'Estate di San Martino* (1961) the Premio Montefeltro and the Dante Alighieri gold medal.

Boccaccio, Giovanni (1313–1375). Although he is best known throughout the world for his prose masterpiece, the *Decameron*, Boccaccio also wrote fine narrative and lyrical poems. The son of a Florentine merchant, he led a carefree life as a young man in Naples, then returned to Florence, where he met Petrarch in 1350. He later lectured on the *Divine Comedy* of Dante in the church of the Badia above Florence until shortly before his death.

Boiardo, Matteo Maria (1441-1494). Count of Scandiano; born near Reggio in Emilia. Although Boiardo made his career in politics, he wrote many poems including *Orlando Innamorato*, the story which Ariosto continued in *Orlando Furioso*.

Campana, Dino (1885—1932). Born in Marradi, north of Florence; studied chemistry briefly at the University of Bologna before being expelled. Campana spent years as a vagabond through Europe and Latin America. He served briefly in the Italian army during the First World War but was soon confined to an insane asylum where he spent the rest of his life. His major reputation in Italian literature rests on one book, his *Canti Orfici* (1914).

Campanella, Tommaso (1568-1639). Entered the Dominican order in 1582. His philosophical works brought him into frequent conflict with the church. He was imprisoned for political conspiracy against the kingdom of Naples and for his heretical views. In 1626 was released through the intervention of the Pope, but shortly afterwards had to flee to France to escape new imprisonment. Died in Paris. Was the author of works on theology, science, and political philosophy as well as poetry.

Carducci, Giosuè (1835–1907). Born in a little village in Tuscany; was appointed professor of Italian literature at the University of Bologna in 1860, and taught there for a quarter of a century. After years of bitter literary and political polemics, he renounced republicanism and became the official poet of a united Italy. He was named a senator of the Italian kingdom in 1890, and received the Nobel prize for literature in 1906.

Cavalcanti, Guido (c. 1255–1300). Belonged to the White faction of the Guelphs in Florence, was exiled to Sarzana, where he fell ill; died shortly after his return to Florence. He and Dante, who dedicated his *Vita Nuova* to him, are the greatest poets of the Florentine school. His philosophical theory of love is demonstrated in a number of his famous *canzoni*, particularly in "Donna mi prega," translated by Ezra Pound, who edited Cavalcanti's *Rime*.

Chiabrera, Gabriello (1552—1638). Born in Savona near Genoa; spent his youth in Rome; served as a diplomat and public official. Chiabrera resisted the fashionable influence of Marino's baroque poetry and created a classical style based on Latin and Greek models.

Cino da Pistoia (1270–1336). Born at Pistoia of a noble family (his full name was Guittoncino dei Sinibaldi); was a friend of Dante and Petrarch, a jurist as well as a poet.

Colonna, Vittoria (1492–1547). Born at Marino; married in 1509 the Marchese di Pescara, and after his death in 1525, retired to her castle on the island of Ischia, near Naples, and later to convents in Rome, Viterbo, and Orvieto. Among her many famous friends was Michelangelo, who dedicated a number of his sonnets to her.

Costanzo, Angelo di (1507–1591). Born and died at Naples, of which he wrote a history in twenty volumes (1581). His poems, admired by his contemporaries, were even more appreciated by the poets of the eighteenth century when they were published in 1709 at Bologna.

D'Annunzio, Gabriele (1863–1938). A soldier-poet (an aviator in World War I), who became a hero of the Fascist movement. Produced many novels, poems, and plays. Out of his vast output, it is doubtful that much will survive, but his best poems display a force and sensuality, and a baroque mastery of language.

Dante Alighieri (1265-1321). With the *Divine Comedy*, which he composed during his exile from Florence, Dante established Tuscan as the language of Italian literature. His *Vita Nuova*, from which two sonnets are quoted here, celebrates his love of Beatrice. Dante was influenced by Brunetto Latini and Guido Cavalcanti. Became opposed to the power of Pope Boniface VIII, and after the victory of the Black Guelph faction in Florence was exiled. Died at the court of Guido da Polenta in Ravenna.

Filicaia, Vincenzo da (1642-1707). Born in Florence, da Filicaia studied law and eventually became governor of Volterra and later of Pisa. His reputation is based on his sonorous patriotic and religious poems, especially "Italia" which Byron freely rendered in *Childe Harold's Pilgrimage*.

Folgore da San Gimignano (1250?-?1317). The poet, whose real name was Giacomo di Michele, was a soldier and courtier in the walled city of San Gimignano. His two cycles of sonnets on the months of the year and the days of the week give a delightful account of the manners of his time.

Foscolo, Ugo (1778-1827). Born in the Ionian Islands; campaigned with the French armies, then became disillusioned with Napoleon. In 1813 fled to Switzerland, after refusing to swear allegiance to the Austrians, and then to London. Died in England. As well as poetry, wrote critical essays, tragedies, and a novel, *The Last Letters of Jacopo Ortis*, which influenced later writers.

Francesco d'Assisi, San (c. 1182-1226). After an early life of pleasure, founded the Franciscan order. His famous canticle exemplifies his ideal of humility and the simple love of nature. Was canonized in 1228 by Gregory IX.

Giusti, Giuseppe (1809-1850). Poet and patriot of the Risorgimento. Born at Monsummeno in Tuscany, and died at Florence. His burlesques and political satires, directed against the Austrian authorities and their Italian collaborators, had immense success.

Govoni, Corrado (1884-1965). Born at Tàmara (Ferrara). Showed the influence of the so-called *crepuscolari* ("twilight poets"), who wrote in a subdued manner in reaction against the excesses of romanticism which had preceded them. His *Selected Poems* was published in 1919.

Gozzano, Guido (1883–1916). Born in Piedmont; had an early success with poems published in various magazines and newspapers. Traveled to India (1912–1913), and returned to Piedmont, where he died of tuberculosis. Was one of "the twilight poets."

Guarini, Giovanni Battista (1538–1612). Born at Ferrara; studied at Padua. Joined the court of Ferrara, and became a friend of Tasso, with whom he later quarreled. Lived in Mantua, Ferrara, Padua, and Venice, where he died. His chief work is the *Pastor Fido,* a pastoral tragicomedy, published in 1590 and acted for the first time in 1596.

Guinizelli, Guido (c. 1235-1276). Born in Bologna; a lawyer by training; exiled when the Guelfs rose to power in 1274; died in exile. A generation older than Dante, Guinizelli was a precursor of *"il dolce stil nuovo."* Dante greatly admired Guinizelli's work and in the *Purgatorio* calls him *"il padre mio"* when he meets the poet's shade among the Lustful.

Jacopo da Lentini (fl. c. 1200–1250). A notary at the court of Frederick II of Sicily. Is referred to by Dante, *Purgatorio* XXIV, 56; is said to have invented the sonnet.

Jacopone da Todi (1230?–1306). Born at Todi; his name was originally Jacopo Benedetti. After the sudden death of his wife (c. 1268), renounced his career as a lawyer and became a Franciscan. Author of *Laudi,* mystical religious poems, and perhaps of the hymn *Stabat Mater Dolorosa.*

Leopardi, Giacomo (1798–1837). Italy's greatest modern poet. Born at Recanati, near Ancona, of a noble family; was educated by his father and at an early age had mastered Greek and Latin. At thirteen wrote a tragedy, at fifteen had prepared a philological study of 350 pages, and at eighteen translated a part of the *Odyssey.* At twenty-three broken in health and an invalid for the rest of his life, escaped from the confinement of his family. His *Canti,* tinged with pessimism, appeared at Florence in 1831.

Luzi, Mario (1914–   ). Born at Florence, where he is now professor of French literature at the university. One of the principal poets of the middle generation after Ungaretti and Montale, has published a number of volumes of poems and of essays. Has also translated Coleridge.

Machiavelli, Niccolò (1469–1527). Born at Florence of a distinguished family; more noted for his political writings including the famous *The Prince,* in which he describes how an ideal prince may employ any means, however unscrupulous, to maintain a strong government. The adjective "Machiavellian" has come to mean political cunning or bad faith. Machiavelli wrote a number of plays, from one of which this lyric is taken.

Marinetti, Filippo Tommaso (1876-1944). Born in Egypt, Marinetti achieved international notoriety by publishing his Futurist Manifesto on the front page of the Parisian *Le Figaro* in 1909. Marinetti's Futurist movement advocated the destruction of the past including museums and libraries, the rejection of conventional morality, and the idealization of machinery. His own poetry is generally poor, but his influence on the theory of the *avant-garde* remains important to this day.

Marino, Giovan Battista (1569-1625). Born in Naples, Marino was considered one of the greatest Italian poets of all time during his lifetime and enjoyed the patronage of kings. His extravagant use of metaphorical conceits created a literary fashion in baroque Italy and Spain which was called *marinismo.* English poets like Drummond, Carew, and Crashaw were also influenced by his style.

Medici, Lorenzo de' (1449–1492). As head of the Medici family, succeeded his father Piero de' Medici as ruler of Florence, where he established himself as a brilliant statesman, scholar, and patron of the arts. He is celebrated for his *Canti Carnascialeschi (Carnival Songs).*

Michelangelo Buonarotti (1475–1564). Born at Caprese, Michelangelo, as sculptor, painter, architect, and poet, is one of the giants of the Renaissance. Was befriended by Lorenzo de' Medici, and in 1501 sculpted for Florence the huge statue of David. Also painted the Sistine Chapel from 1508 to 1512; designed the Library of San Lorenzo and the Medici Chapel in Florence; became the architect of St. Peter's in Rome, where he died. Is buried in Santa Croce in Florence. His poetry has something of the passionate intensity and muscularity of his sculpture and painting.

Montale, Eugenio (1896-1981). Born at Genoa; his first volume *Ossi di seppia* (1925) shows the influence of the Ligurian coast. Became director of the Gabinetto Vieusseux in Florence in 1927 and served until 1938, when he was dismissed for refusing to join the

Fascist party. Had been a contributing editor to the *Corriere della Sera* in Milan from 1947 till his death. With Ungaretti he was identified with "the hermetic school," and in the pessimistic cast of his work resembles Leopardi. Also shows a close affinity for T. S. Eliot, although the spiritual wasteland Montale depicts is not redeemed through Christian faith.

Palazzeschi, Aldo (1885-1974). Pen name of Aldo Giurlani. Born at Florence; was one of the early members of the futurist group, with which he broke in 1914. Became famous for his novels, *The Materassi Sisters* (1934) and *The Cuccoli Brothers* (1948).

Pascoli, Giovanni (1855-1912). Succeeded Carducci as professor of literature at the University of Bologna (1905). The sadness of his life (his father was murdered when he was twelve years old and his mother died a year later) is reflected in gentle pastoral poetry which prompted him to be called the son of Vergil.

Pasolini, Pier Paolo (1922-1975). Born in Bologna, Pasolini was an internationally acclaimed film-director and novelist as well as a poet. Influenced by both Catholicism and Marxism, he was committed to the ideals of popular art stripped of traditional literary trappings and was widely considered Italy's leading neo-realist poet. He was murdered in Rome by a homosexual prostitute in 1975 under circumstances still unclear.

Pavese, Cesare (1908-1950). Born near Turin where he spent most of his life except for a year of political banishment to Calabria under the fascist regime. Pavese's international reputation was won primarily by his bleakly realistic novels. He committed suicide a few weeks after receiving Italy's prestigious Strega Prize.

Penna, Sandro (1906-1977). Born at Perugia. In his poetry he is adept at catching sensations and recording impressions.

Petrarca (Petrarch), Francesco (1304-1374). Born at Arezzo, the son of a Florentine lawyer who had been exiled with the White Guelphs in 1302; studied at the universities of Montpellier and Bologna. His poetry celebrates his love of Laura, whom he first saw on April 6, 1327, at church in Avignon. His love for her lasted even after her death. After extensive travels in Europe, he retired to Vaucluse, but spent his last years at Arquà, where he is buried. Perfected the sonnet form.

446

Piccolo, Lucio (1903—1969). Born in Palermo, Piccolo was a Sicilian nobleman, the Baron of Calanovella. He was also the cousin of Giuseppe di Lampedusa, author of *The Leopard*. His aristocratic upbringing combined with a taciturn temperament led him to eschew the Italian literary world and not seek publication of his own work until late in his life.

Poliziano, Angelo (1454–1494). Called himself after his birthplace, Montepulciano; his real name was Ambrogini. Came to Florence to study and later became the tutor of Giuliano de' Medici, for whom he wrote *Stanze per la giostra di Giuliano*. Later became professor of Greek and Latin at the University of Florence. Wrote a masque *Orfeo*, which anticipated the libretto in the modern sense.

Pulci, Luigi (1432-1484). Born in Florence; sponsored as a young man by the Medici family. Pulci's epic poem on Charlemagne and Roland, the *Morgante*, is a classic of Italian literature.

Quasimodo, Salvatore (1901-1968). Born at Syracuse; became an employee of the State Civil Engineers Bureau, and travelled throughout Italy. At twenty-two he began his studies of the classics, especially of Greek. Translated Greek lyric poetry, and it was an important influence on his work. Settled in Milan in 1938, devoted much of his time to literary journalism. Evoked the landscape of his native Sicily in the best of his poetry, which was deepened by his experience of World War II and the Resistance which accompanied it. He received the Nobel prize for literature in 1959.

Redi, Francesco (1626–1698). Born at Arezzo; studied medicine at the University of Pisa, and in 1654 was appointed physician to the Duke of Tuscany. Wrote numerous scientific works as well as poems, the best known of which is his dithyramb, *Bacco in Toscana* (1685), from which the passages here given are excerpted.

Risi, Nelo (1920—   ). Born in Milan; took a degree in medicine but never practiced; has had a distinguished career in journalism and film-making. Risi is the most distinguished living practitioner of Italy's long tradition of satiric poets. His acutely impartial intelligence and savage sense of irony have created a poetry of unusual moral force.

Rustico di Filippo (1200?–1270). Born at Florence; a friend of Brunetto Latini, one of the first to use the Tuscan dialect. Most of his sonnets, of which about sixty are extant, are, like the one cited here, in the burlesque vein.

447

Saba, Umberto (1883–1957). Born into the Jewish community of Trieste (the city was not reunited with Italy until 1918); was close in spirit to "the twilight poets," but his lyricism was much more personal. His most important work is the *Canzonieri* (1921).

Scotellaro, Rocco (1923—1953). Born in Tricarico, Lucania; became mayor of his native village at 23; unjustly jailed for embezzlement; upon liberation he left for Portici where he died three years later. Scotellaro's reputation is based on one posthumous volume of poems *E Fatto Giorno* (*Day is Come*, 1954).

Sereni, Vittorio (1913-1983). Born at Luino, near Milan; taught in various cities in the north, then became one of the directors of the publishing house of Mondadori. Translated Pound, Valéry, and William Carlos Williams. In World War II fought in Greece and Sicily, and was for two years a prisoner of the Allies in Algeria and Morocco. His war experience greatly influenced his poetry.

Stampa, Gaspara (c. 1523-1554). Born in Padua of a noble family. While living in Venice, Stampa fell in love with a young nobleman who eventually abandoned her for another woman. Her sonnets, madrigals, and elegies, much admired by Rilke, passionately chronicle tragic romance with a candor and directness unique in women poets of the Renaissance.

Tasso, Torquato (1544-1595). The great epic poet wrote the sonnet on cats, which is here translated, while confined for seven years in the asylum of Santa Anna in Ferrara. Born at Sorrento, educated by the Jesuits at Naples and at the Universities of Padua and Bologna. Had almost finished his major work *Jerusalem Delivered*, which celebrates the First Crusade, when in 1575 he became mentally ill. He wrote letters, dialogues, and many lyrics. After years of wandering, died in Rome at the monastery of St. Onofrio just before Clement VIII was to crown him poet laureate on the Capitol.

Ungaretti, Giuseppe (1888-1970). Born at Alexandria, Egypt; pursued his studies in Paris until 1914. During World War I served in the Italian army in France and Italy, and his war experience marked his poetry. In 1936 became professor of Italian literature at São Paulo, and returned to Italy as professor of modern literature at the University of Rome in 1943. Has been called the creator of "the hermetic school" of poets; his clean, spare style won him international renown. Died just after accepting the first international prize awarded by Books Abroad (the University of Oklahoma).

Valeri, Deigo (1887-1976). For some years was professor of French at the University of Padua; then became superintendent of the Belli Arti in Venice, the city he celebrates in his poetry. The title of his first collection, *Le Gaie Tristezze* ("The Gay Sadnesses"), sets the tone of much of his work. He received the Etna-Taormina prize in 1959.

Vittorelli, Jacopo (1749–1835). Author of many musical lyrics. Born and died at Bassano; lived also in Venice, where he held public office.

INDEX OF POETS

INDEX OF TRANSLATORS

ACKNOWLEDGEMENTS

ૠ

The compilers of *Poems from Italy* and New Rivers Press wish to thank the following authors, translators, editors, publishers, and agents for permission to reprint copyrighted material. Every possible effort has been made to trace ownership of each poem and translation included. If any errors or omissions have occurred, and the publisher is notified of their existence, correction will be made in subsequent editions.

Anvil Press for Jack Bevan's translations of Quasimodo, from *Complete Poems*, copyright © Anvil Press Poetry, London, 1983; Schocken Books, New York 1984. Reprinted by permission of Anvil Press Poetry, Ltd.

William Arrowsmith for his translation of Pavese.

Atheneum Publishers for W.S. Merwin's translation of Buonarotti's "To Pope Julius II" from *Selected Translations: 1948-1968*. Copyright © 1968 by W.S. Merwin. Reprinted with the permission of Atheneum Publishers.

Thomas G. Bergin for his translations: of d'Aquino's "Lament" and Boccaccio's "To The Fair Kingdom," published by L.R. Lind in *Lyric Poetry of the Italian Renaissance*, copyright © 1954 Yale University Press; of Petrarch's "I Find no Peace" which first appeared in *Translations from Petrarch, A Selection Compiled by T.G. Bergin*, published by Oliver and Boyd Inc., Edinburgh and London, 1954; and of Saba's "The Goat" which first appeared in *The Promised Land and Other Poems*, edited by S.F. Vanni, New York 1957. All reprinted here by permission of Mr. Bergin.

BOA Editions, Ltd. for Isabella Gardner's translation of Giuseppe Ungaretti's "Feeling of Time" from *That Was Then: New and Selected Poems*, copyright © 1980 by Isabella Gardner and reprinted with the permission of BOA Editions, Ltd.

Anthony Burgess for his translations of Belli's "Annunciation" and "The Last Judgement," copyright © Liana Burgess, 1984. Reprinted by permission of Mr. Burgess.

John Ciardi for his translation of an excerpt of Dante's *Purgatory*, published by N.A.L. Translation copyright © 1959, 1960, 1961, 1965, 1970 by John Ciardi. Reprinted by permission of Mr. Ciardi.

Alfred Corn for his translation of Montale.

Patrick Creagh for his translations of Ungaretti and Leopardi.

Noman Thomas Di Giovanni for his translation of Pavese.

Guilio Einaudi Editore for Pasolini's "Il Pianto della Scavatrice" from *Le Ceneri di Gramsci* by Pier Paolo Pasolini, copyright © 1981 Giulio Einaudi Editore, Torino; and for Cesare Pavese's poems. Reprinted by permission of Giulio Einaudi Editore.

Gavin Ewart and London Magazine for his translation of Risi.

453

454

Peter Russell for his translation of Matteo Maria Boiardo, which first appeared in *Nine*, London. Reprinted by permission of Mr. Russell.

Martin Secker & Warburg Ltd. for E.J. Scovell's translation of Pascoli from *The Space Between*, by E.J. Scovell, published by Martin Secker & Warburg. Reprinted by permission of Martin Secker & Warburg, Ltd.

C.H. Sisson for his translation of an excerpt from Dante's *Purgatory*. Copyright © 1980 by C.H. Sisson. Reprinted by permission of Mr. Sisson.

Felix Stefanile for his translations of Angiolieri; of Saba's "One Night," and "The Boy and the Shrike," from *Umberto Saba: 31 Poems*, copyright © 1978, Elizabeth Press; of Marinetti, Govoni and Palazzeschi from *The Blue Moustache*, copyright © 1980, the Elizabeth Press. Reprinted by permission of Mr. Stefanile.

Henry Taylor for his seven translations, all of which appeared in *Poems from Italy*, compiled by William Jay Smith, Thomas Y. Crowell Press, copyright © 1972. Two translations, St. Francis of Assisi's "Canticle of Created Things" and Ungaretti's "In Memoriam" since appeared in *An Afternoon of Pocket Billards*, copyright © 1975 by Henry Taylor, published by the University of Utah Press. Reprinted by permission of Mr. Taylor.

Joseph Tusiani for his translation of Boccaccio from *Nymphs of Fiesole*, translated by Joseph Tusiani, Fairleigh Dickinson University Press, copyright © by the translator; and of Stampa from *Italian Poets of the Renaissance*, translated by Joseph Tusianai, copyright by the translator. Reprinted by permission of Mr. Tusiani.

University of California Press for Lawrence Smith's translation of Risi from *The New Italian Poetry, 1945 to Present, a Bilingual Anthology* edited by Lawrence Smith, published by the University of California Press, copyright © 1981 the Regents of the University of California; and for Carlo Golino's translations of Gozzano's "The Difference," and Govoni's "The Little Trumpet" from *Contemporary Poetry: Anthology*, edited by Carlo Golino, 1962, University of California Press, copyright © 1962 the Regents of the University of California. All are reprinted with the permission of the University of California Press.

Paul Vangelisti for his translations.

Richard Wilbur for his translations of Ungaretti's "Weightless Now" and Quasimodo's "The Agrigentum Road." Reprinted from *Advice to a Prophet and Other Poems* by Richard Wilbur, with the permission of Mr. Wilbur.

William Weaver for his translations.

David Wright for his translation of di Costanzo's "The Death of Virgil" from *Moral Stories*, Deutsch, London, 1954. Reprinted by permission of Mr. Wright.